IMAGES
of America

NEW CASTLE

CHAPPAQUA AND MILLWOOD

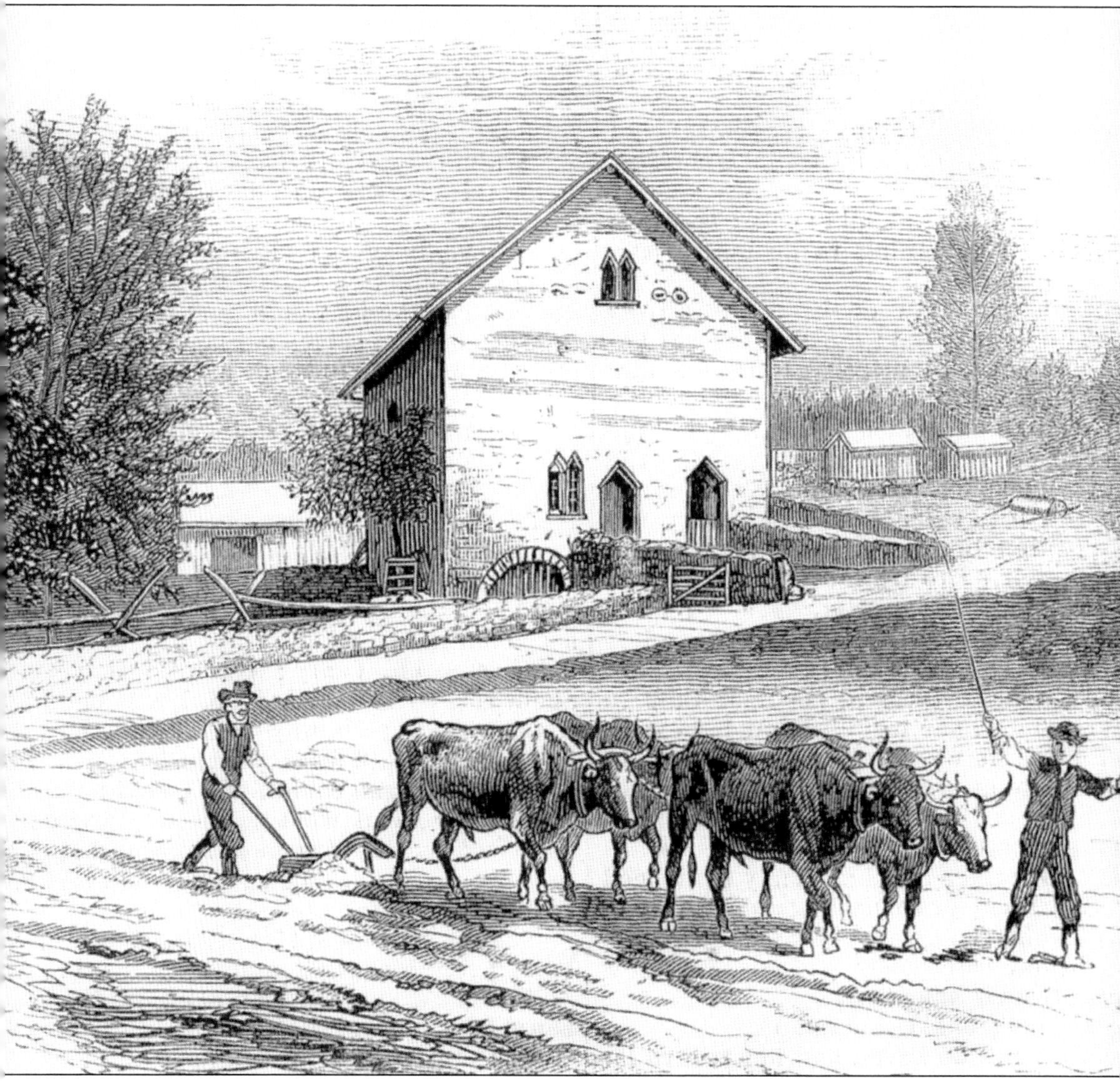

In this 1872 wood engraving, Horace Greeley is depicted at the plow by his concrete barn.

On the cover: Please see page 122. (Courtesy of the New Castle Historical Society.)

IMAGES
of America

NEW CASTLE
CHAPPAQUA AND MILLWOOD

The Chappaqua History Committee
and Gray Williams
Foreword by Pres. Bill Clinton

ARCADIA
PUBLISHING

ISBN 978-0-7385-3928-7

Published by Arcadia Publishing
Charleston, South Carolina

Printed in the United States of America

Library of Congress Catalog Card Number: 2005931670

For all general information contact Arcadia Publishing at:
Telephone 843-853-2070
Fax 843-853-0044
E-mail sales@arcadiapublishing.com
For customer service and orders:
Toll-Free 1-888-313-2665

Visit us on the Internet at www.arcadiapublishing.com

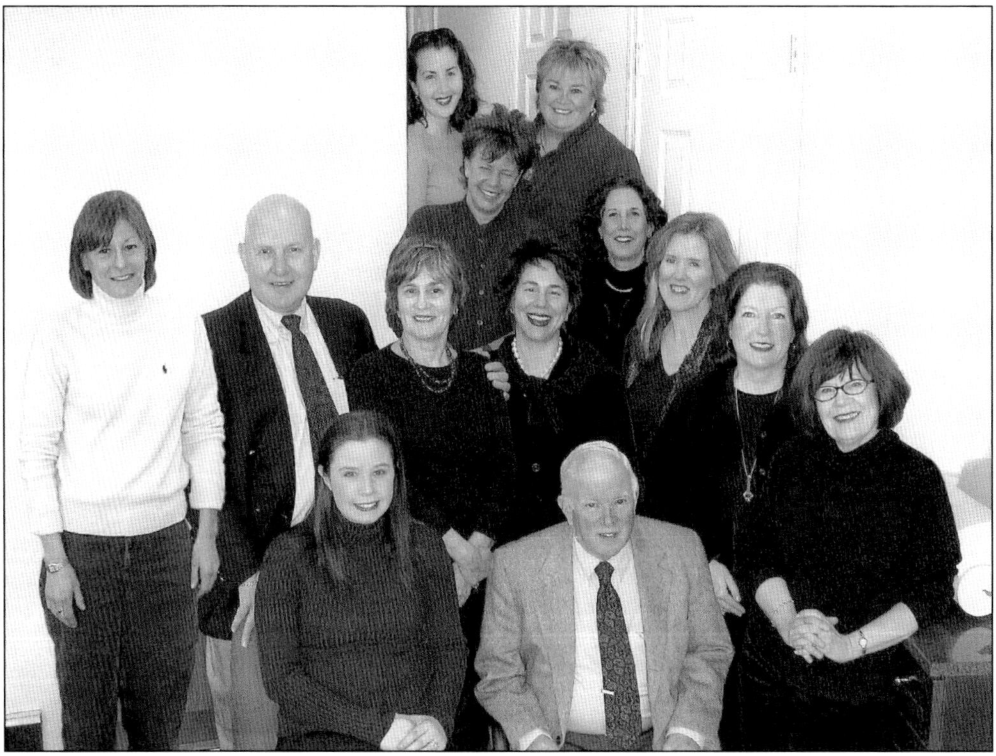

Shown are, from left to right, members of the Chappaqua History Committee (first row) Maura Dunn and Gray Williams; (second row) Lynne White, Karl Weydig, Pat Gerard, Joanna Rizoulis, Helen Escoffier, Janet Short, and Nancy Hutchens; (third row) Jean Cameron-Smith and Tina Plesset; (fourth row) Rose Marina and Phyllis Weydig. Missing are Emma Hoy, Stacy Levey, and Eric Rosenfeld. (Photograph by Michael Fields.)

Contents

FOREWORD

New Castle, like the rest of this part of the country, was first home to Native Americans. The township was settled by farmers and then became part of the manufacturing boom that America discovered in the late 1800s and early 1900s. Descriptive street names still identify the places where farms, orchards, and mills once stood. Today New Castle, with its hamlets of Chappaqua and Millwood, is largely a residential area serviced by a large variety of small business, its history reflected in old buildings and stone fences of a bygone era, its beauty preserved in wooded parks and walking trails.

Chappaqua, where Hillary and I live, was established by Quakers in the mid-1700s, and the 1753 Meeting House still stands, one of the oldest remaining structures in the town. A century later, Horace Greeley, the famed newspaper editor and Democratic presidential candidate, moved there. His house is a museum that offers an interesting glimpse into the important times in which he lived.

Today, New Castle's inhabitants reflect the social, political, and religious diversity of America, with new immigrants from Latin America, Asia, and Africa living and working with people whose families have been here for generations. However, in spite of all the changes, the town retains the feel of an earlier era and its traditional values. The people are friendly. The schools are good. Life is organized around work and family. Children are everywhere, with lots of teams to join, parks to play in, space to grow up in. Hillary and I like living here, a place where past and present meet.

Bill Clinton

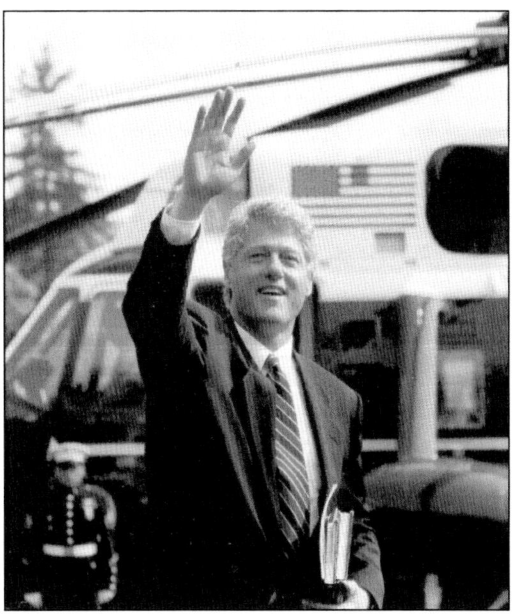

Bill and Hillary Clinton moved to Chappaqua in January 2000, after spending eight years in the White House. Bill now commutes to his office in Harlem.

Introduction

Our appreciation for the beautiful and picturesque suburban town of New Castle, and of its hamlets, Chappaqua and Millwood, is greatly enriched by our knowledge of its past. And it is even further enriched when we can envision what that past looked like. This book in the Images of America series brings the history of New Castle alive, through drawings, prints, photographs, and maps—all demonstrating how much our present is rooted in our past.

The story of New Castle begins with its earliest European settlers—mostly Quaker homesteaders migrating from Long Island and southern Westchester. Our earliest recorded landmarks are the Quaker meetinghouse and its surrounding graveyard, dating from the mid-1700s. The meetinghouse was the nucleus of the original village of Chappaqua, and several of its homes and shops still exist in the neighborhood along Quaker Street.

The arrival of the railroad brought about far-reaching changes, especially in Chappaqua, where a station stop of the New York and Harlem Railroad was established in 1846. The center of Chappaqua moved from the Quaker meetinghouse to the railroad crossing, initiating a period of rapid growth and increasing prosperity. The economy of New Castle changed as well. Its original subsistence farms became transformed into market farms, specializing in dairy and apple products that could be shipped quickly by rail to New York City.

Railroad service to Millwood did not arrive until 1881, and the community remained smaller and more rural than Chappaqua through much of the 1900s. Nonetheless, Millwood was located on a major highway, the Somerstown Road, and its principal inn and tavern, the Granite House, was during the 1800s a community center not only for Millwood but also for New Castle as a whole. Like Chappaqua, Millwood retains several fine old farmhouses and other relics of its rural past.

Other monuments of the past include the churches and churchyards of the many other religious denominations besides the Quakers who have found a welcome in New Castle. These range in time from the churchyard of St. George's Episcopal Church, founded before the Revolution, to Temple Beth El, designed by famed modern architect Louis I. Kahn and completed in 1972. There are also a few survivors of the one- or two-room "common" schools that used to provide the only public education in New Castle. They were largely supplanted by the comprehensive Horace Greeley School in the 1920s, beginning a period of growth and progress that have made the Chappaqua Central School District one of the most outstanding in the country.

By the end of the 1800s, farming in New Castle had declined, and much of the former farmland was bought up by wealthy New Yorkers and assembled into large estates. Many of these estate owners built imposing mansions on the highest prominences of their properties and were familiarly known as hilltoppers. The Depression of the 1930s brought an end to the estate era and hastened what was already a major transition toward suburbanization.

Since the end of World War II, New Castle has become entirely suburban. Its last farm was sold for subdivision in 1997. Nonetheless, as this book shows, our suburban present has been substantially shaped by our rural past, and respect for our past can help us plan for a better future.

—Gray Williams
Town Historian

ACKNOWLEDGMENTS

This book would not have been possible without the cooperative effort of many people.

First, thanks go to Gray Williams, the New Castle town historian, who labored many, many long hours to edit the material and ensure the facts contained in *New Castle: Chappaqua and Millwood* are accurate. We are indebted to him for his support and time spent with the Chappaqua History Committee, a group of volunteers dedicated to preserving the history of our wonderful community.

Members of the committee—associates of the Julia B. Fee Real Estate company—are Joanna Rizoulis, managing director of the Chappaqua and Katonah offices; administrators Rose Marina and Maura Dunn; and agents Helen Escoffier, Pat Gerard, Emma Hoy, Nancy Hutchens, Stacey Levey, Tina Plesset, Eric Rosenfeld, Janet Short, Karl Weydig, Phyllis Weydig, Lynne White, and Jean Cameron-Smith, who deserves a special thank-you for her vision and perseverance, which made this project come to life.

We especially thank Betsy Towl and the staff of the New Castle Historical Society for sharing the society's photograph collection, as well as for their patience and assistance with the committee. Unless otherwise credited, all photographs and documents in *New Castle: Chappaqua and Millwood* are from the society's extensive archives.

For their contributions of time and material, we thank Stuart Bradley, Phil Chadeayne, John Crabtree, Corinne Cardoff Dailey, Frances Turner Davidson, Michael Fields, Richard Pogact, Jane Stewart of the Mount Kisco Historical Society, and Katie Hite, Elizabeth Fuller, and Chris Marinaro of the Westchester County Historical Society. Thanks also go to those families who opened their personal albums and shared their memories.

Finally, my wife and I consider ourselves quite blessed to have the opportunity to raise our family in New Castle. Although she and I come from diverse backgrounds, we have both found New Castle to be a place to call home. We are eternally grateful for all those who came before us, from the founding Quakers to our present neighbors and friends who contribute countless hours every day toward making this a true community. We will ever be indebted to those who have preserved the rich history that has made this town so special.

—Randy Katchis

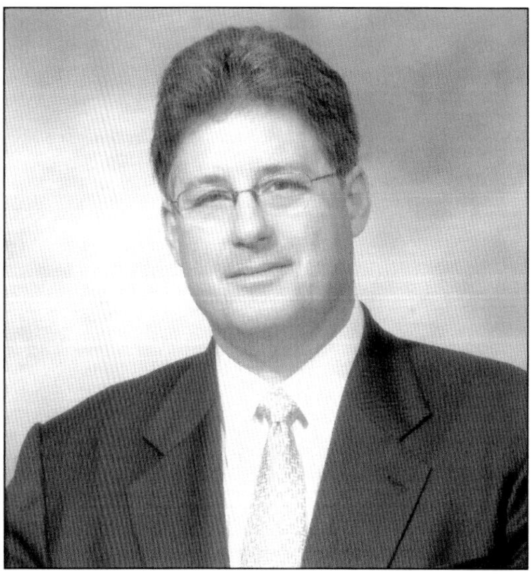

Randy Katchis is delighted to have taken part in this important project, recounting and preserving the development of New Castle. He is the owner of Julia B. Fee Real Estate. The company was founded by Julia B. Fee, a formidable businessperson who instilled in her agents a commitment to community.

One

Early New Castle and the Quaker Heritage

The first European settlers in the New Castle area were mainly members of the Religious Society of Friends, or Quakers. They believed that every human being shared a part of the divine spirit, the Light Within; that all people were equal regardless of race or gender; and that taking part in war was sinful. In the early 1730s, Quaker families made their way into northwest North Castle, which later became New Castle. Among these pioneers was Abel Weeks, whose family had originally come to Westchester from Long Island. He built a house on Armonk Road (Route 128), north of Wampus Pond. Soon he and his Quaker neighbors were holding meetings there rather than traveling several miles to the meetinghouse in Purchase.

By 1753, the local Quakers began a small meetinghouse of their own in an area of North Castle they called Shapiqua. Weeks, John Cornell, and Moses Quinby were appointed to supervise the construction. The meetinghouse became the nucleus of the first village of Chappaqua.

The Quakers, as pacifists, provided no soldiers for the militia during the Revolution and, consequently, were heavily taxed. New Castle was in what was euphemistically called the Neutral Ground, between British forces to the south and the Continental army to the north. This area became prey to bandits and cattle thieves, called Cowboys and Skinners, from both sides. Important figures including George Washington, Alexander Hamilton, Comte de Rochambeau, and British spy John André passed through the community, and in 1781, Rochambeau's expeditionary army camped at North Castle Corners, now the intersection of Main Street (Route 117) and Bedford Road (Route 172) in Mount Kisco.

In 1791, the town of New Castle was split from North Castle, and the town entered a 50-year period of slow growth until the New York and Harlem Railroad reached Chappaqua in 1846.

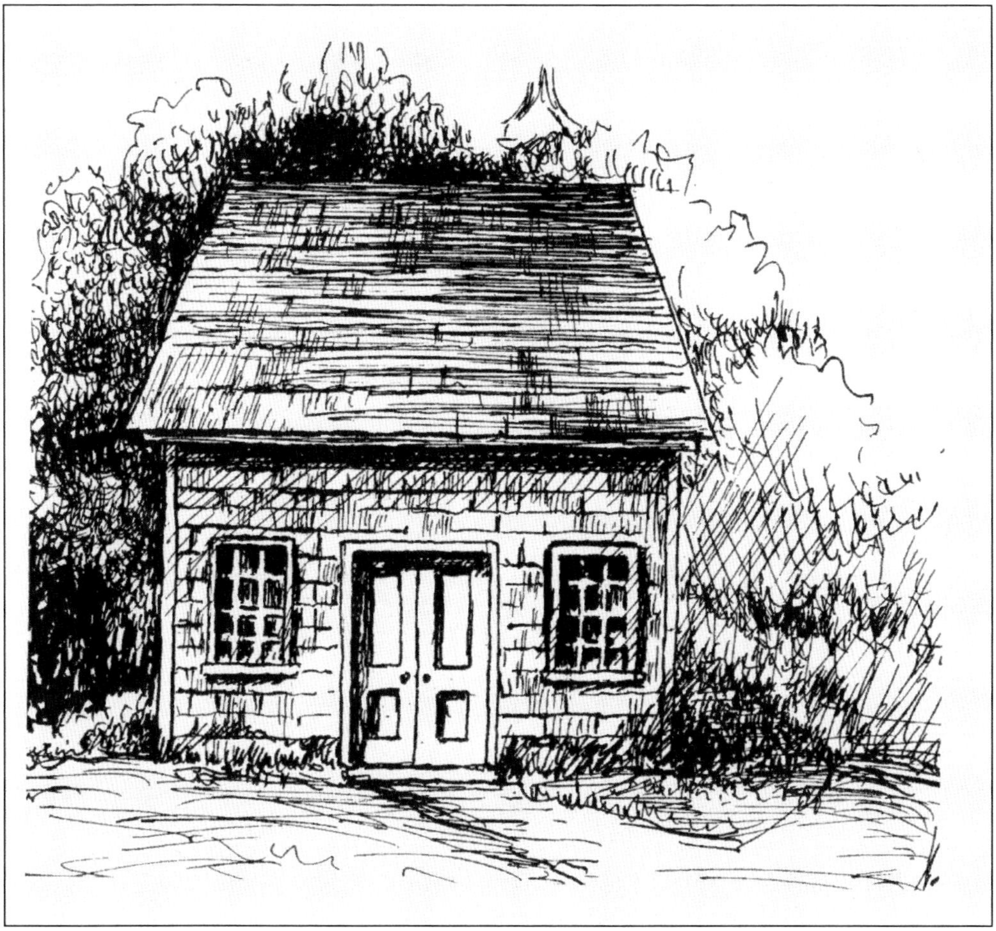

The Quakers built their first meetinghouse in the area between 1753 and 1754, under the supervision of Abel Weeks, John Cornell, and Moses Quinby. The small building was located in the area of North Castle that the Quakers called Shapiqua, and it became the nucleus of the first village of Chappaqua. This sketch shows what the original meetinghouse may have looked like before it was enlarged. (Drawing by Toni Hutin.)

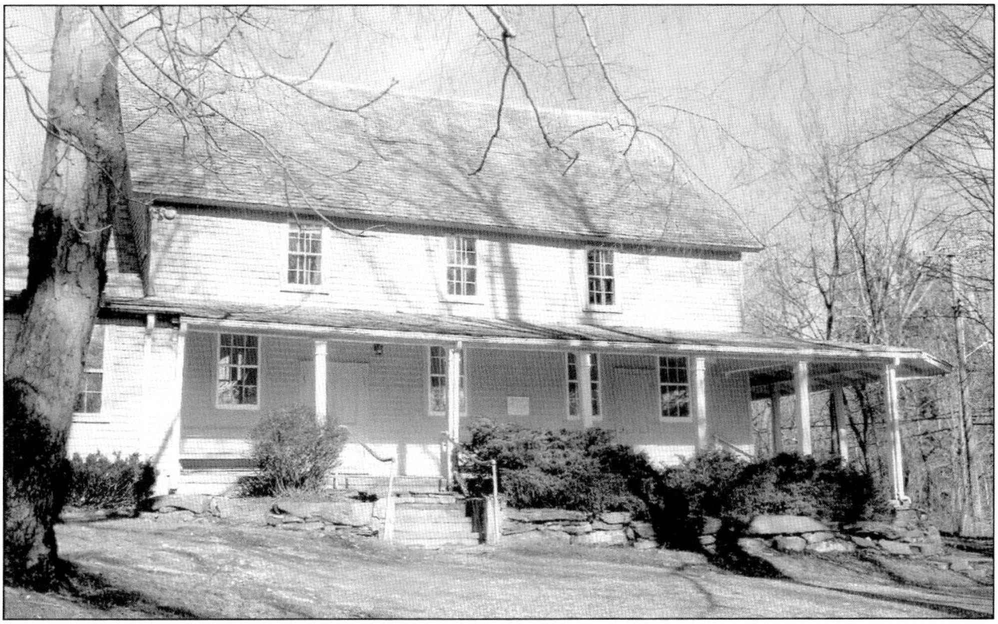

The earliest documented building in New Castle is the Chappaqua Friends Meeting House, which was enlarged after the Revolution and still exists, together with several of the early Quaker homes along Quaker Street (Route 120). Outside, it resembles a simple farmhouse, except that it has two front doors. Formerly, men and women entered the building by separate entrances. (Photograph by Gray Williams.)

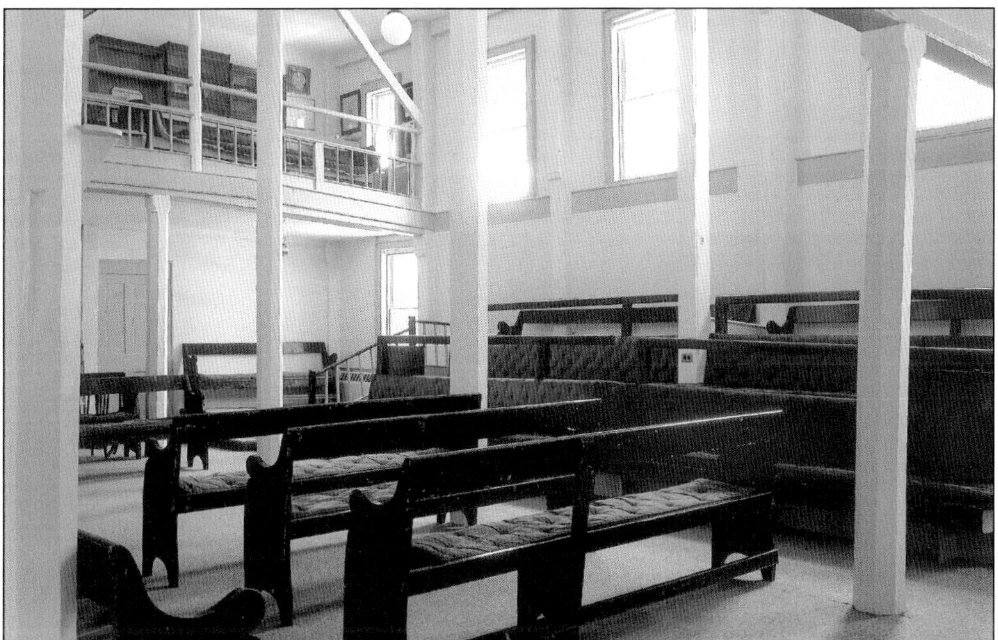

Inside the meetinghouse, men and women no longer sit apart or conduct separate business meetings. Otherwise the interior is arranged much as it was in the 1800s. Most of the congregation sits on plain benches situated on the floor. The few raised rows in the back are reserved for meeting officers and other "weighty" members. (Photograph by Gray Williams.)

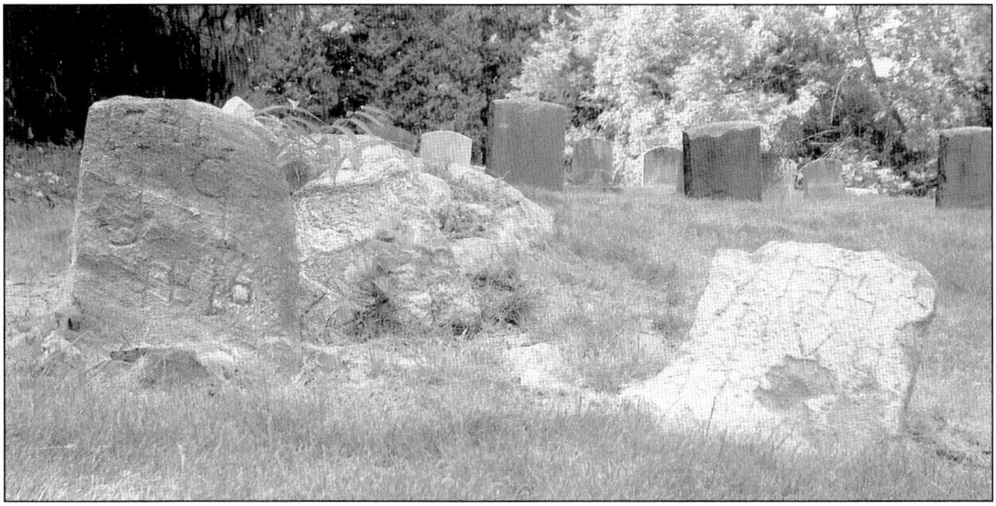

The meetinghouse is located within an even earlier graveyard. Its two acres were donated in 1745 by John Reynolds, from his Quaker Street farm. The earliest grave markers were oblong pieces of fieldstone, some unmarked, some inscribed with initials, and some identified with initials and dates. The earliest dated stones are those of Phoebe Vail Quinby (1745–1776) and her husband, Josiah Quinby (1741–1816), whose farm was at the intersection of Millwood and Seven Bridges Roads. Some Quaker families have monuments for several generations: Carpenter (20 monuments), Haight (30), Hallock (15), Halstead (19), Kipp (42), Pierce (30), Quinby (25), Sarles (16), Thorn (26), Tompkins (12), Underhill (22), Van Tassell (12), Washburn (30), and Weeks (14). (Photograph by Gray Williams.)

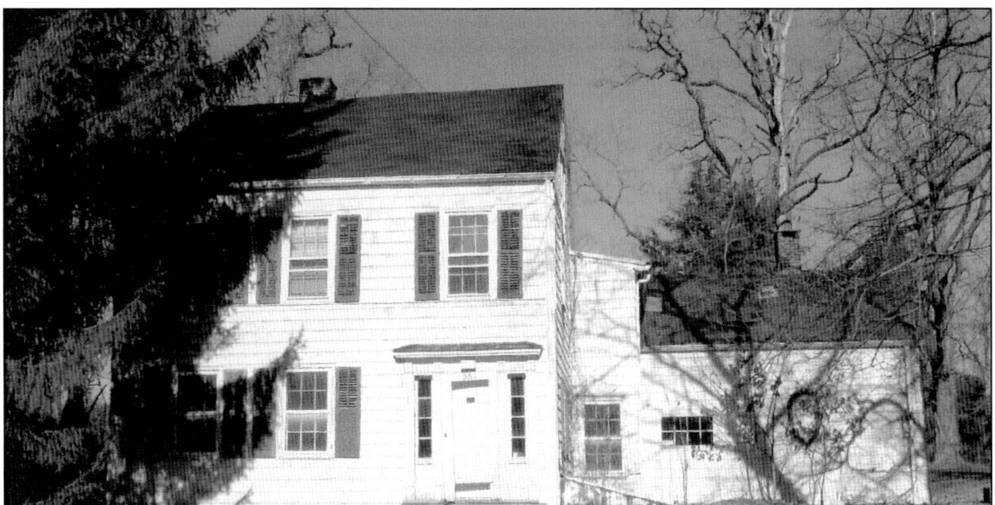

Most Colonial period Quaker homes have been lost or so altered that their original forms are hard to envision. The Haight-Sutton farmhouse on Whippoorwill Road is an exception. The low section (right), with a keeping room and a kitchen on the first floor and a sleeping loft above, appears to have been the original home of Caleb Haight (1730–1820) as early as 1758. The two-story wing existed by the date of Haight's will in 1817. The farmstead remained in the family until the death of Haight's grandson in 1872, when it was acquired by Haight descendant Walter Sutton. It was the last working farm in New Castle until the 1990s, when it was sold and subdivided. The house and its ancient trees have been preserved. (Photograph by Gray Williams.)

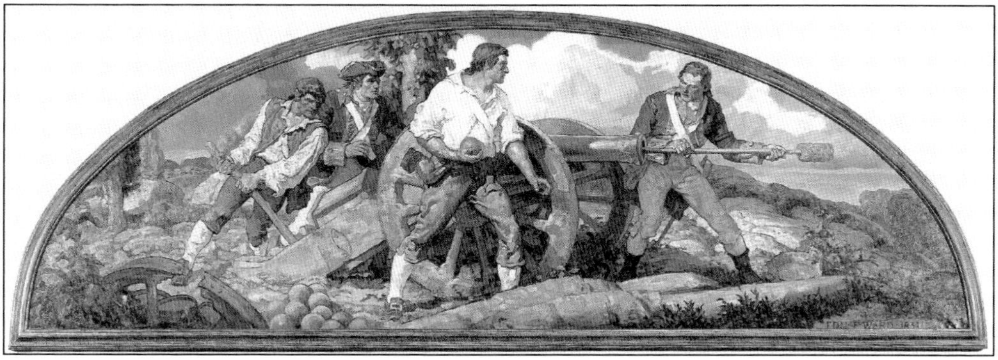

After the indecisive Battle of White Plains in late October 1776, Gen. George Washington's troops retreated north through North Castle. Some of his sick and wounded soldiers were likely cared for in the Quaker meetinghouse in Chappaqua and others in St. George's Episcopal Church in Mount Kisco. Sutton Reynolds Jr. provided the only documentary evidence of these events in his 1865 reminiscences: "In the time of the Revolution War the matrician [American] army left wite plains and march north. They stuck their tents around the meeting house for a hospital and bayed [buried] the dead in north side of meeting house." Physical evidence was found during construction of the horse shed north of the meetinghouse; fragments of bone and uniform buttons were unearthed. (Mural by Edmund F. Ward, White Plains Public Library; photograph by John Maggiotto for Westchester County Historical Society.)

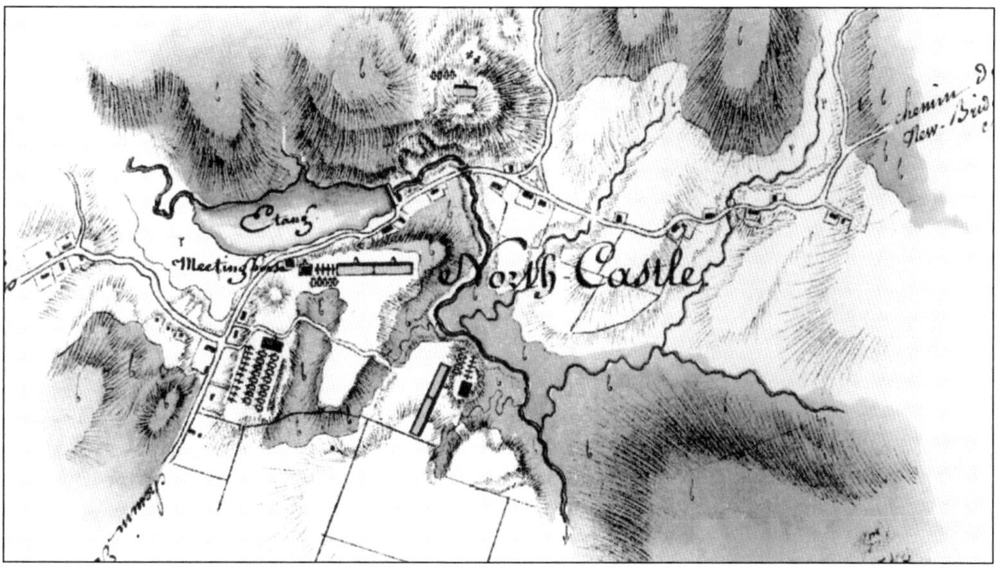

The most important Revolutionary event to take place in New Castle was not a battle, but a meeting. In the summer of 1781, Washington summoned from Rhode Island General Rochambeau's 5,000 French troops to join him in a campaign against the British. The French marched across Connecticut to North Castle Corners and encamped near the site of the present Northern Westchester Medical Center. On July 5, Washington met and reviewed the troops, who then marched south to a joint encampment near Hartsdale. The British thought an attack on New York City was imminent. But the troops doubled back to Verplanck, crossed the Hudson, and proceeded to Virginia. There they joined Lafayette's forces, and besieged the British at Yorktown, forcing the surrender of General Cornwallis and effectively ending the war. The water shown here was once a lake, since drained and transformed into Leonard Park. (Map from Rochambeau officer's journal.)

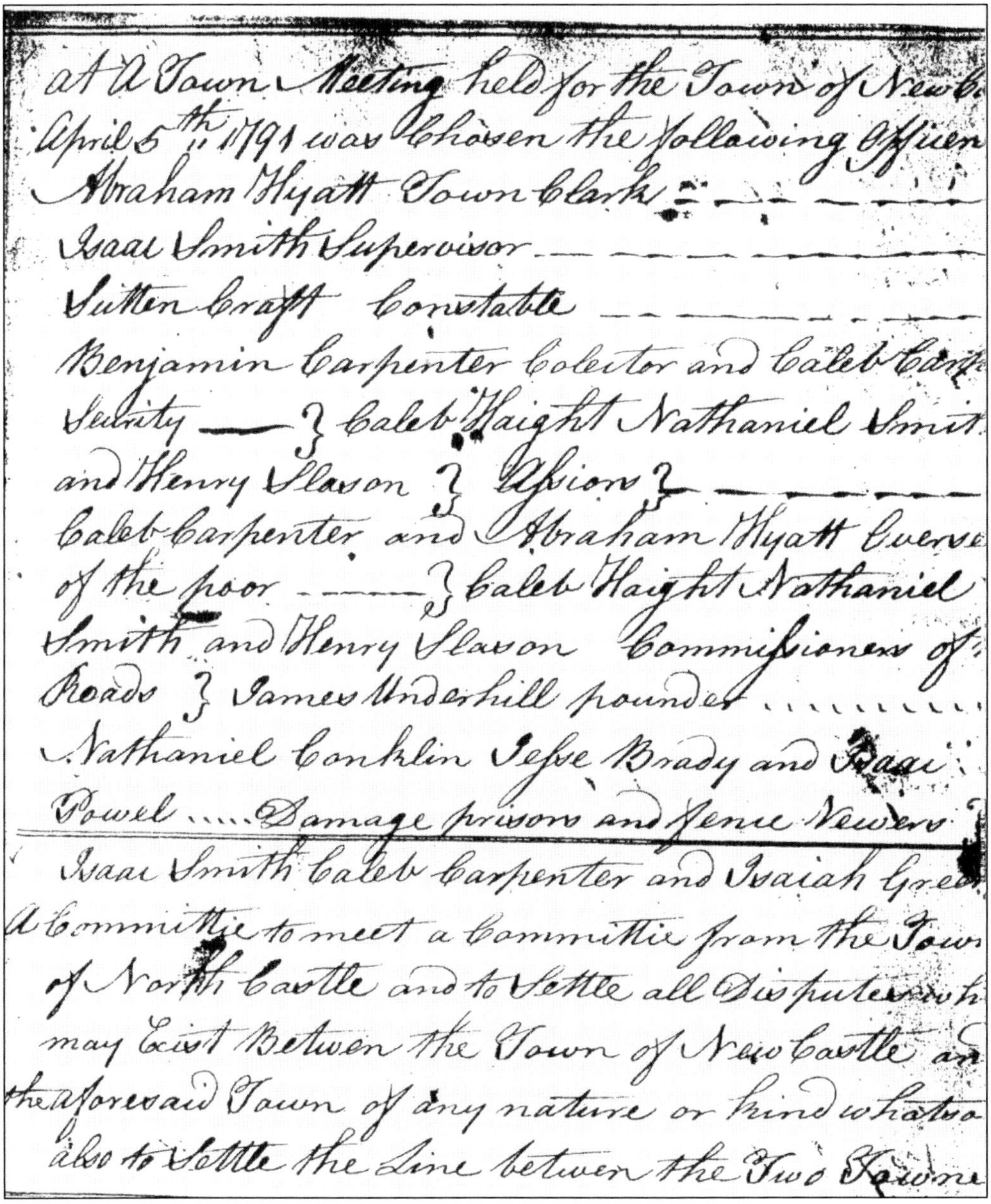
at A Town Meeting held for the Town of New C
April 5th 1791 was Chosen the following Officers
Abraham Hyatt Town Clark
Isaac Smith Supervisor
Sutten Craft Constable
Benjamin Carpenter Colector and Caleb Carp
Security — } Caleb Haight Nathaniel Smit
and Henry Slason } Assesors }
Caleb Carpenter and Abraham Hyatt Overse
of the poor — } Caleb Haight Nathaniel
Smith and Henry Slason Commissioners of
Roads } James Underhill pounder
Nathaniel Conklin Jesse Brady and Isaac
Powel ..... Damage prisors and fence Viewers
Isaac Smith Caleb Carpenter and Isaiah Gree
A Committie to meet a Committie from the Town
of North Castle and to Settle all Disputes wh
may Exist Betwen the Town of New Castle an
the aforesaid Town of any nature or kind whatso
also to Settle the Line betwen the Two Towns

In 1791, the state legislature divided North Castle roughly in half, and the northern portion became New Castle. On April 5, New Castle held its first annual town meeting and elected officers for the coming year. Abraham Hyatt was elected "Clark" (clerk) and Isaac Smith, supervisor. Smith, a physician, was reelected in 1792, but his tenure was cut short. Also a deputy sheriff for Westchester County, Smith was fatally shot while trying to arrest John Ryer, a "worthless character . . . wanted on some trivial offense." Ryer was apprehended in Canada, brought back to Westchester, tried and convicted at Bedford Courthouse, and hanged. An "Extory" (extraordinary) town meeting was held on May 26, 1792, "for the Purpose of Chuseing A Supervisor in the place of Doctor Isaac Smith Decesed."

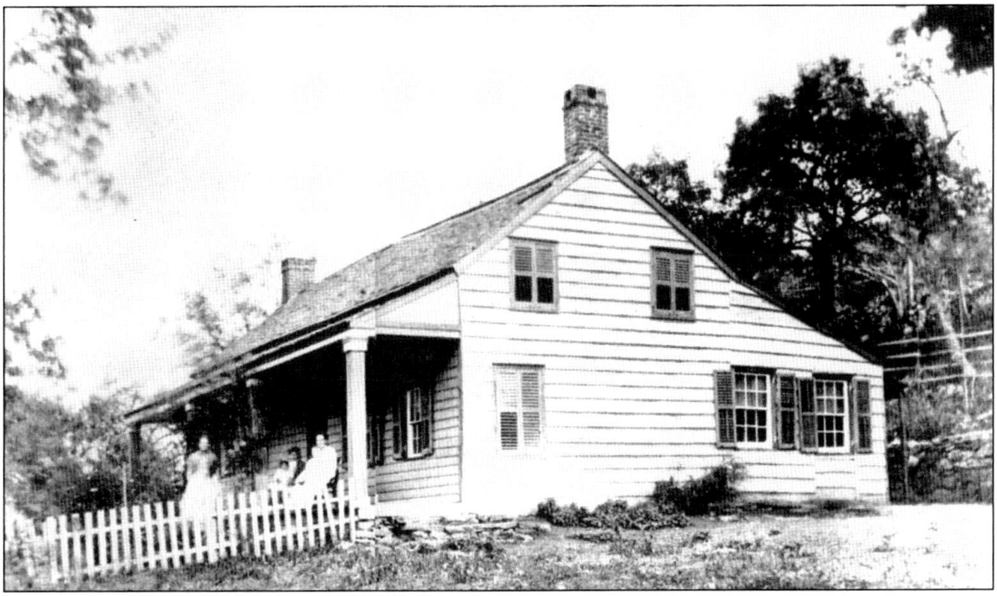

For several decades, it was customary to hold annual town meetings in the public rooms of taverns. The Aaron Mabee house and tavern on Roaring Brook Road was the location for town meetings from 1811 to 1819. Its architectural style, with the roof extending to form a front porch, suggests that it may originally have been built in Colonial times. The house has since been enlarged, but the exterior has been changed relatively little. (Courtesy of George and Janet Short.)

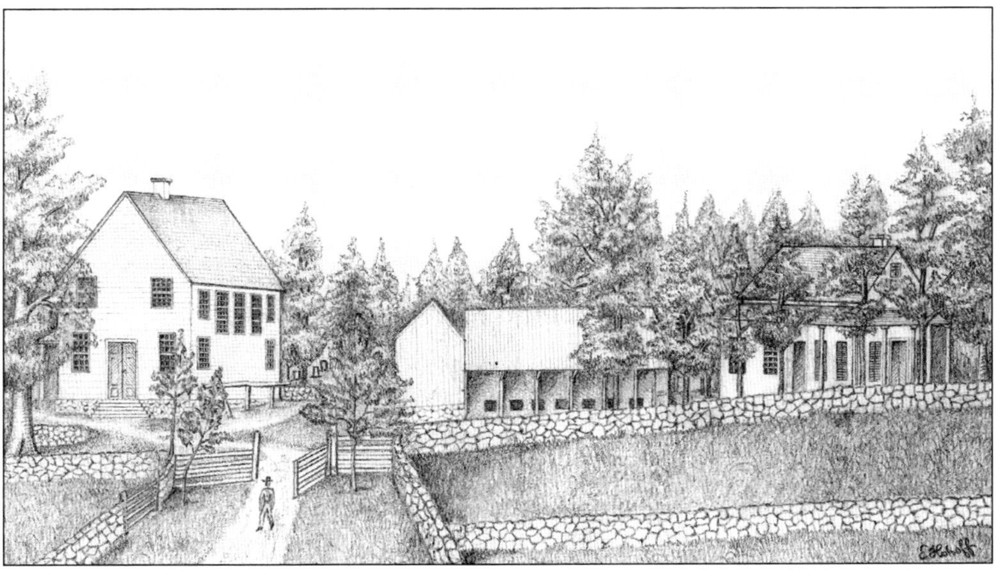

In 1828, a doctrinal conflict among the Religious Society of Friends caused a division between two separate groups, the Orthodox and the Hicksites (named after Long Island preacher Elias Hicks). The Chappaqua meetinghouse continued in the possession of the Hicksites, while the Orthodox built a second meetinghouse at the northern end of the graveyard. Between the two buildings, a single horse shed served both congregations. In the late 1880s, the Orthodox meetinghouse was taken down and moved to King Street, near the center of Chappaqua. The schism finally ended after World War II, and the Orthodox meetinghouse is now the Village Nursery School. (Courtesy of Chappaqua Friends Meeting.)

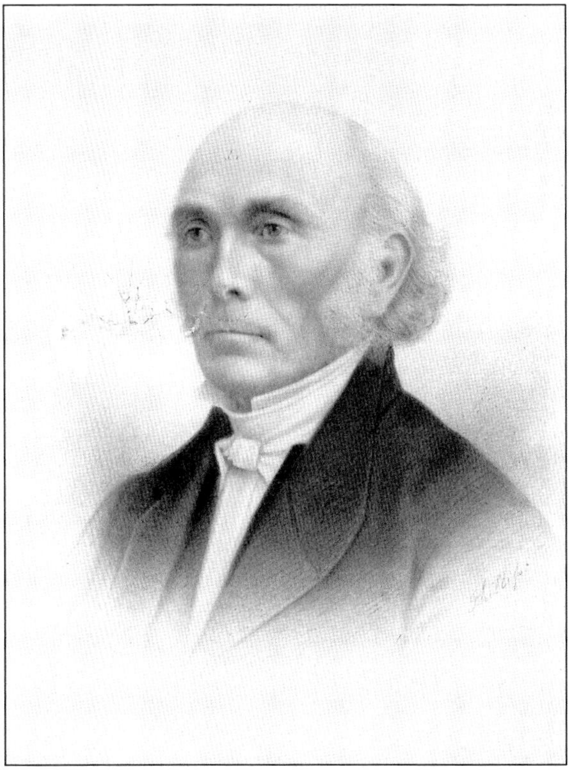

Moses Pierce (1816–1886) and his wife, Esther Pierce (1815–1900), were prominent and active members of the Chappaqua meeting. Moses Pierce scrupulously followed the Quaker Peace Testimony and as a young man was imprisoned briefly for refusing to serve in the militia. Like Quakers generally, the Pierces opposed slavery and, according to tradition, maintained an Underground Railway station at their farm on Bedford Road, just over the New Castle line in Pleasantville. They were also founders of the local temperance society. (Courtesy of Chappaqua Friends Meeting.)

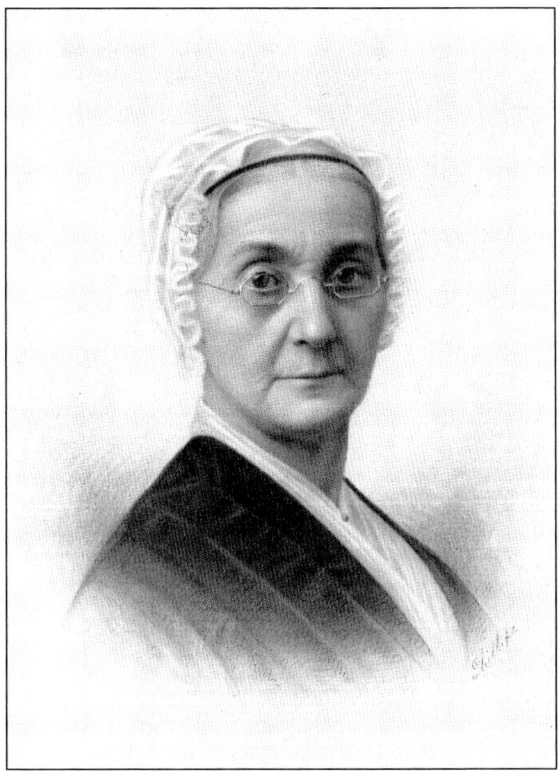

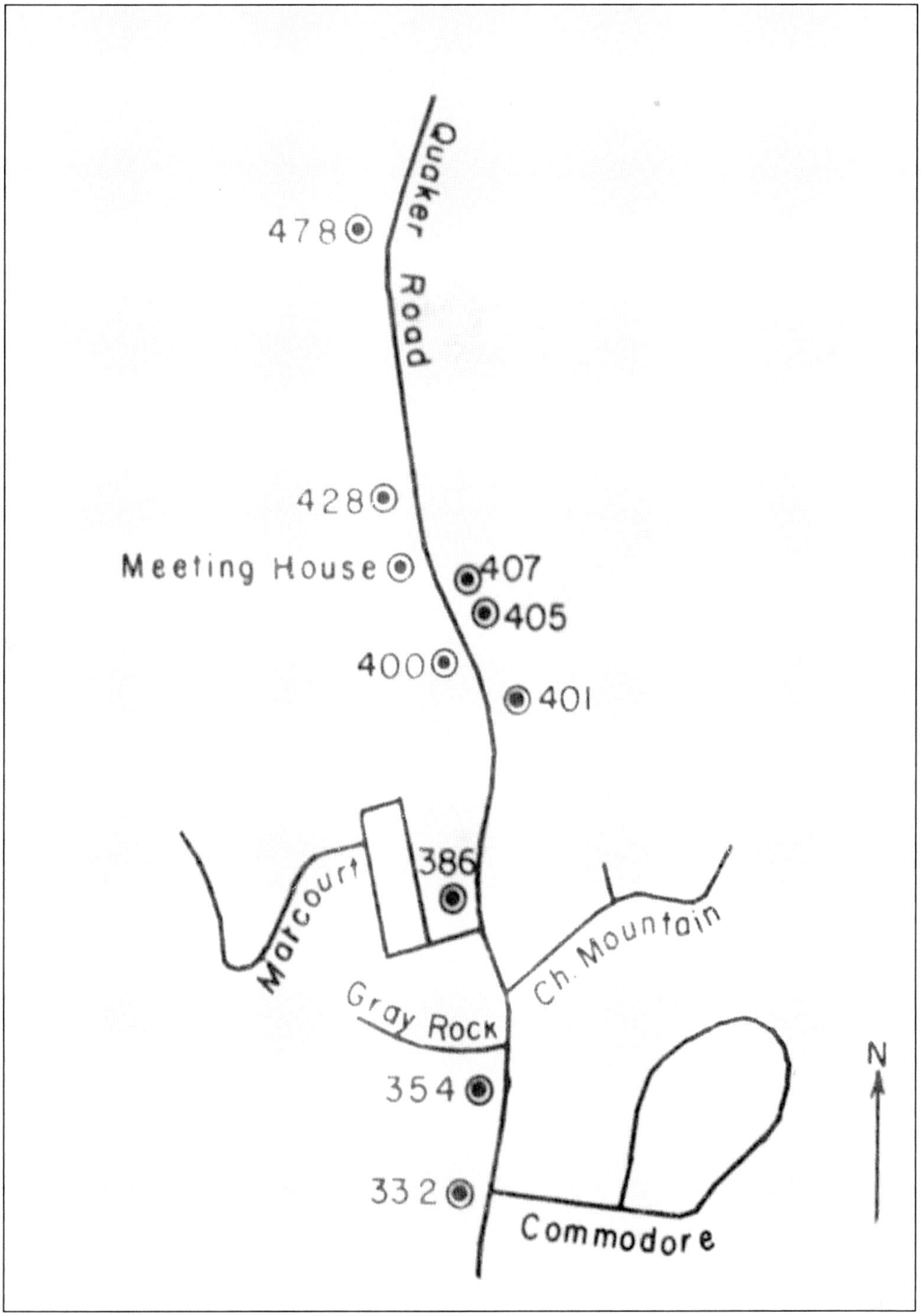

The original hamlet of Chappaqua was centered near the Quaker meetinghouse on Quaker Street. Several of its buildings comprise a historic district that is listed on the National Register of Historic Places. All of the houses have been enlarged or altered over the years, but they nevertheless give a vivid impression of the modest, primarily Quaker village in the early 1800s.

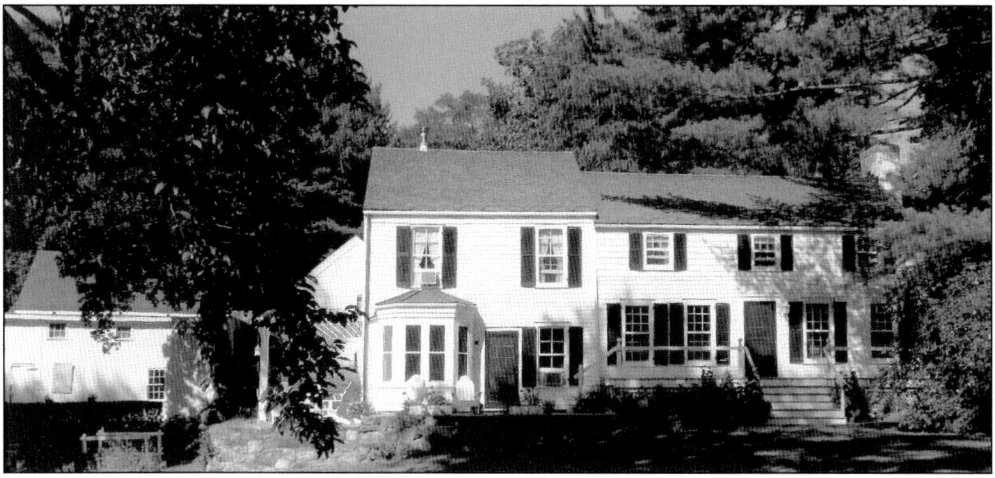

The Reynolds-Carpenter farmhouse (332 Quaker Street) was built by Sutton Reynolds Jr.'s grandfather. Reynolds wrote, "About the year 1698 or 9 my grandfather was born his name John Reynolds his wife name Hannah they moved from Long Island about the year 1740 and settled near mill pond he bough severl hundred acres of new land from the pond [now a wetland] up Shappaqua street to the North road that lead to Sing Sing." The farm extended from Kipp Street north on both sides of Quaker Street at least as far as the Quaker cemetery and meetinghouse, for around 1745, John Reynolds donated these two acres to the Religious Society of Friends. In 1846, Sutton Reynolds sold part of the farm, including this house, to Robert Carpenter, whose family occupied it for almost a century. The oldest part is to the right. The other half was added in 1850. Both have been modified over the years. (Photograph by Gray Williams.)

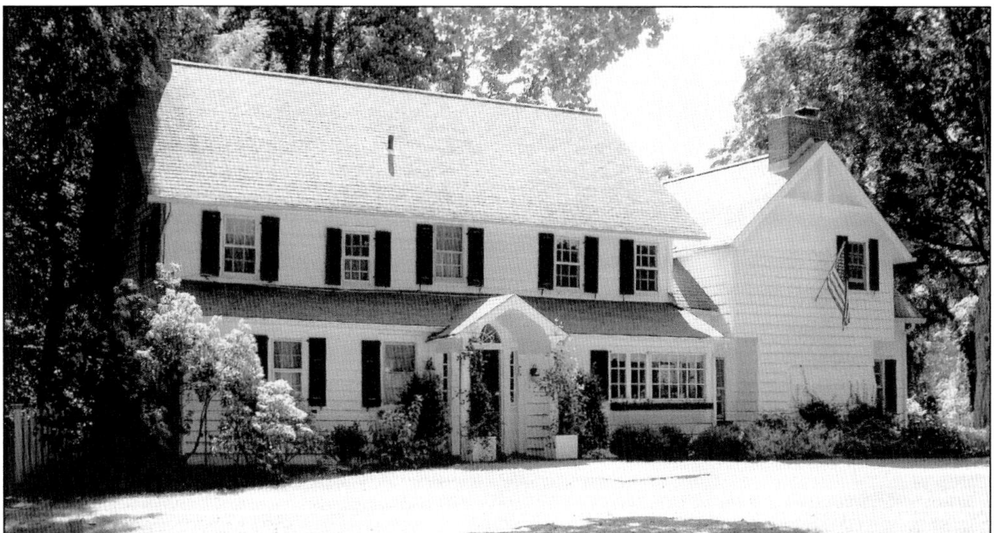

The Sutton Reynolds house (354 Quaker Street) is the second of two houses located on the old Reynolds farm. Part of the house—probably the part to the far left—was built in the late 1700s. It eventually became the home of Sutton Reynolds Jr. In 1869, the property, including land on the other side of Quaker Street, was bought by Alfred Underhill, who had four successive wives, the last of whom became his widow. He also kept a flock of sheep, guarded by shepherds, on the western slope of Chappaqua Mountain, where Chappaqua Mountain Road and Cross Ridge Road are now. (Photograph by Gray Williams.)

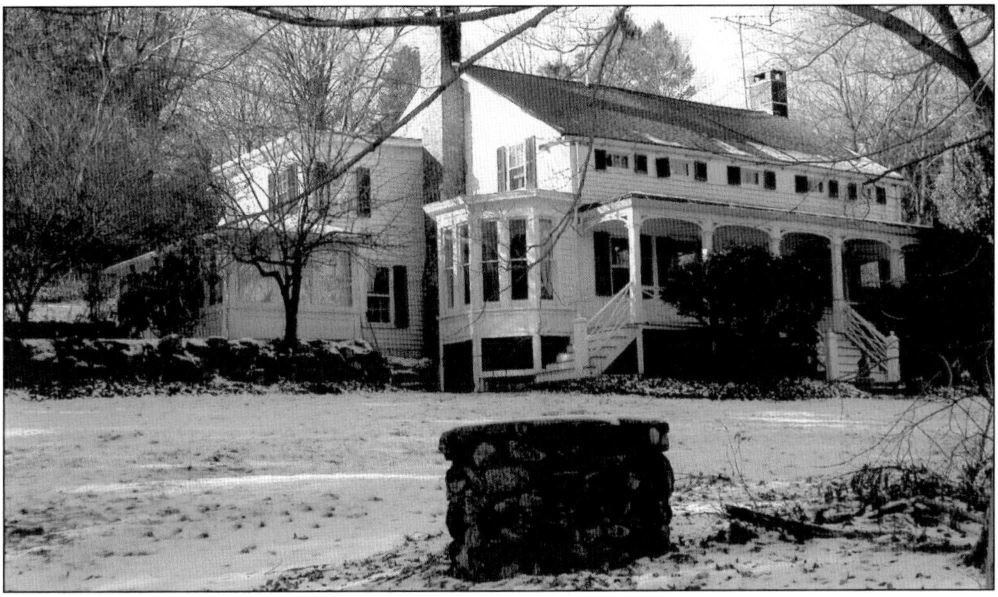

The Thorn-Dodge house (386 Quaker Road) was built in two stages, at very different times. The small original house, probably built before the Revolution, once stood by the well close to the road. The owner was Elnathan Thorn, who died in 1789. Henry Dodge, son of Thomas Dodge, acquired the property in 1848, and in 1852, he and his wife, Rebeccah, built a large Victorian house farther back on the hillside and moved the original cottage to form a rear wing. (Photograph by Jean Cameron-Smith.)

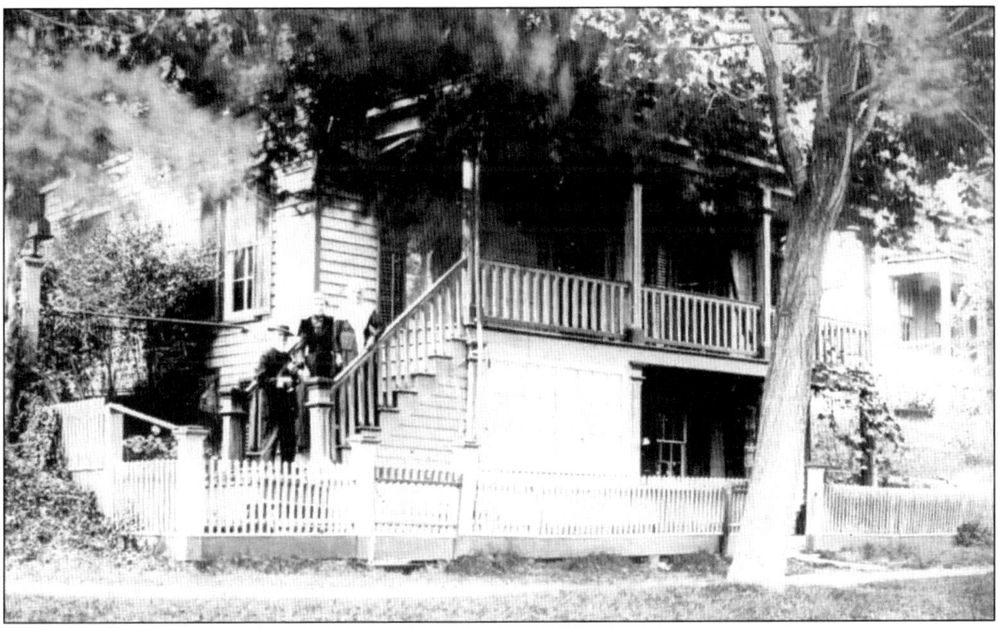

The Samuel Allen currying shop (400 Quaker Road), for the processing of hides into leather, is mentioned in a neighbor's deed of 1825. This photograph from about 1900 shows it once had a two-story front porch, an architectural feature that was characteristic of Colonial houses built on a hillside, with the main living quarters on the second floor. The ground floor might be used for a kitchen or for storage, or, as here, for a workshop. (Courtesy of Albert V. Hutin Jr.)

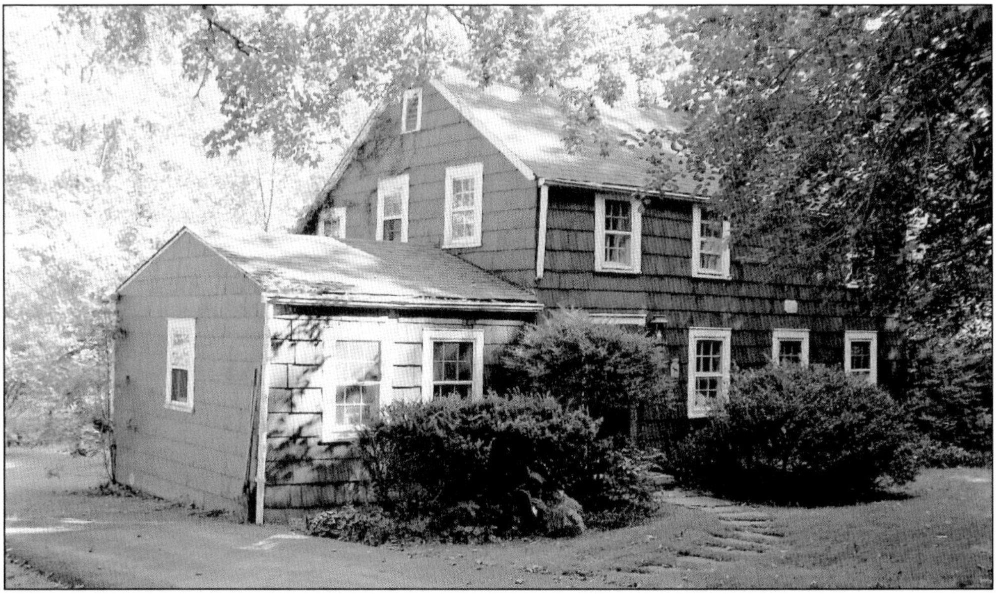

The Old Barn (401 Quaker Road) was built on the Samuel Allen farm in the early 19th century. The date 1833 is carved into a stone at the entrance. The sturdiness of the structure and its low but solid cellar suggest it may have served as a living space for human beings as well as a barn for animals. It was enlarged and converted entirely to a home early in the 20th century. (Photograph by Gray Williams.)

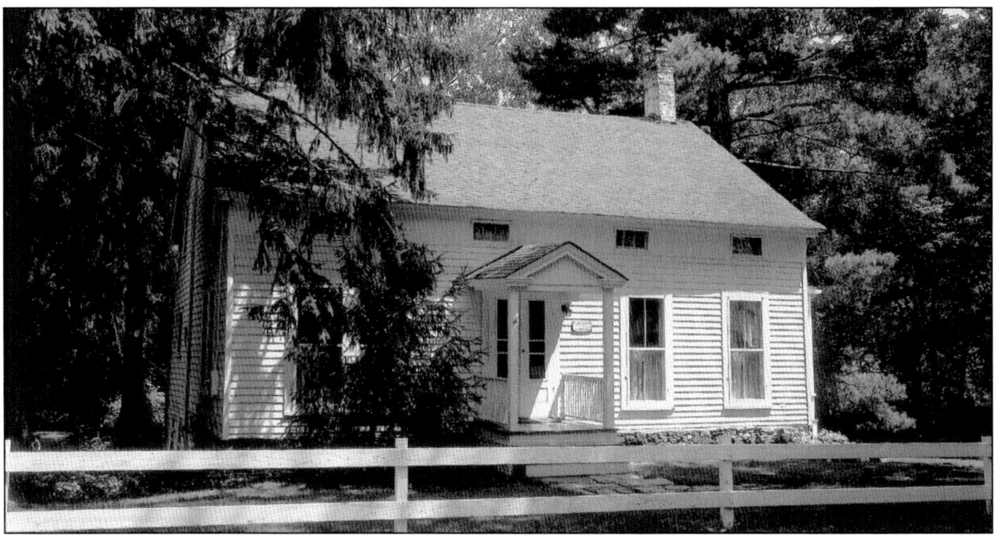

The Samuel Allen house (405 Quaker Road), built around 1830, was originally on a 63-acre farm that Samuel Allen (1794–1880) purchased in stages from the Underhill family, starting about 1824. Like many other farms of the period, it contained a complex of buildings: this house, the nearby currying shop, a barn, and a tenant house. The cultivated areas included an orchard and a nursery garden that Allen named, poetically, Ulwine Sylvia. One curious feature of this house is that it has a tree inside: a tall timber, complete with bark and neatly concealed in a casing, with the house built around it. The small, second-story eyebrow windows, wide-plank floors, and hand-hewn beams in the cellar and attic are typical of early Federal houses. (Photograph by Gray Williams.)

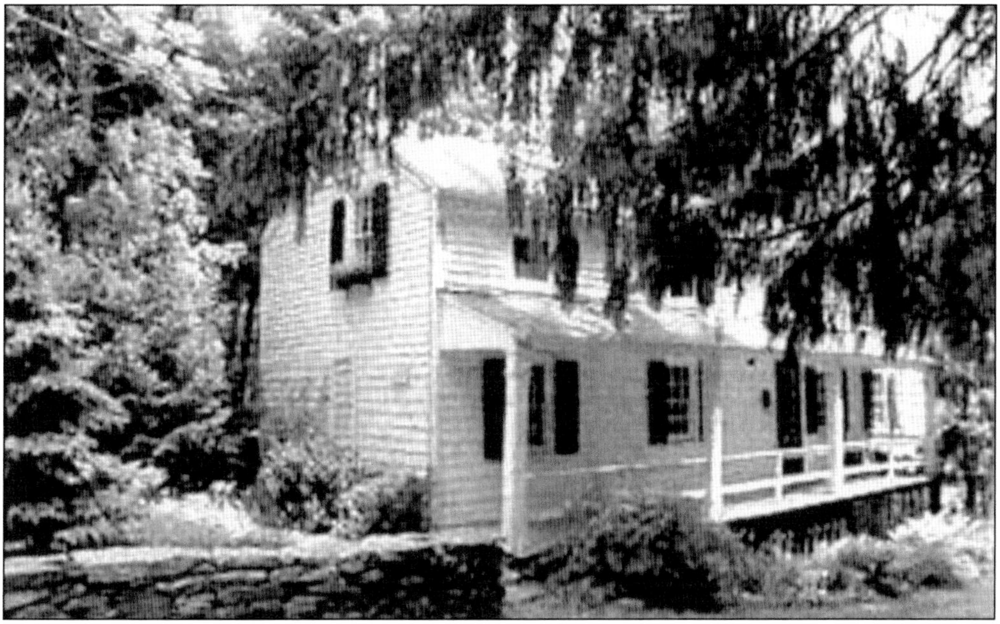

The Allen tenant house (407 Quaker Road), located close to the main Samuel Allen house, is an example of the so-called "tenant houses" frequently referred to in early town minutes. Such auxiliary buildings could be used to house members of the family or hired workers, or they might be rented out for extra income. This house appears to have been built about 1850 on the foundation of a much earlier structure.

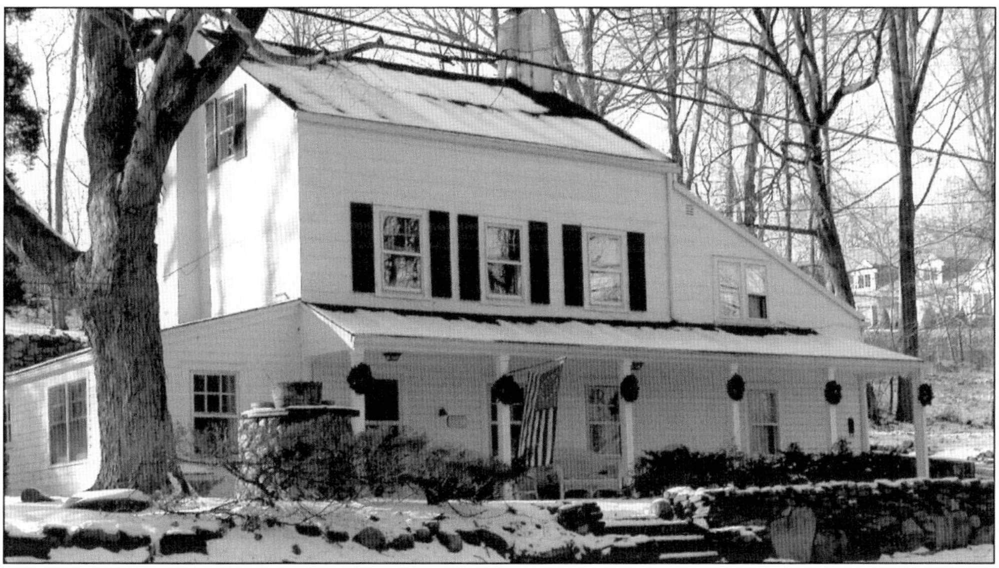

The Thomas Dodge house (428 Quaker Road) may have been built in the 1700s, and can be traced back to one of Chappaqua's oldest Quaker families, the Dodges—specifically Thomas Dodge (1778–1856) and his wife, Hannah (1779–after 1856). Dodge was a farmer, a cabinetmaker, the caretaker of the neighboring Quaker cemetery, and (perhaps most important) a coffin maker. He and his descendants kept a *Book of Deaths*, which listed coffin commissions by date of burial for some 2,300 individuals, mostly Quakers. It is one of the most valuable primary documents of New Castle history. (Photograph by Jean Cameron-Smith.)

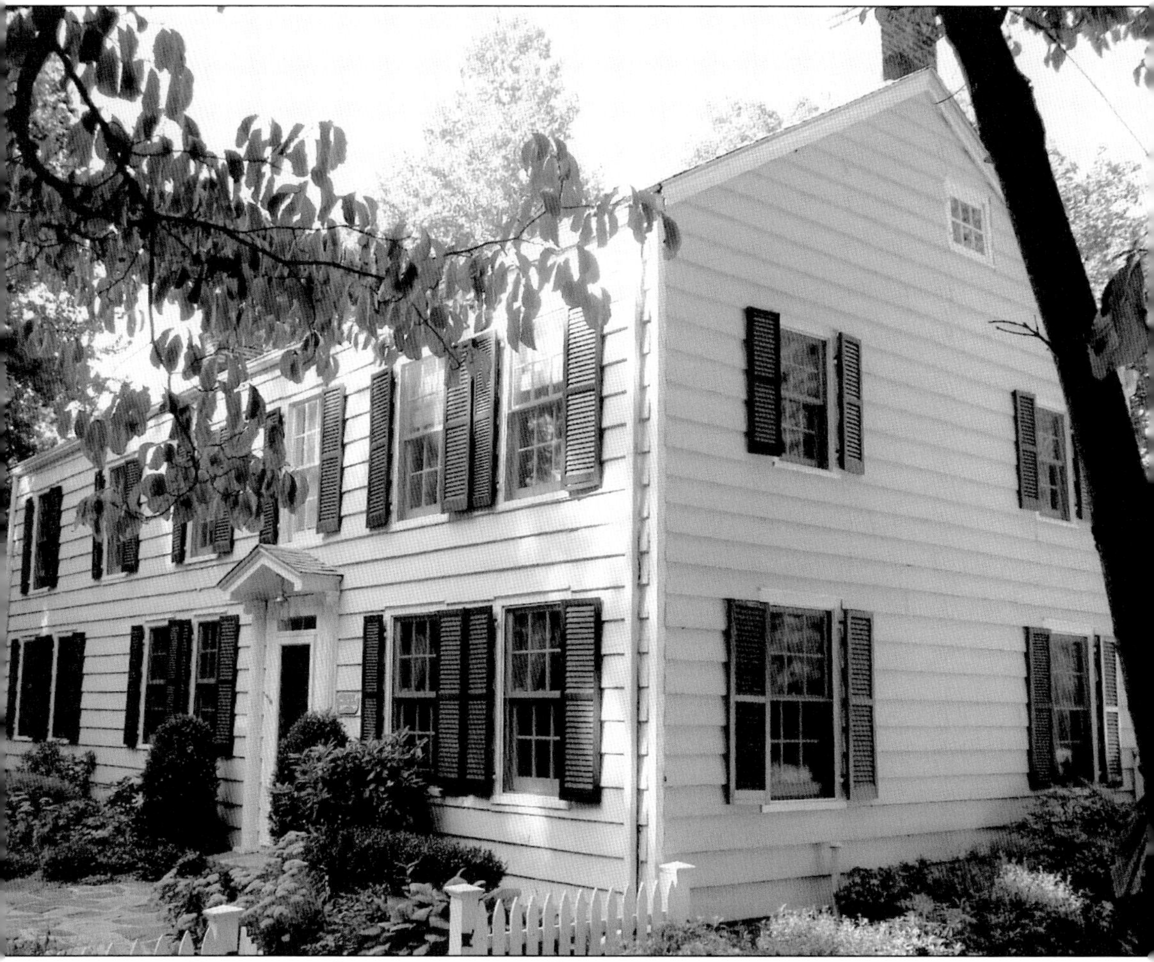

Originally just a small cottage, Stony Hollow Farm (478 Quaker Road) may have been built before 1823, when a reference to "Stony Holler" appears in town records. The name suggests that it was probably not the most fertile farmland. The property belonged to the Bradys, who had large holdings along Quaker Street as far as Hardscrabble Road. It had apple orchards in the back valley and a stream that was dammed to make a pond. Expanded over the years, the house was owned from 1855 to 1900 by Quakers Elijah Collins (1813–1900) and his wife, Eliza (1815–1896). Later occupant Edwin Bedell (editor of the local newspaper, the *Item*) found arrowheads when plowing and speculated that American Indians had once gathered near the stream to hunt the animals that came down to water. (Photograph by Gray Williams.)

Two

MAKING A LIVING

From Colonial times, the economy of New Castle went through four phases. During the first phase, most families made their living on self-sufficient subsistence farms. There were a few stores to provide supplies that could not be raised or made locally, plus a couple of blacksmith shops to fashion tools and nails and horseshoes, sawmills to turn logs into building lumber, and gristmills to grind grain into meal and flour. But by and large, the pioneer farmers produced most of what they needed and sold relatively little to outside markets.

Several of these farms were extensive, comprising of hundreds of acres. But the farmhouses were small, and the local lifestyle tended to be simple and arduous. Characteristic relics of this era are the rough stone walls, still a common feature of the landscape. They were used to mark property boundaries, to anchor fences, and to dispose of the ubiquitous rocks in the glacial soil so that fields could be plowed or mowed.

The second phase was triggered by the arrival of the railroad in 1846. Subsistence farms became market farms, whose main products were milk and apples. The center of Chappaqua shifted from Quaker Street to the railroad crossing, where a hotel and several stores were established. In the late 1800s, a few factories were built, such as the Spencer Optical Manufacturing Company in what is now Mount Kisco and the Chappaqua Shoe Factory on North Greeley Avenue.

In the third phase, agriculture declined and many farms were bought up and consolidated into large estates by wealthy New York City businessmen. This period was transitory, however. In the 1900s, virtually all these estates were sold and subdivided for residential development.

The fourth phase was the transformation of New Castle into a suburb, first of New York City and then of satellite centers in the metropolitan area. During this period the town also became the home of the *Reader's Digest*.

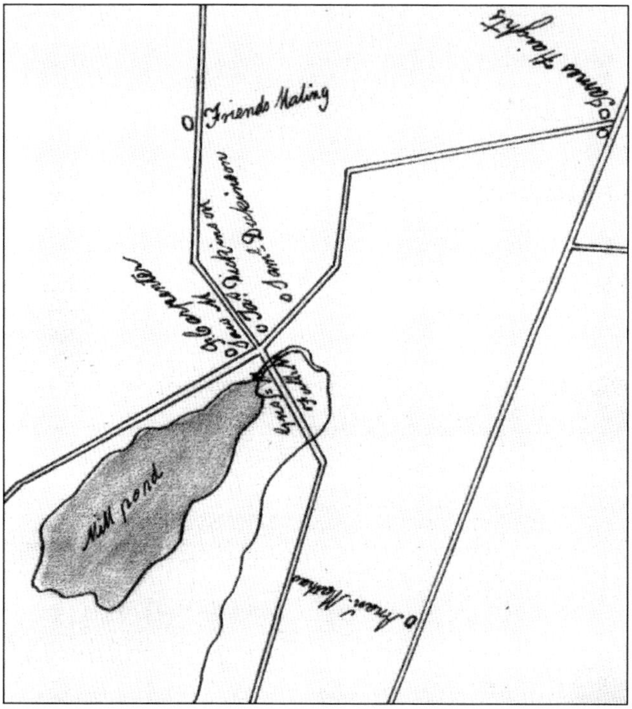

There was very little industry in early New Castle. The main exceptions were water-powered mills, which were in use from Colonial times. This schematic map of 1797 shows three such facilities near the intersection of Quaker and Kipp Streets, all making use of water from a large lake that used to exist there. There was a sawmill, a fulling mill (used in the finishing of wool fabric), and a gristmill. Such mills remained in operation until the late 1800s, when waterpower was finally supplanted by coal-fueled steam. The lake was then drained, leaving only an extensive wetland in its place.

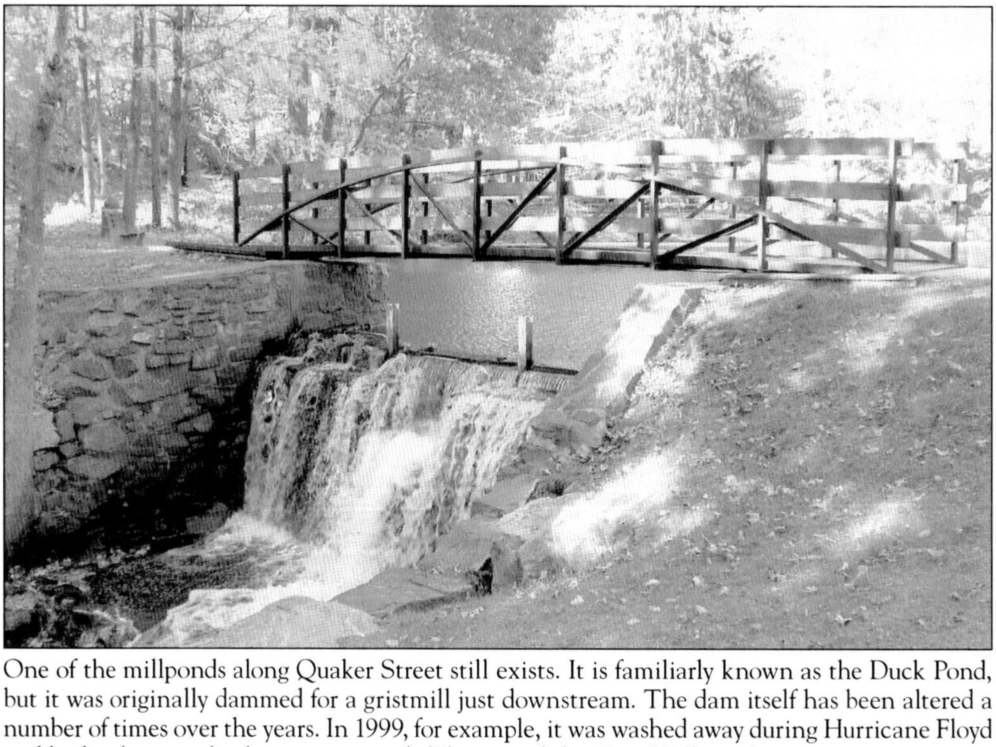

One of the millponds along Quaker Street still exists. It is familiarly known as the Duck Pond, but it was originally dammed for a gristmill just downstream. The dam itself has been altered a number of times over the years. In 1999, for example, it was washed away during Hurricane Floyd and had to be completely reconstructed. (Photograph by Gray Williams.)

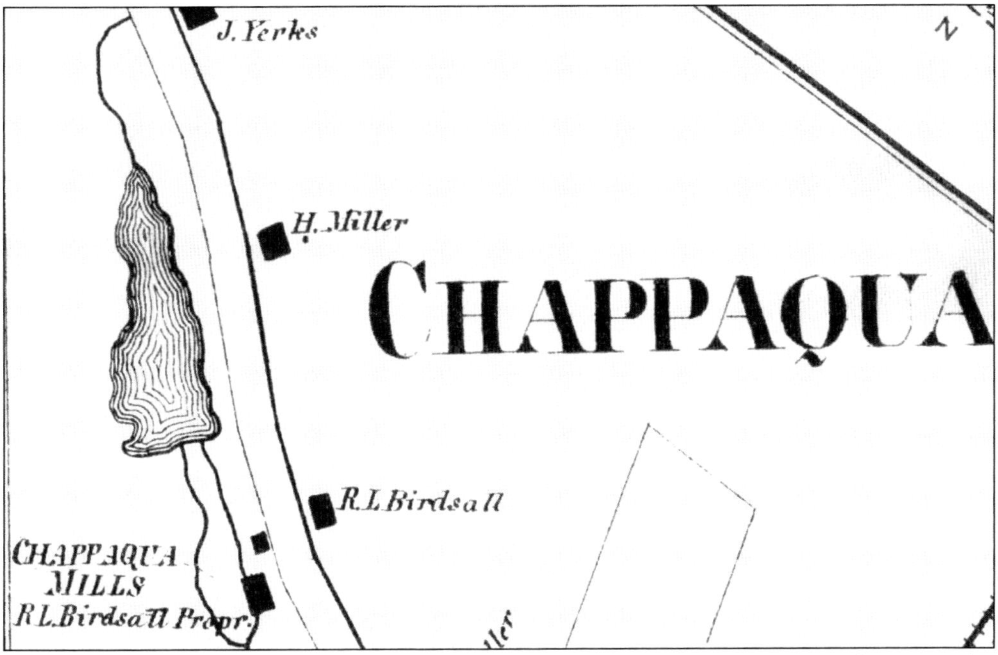

This detail from a map of 1867 shows how the mill drew water from the Duck Pond. Next to the main channel of the river below the dam, a second channel, or millrace, was created, running directly to the mill. A gate controlled the flow through the race—it was opened to set the mill wheel in motion and closed when the mill was not in use.

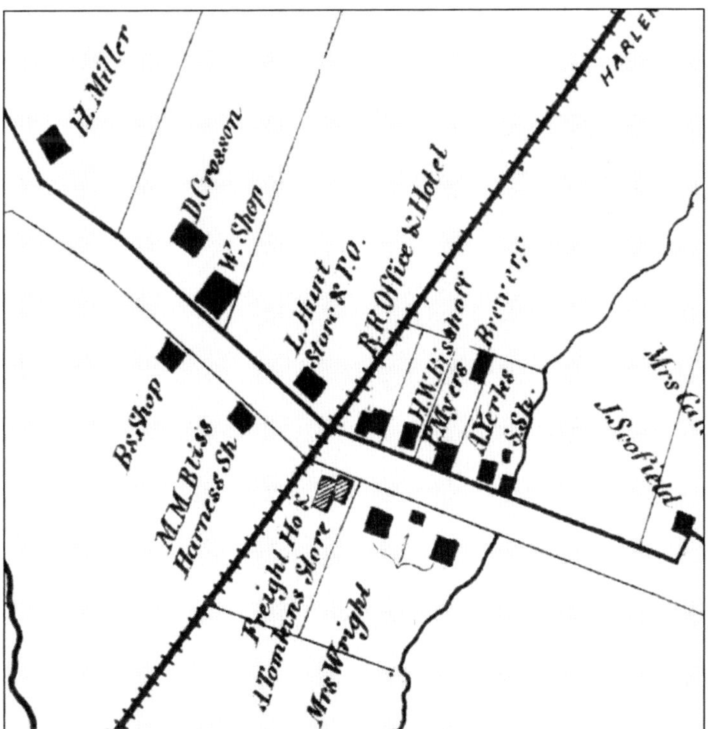

The arrival of the Harlem Valley Railroad in 1846 brought radical changes to the economy of New Castle. The center of Chappaqua moved a mile and a half down Quaker Street toward the railroad. A new Main Street was laid out, running east from the railroad crossing and then turning northeast up what is now King Street. New stores and other businesses arose on either side of the crossing.

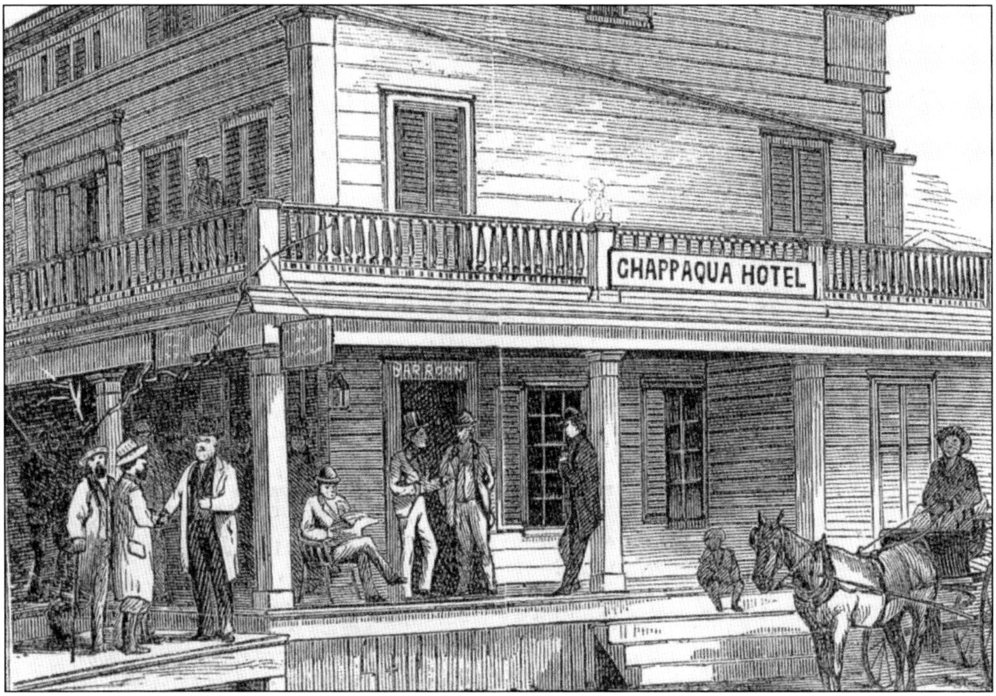

One of the earliest businesses in the new village was the Chappaqua Hotel, built next to the railroad on the north side of Main Street. It also served as the railroad station until the late 1860s, when a new station was built on North Greeley Avenue. The hotel, with its restaurant and barroom, became a major community center. Horace Greeley and his family often dined there and put up their visitors in its rooms.

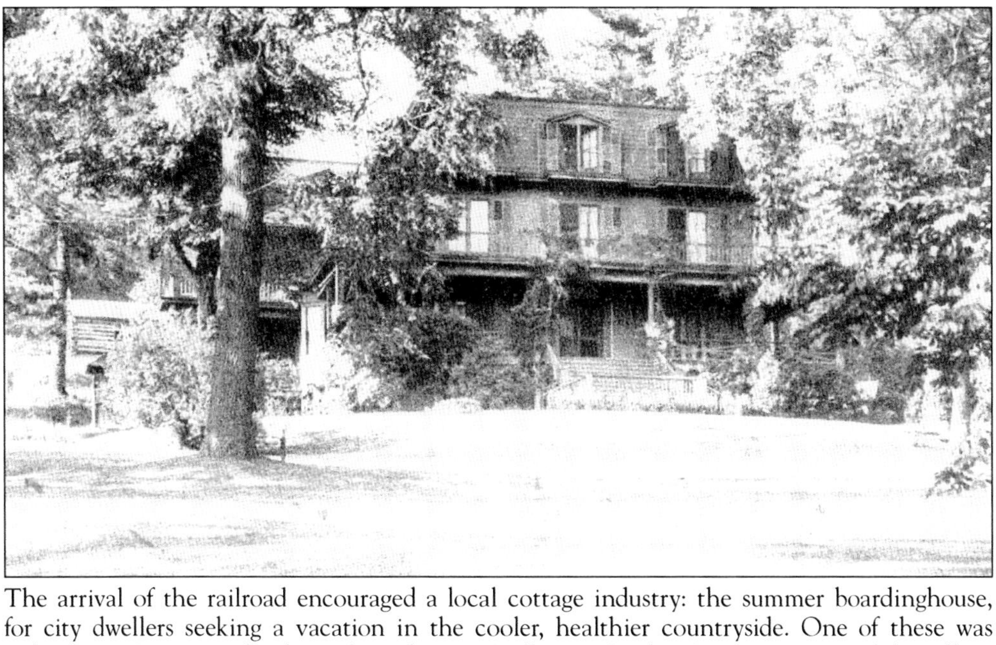

The arrival of the railroad encouraged a local cottage industry: the summer boardinghouse, for city dwellers seeking a vacation in the cooler, healthier countryside. One of these was Whispering Pines, run by the widow of Henry Miller, on Quaker Street just west of the village center. Part of this building complex still exists as a private home.

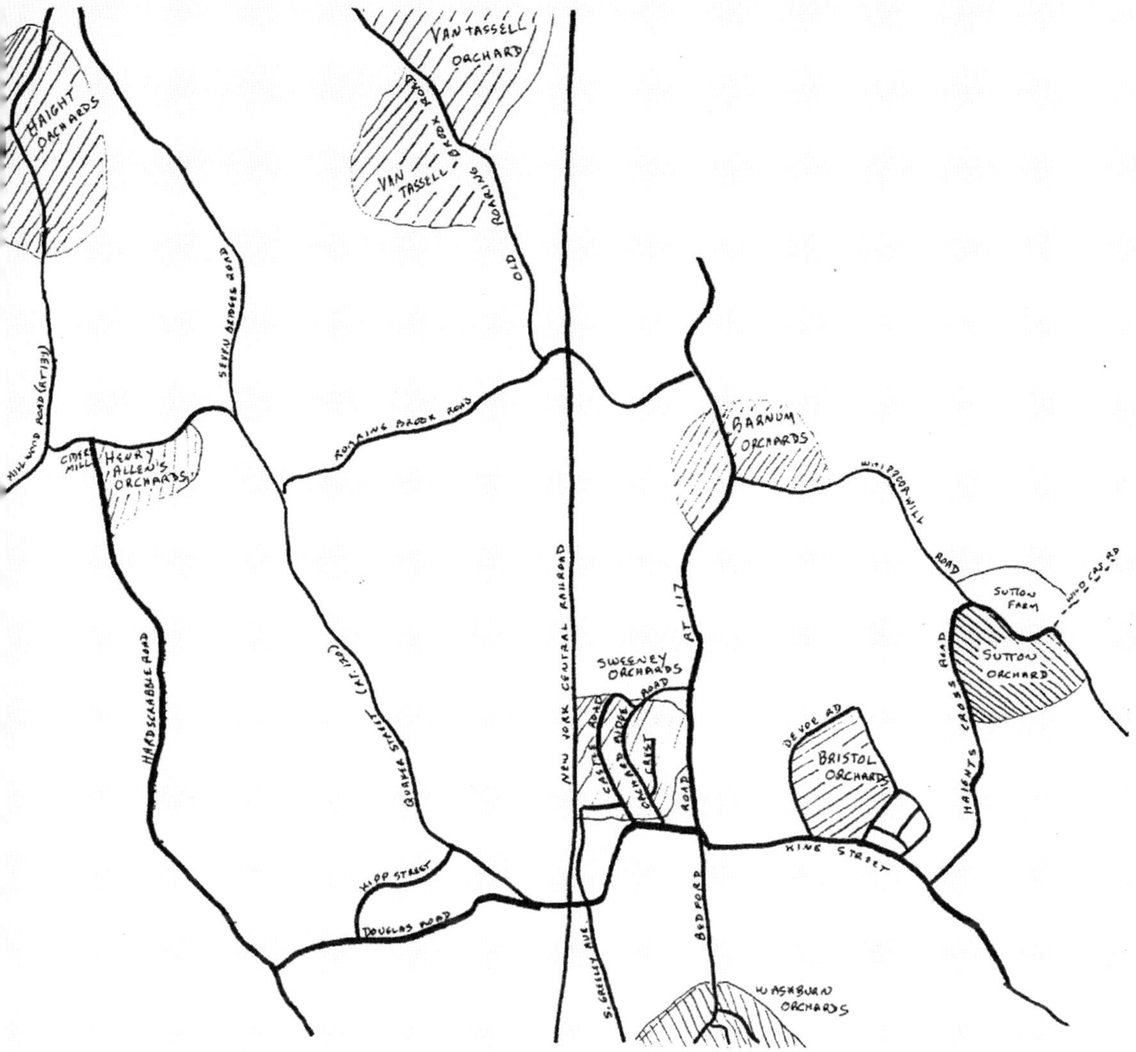

The railroad made it possible to ship perishable farm products quickly to New York City. In New Castle, these fell into two main categories: the first was milk and other dairy products; the second was apples and their by-products—cider, cider vinegar, and pickles. This map shows several of the large orchards that used to be a major feature of the New Castle landscape. All are long gone, but relics of them can be found in a few old buildings and in local street names such as Westorchard Road and Orchard Ridge. (Map from *The Story of the Orchards around Chappaqua As I lived with Them in My Early Life on the Farm*, by Ralph H. Sutton.)

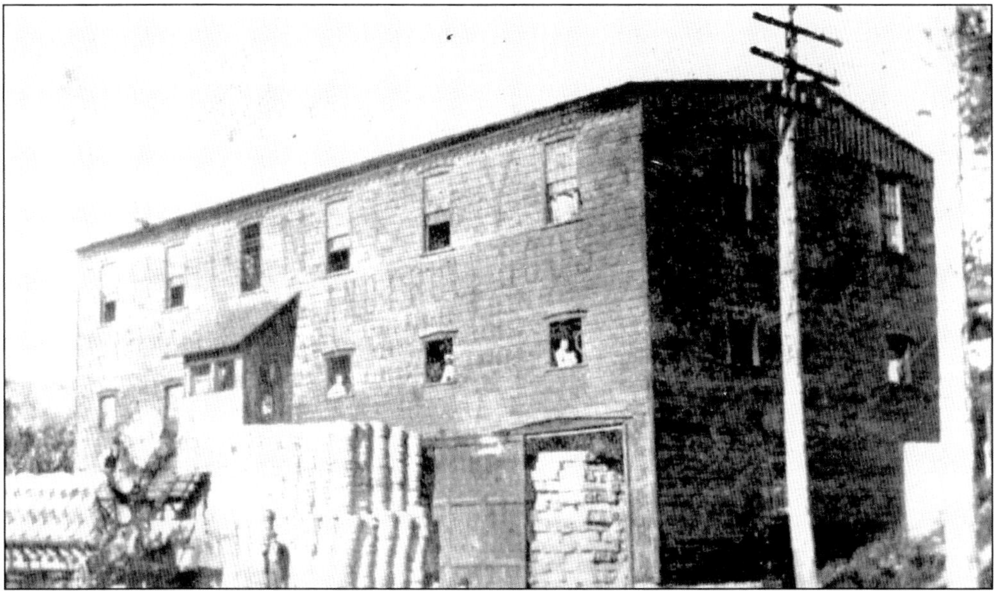

Apples, vinegar, and pickles were customarily packed and shipped in wooden barrels, and at least two barrel factories, known as cooperages, operated in New Castle. This one belonged to the Quinby family, descendants of pioneer Quakers. It was located on Hunt's Lane in Chappaqua, next to the railroad, first in a frame building that burned and then in the concrete structure shown here. In the 1900s, the factory was used to manufacture twine, and in recent years it has been converted to an office.

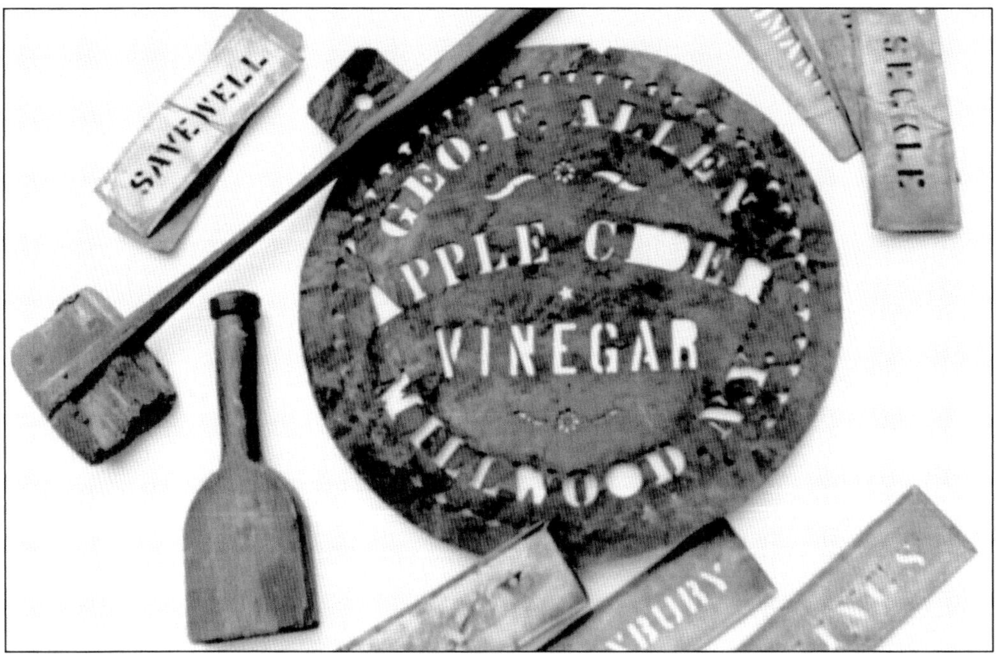

Henry Allen's orchard was near Hardscrabble Road and Quaker Street. His home at the corner still exists, and so does the concrete building across the street that once housed his cider mill and vinegar works. These stencils were used to label the barrels for his cider vinegar and for the varieties of fruit he raised. The tools were used to drive the barrelheads into place.

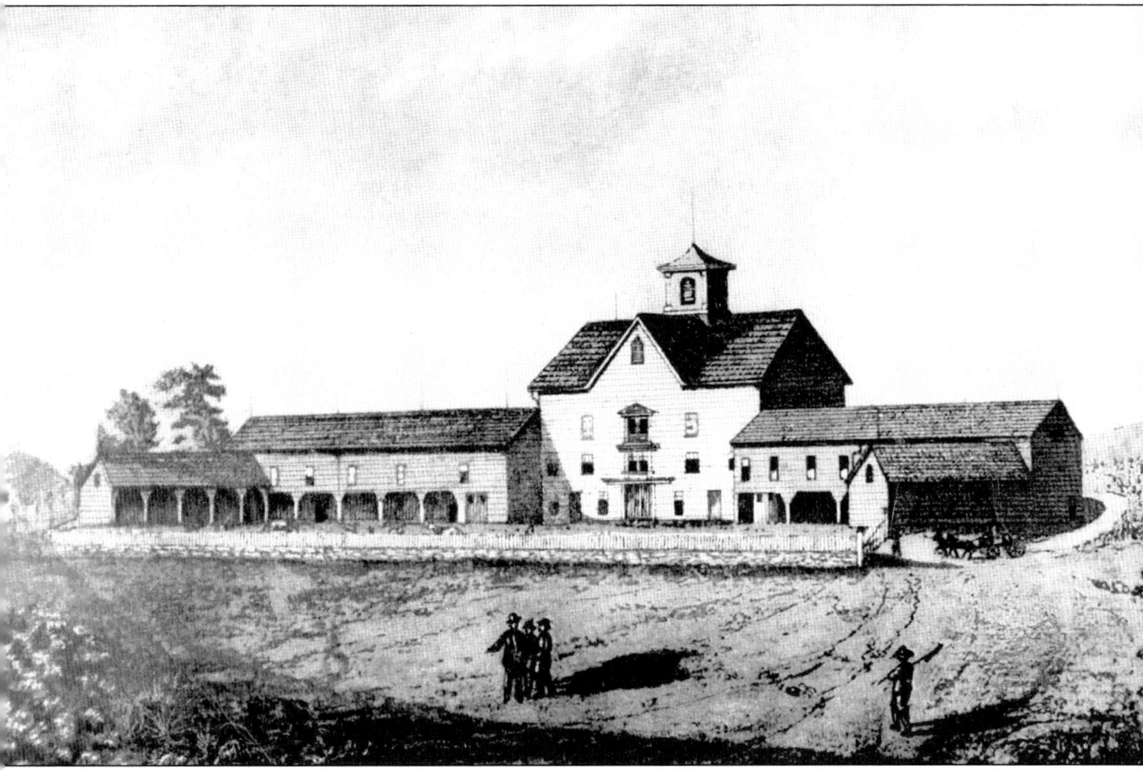

Several varieties of apples were raised in New Castle orchards. Farmers obtained seedlings of them from establishments such as Reisig and Hexamer's Ivy Hill Nursery, near Bedford Road between Chappaqua and New Castle Corners. The nursery appears to have been in business until the late 1800s, when the property was acquired by the Kittle family. It was then purchased by Moses Taylor and absorbed into his large estate, Annandale Farm. Taylor extensively reconstructed this barn into a house for his daughter, but she did not care for the result and instead chose a house in Bedford for her home. The reconstructed barn was then renamed the Kittle House and used by a series of country inns and restaurants, as it is today. (Courtesy of John Crabtree.)

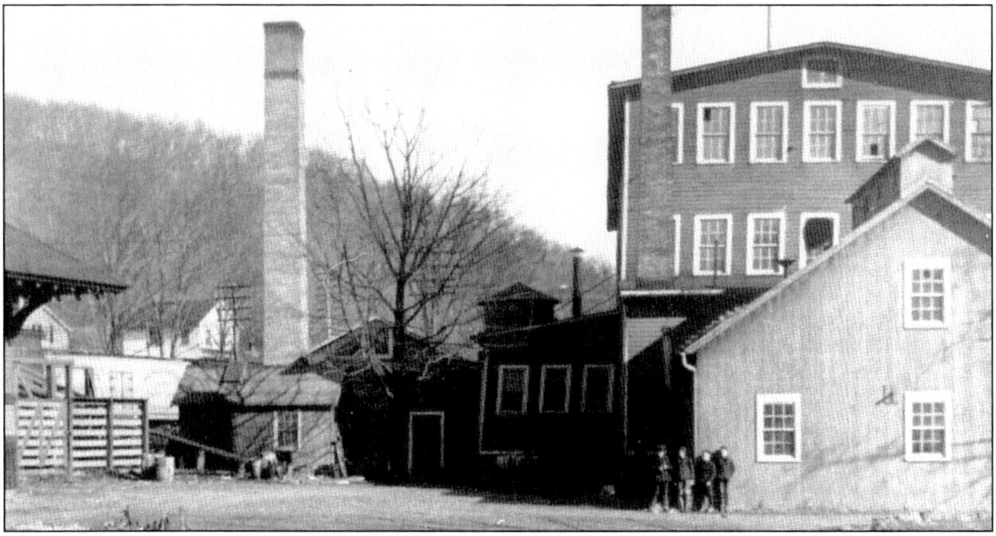

Making shoes was a common cottage industry in farming communities during the winter off-season. In 1868, Henry Bischoff was joined by Remington Farrington and William Bird in turning the cottage industry into a mechanized, year-round enterprise. They established the firm of Farrington, Bischoff, and Bird and built a shoe factory near the railroad station on North Greeley Avenue. The original building burned in 1876, but was quickly rebuilt. In 1885, Bischoff bought out his partners, and Farrington, Bischoff, and Bird became the Chappaqua Shoe Company. It employed up to 75 workers, male and female. The business closed about 1900, and the factory was used by a couple of other manufacturers before being demolished in 1911.

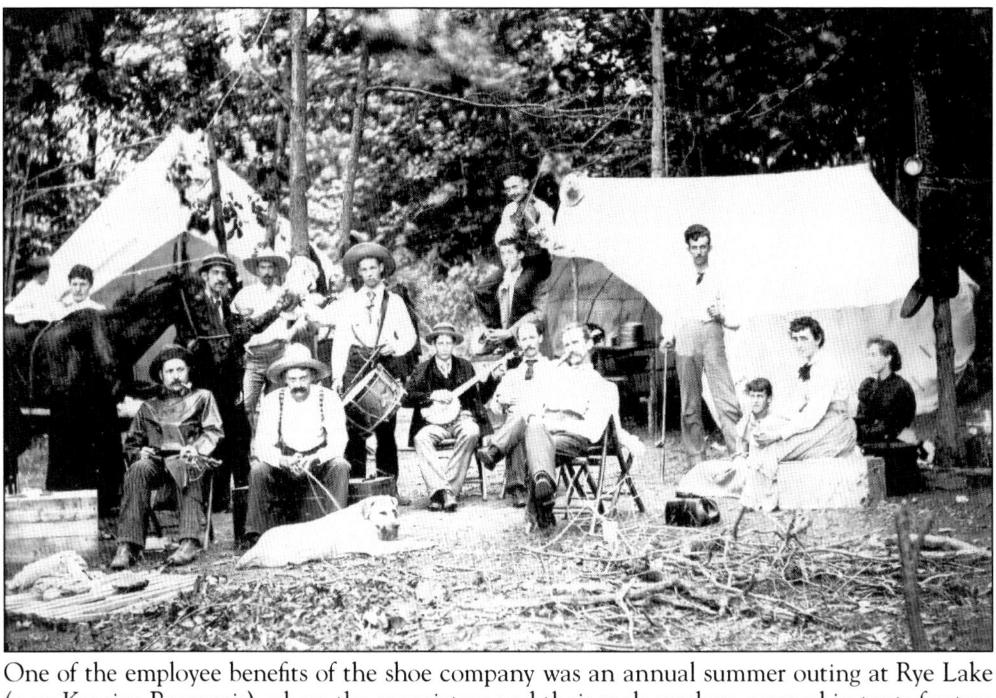

One of the employee benefits of the shoe company was an annual summer outing at Rye Lake (now Kensico Reservoir), where the proprietors and their male workers camped in tents for two weeks, presumably at company expense. For propriety's sake, women and other family members could not stay overnight but were welcome on regular visitors' days.

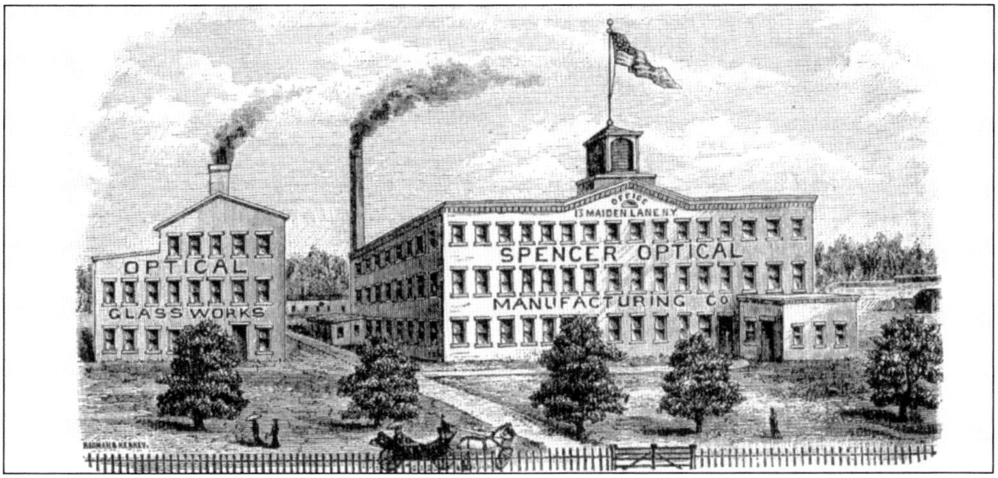

The Spencer Optical Manufacturing Company of New Haven, Connecticut, moved to New Castle Corners in 1874, in part because of Kisco Lake, seen as a reliable water supply to power its machines for grinding and polishing eyeglass lenses. The lake lay on Judge Robert Leonard's property, east of Main Street and south of the Bedford Road intersection. Spencer Optical became the biggest employer in New Castle, with up to 200 employees, and one of the world's largest manufacturers of eyeglasses, producing about 550,000 pairs annually. By 1878, community members had become concerned that the lake might be responsible for the high incidence of malaria in the neighborhood, although they did not know the reason: carrier mosquitoes breeding in the warm, still water. The Leonard family decided to drain the lake. Spencer Optical sued to preserve its water supply but, by 1888, gave up, shut the factory, and moved to Newark, New Jersey. Kisco Lake is now Leonard Park. (Wood engraving from *History of Westchester County*, by J. Thomas Scharf.)

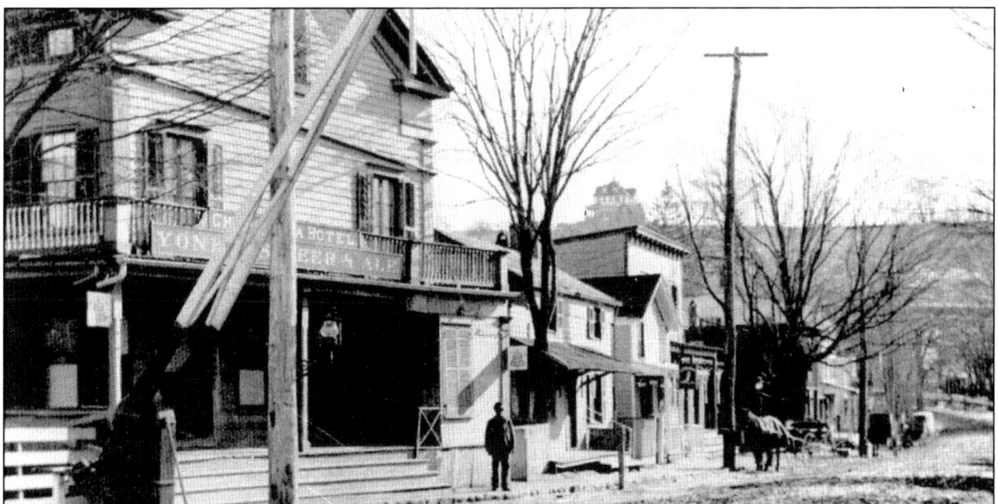

At the beginning of the 20th century, downtown Chappaqua was a small but bustling commercial center, its agricultural economy bolstered by the spending of rich estate owners and a gradually increasing influx of New York City commuters. Shown is the north side of Main Street (now Lower King Street), still unpaved, with virtually all the buildings of wood. The Chappaqua Hotel continued to occupy its strategic location next to the railroad crossing, and a string of stores and residences extended to Greeley Avenue and up King Street.

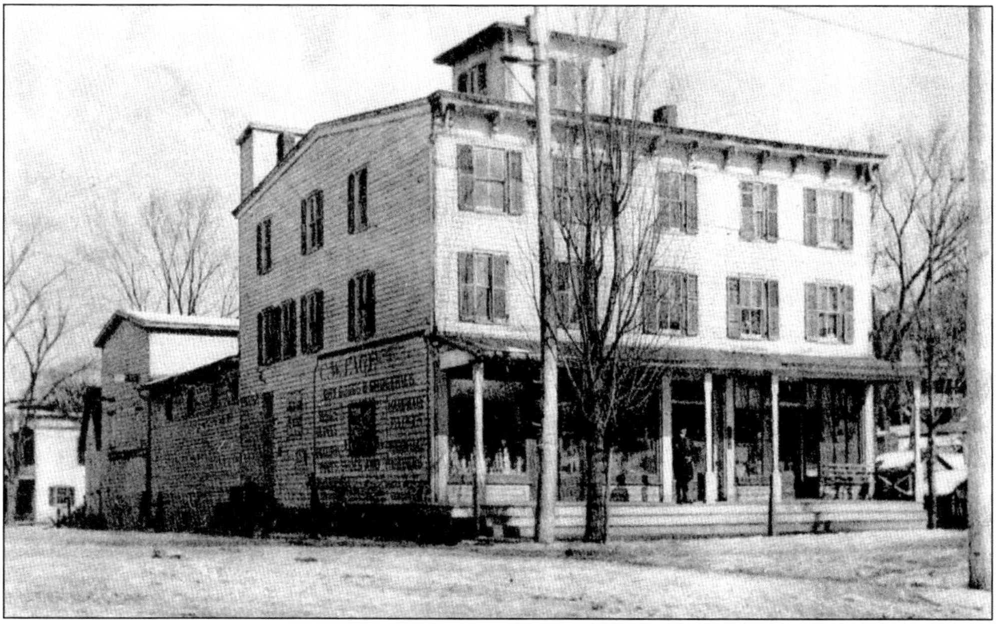

The largest commercial building in Chappaqua was this imposing Italianate structure, rising three full stories, plus a cupola, at the northeast corner of Main Street and North Greeley Avenue. In the 1880s, it was the headquarters of Edward S. Quinby's dealership in agricultural machinery and housewares. By the 1900s, it had become the general store of the Clarence W. Page family. It was replaced by much less picturesque masonry buildings during the 1930s.

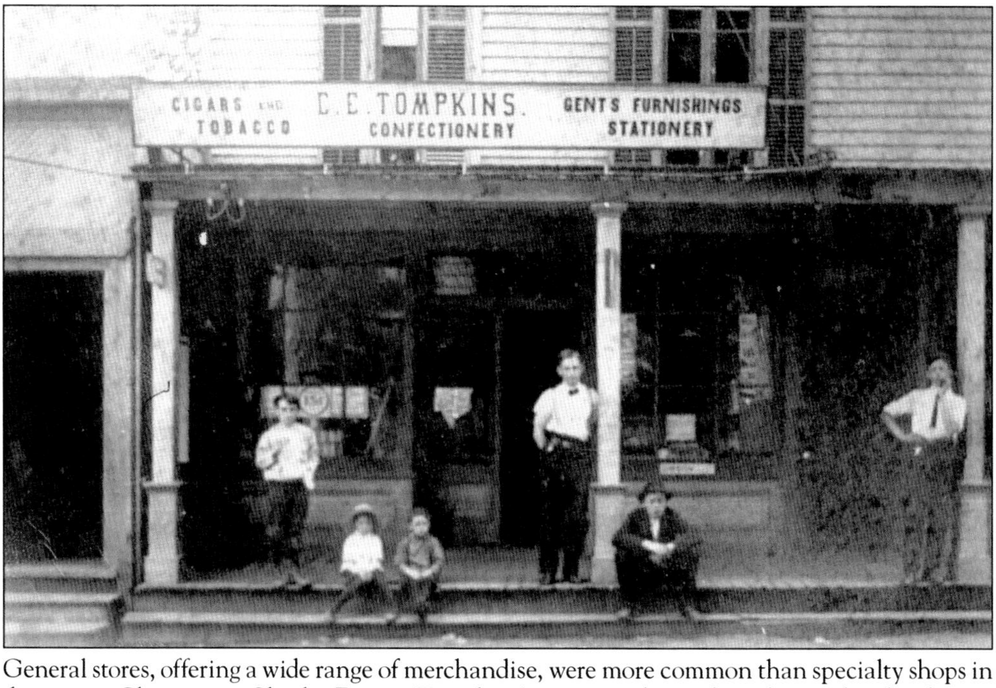

General stores, offering a wide range of merchandise, were more common than specialty shops in downtown Chappaqua. Charles Everett Tompkins's store was located on the south side of Main Street. As the sign proclaims, it sold cigars and tobacco, confectionery (candy), gentlemen's furnishings (haberdashery), and stationery.

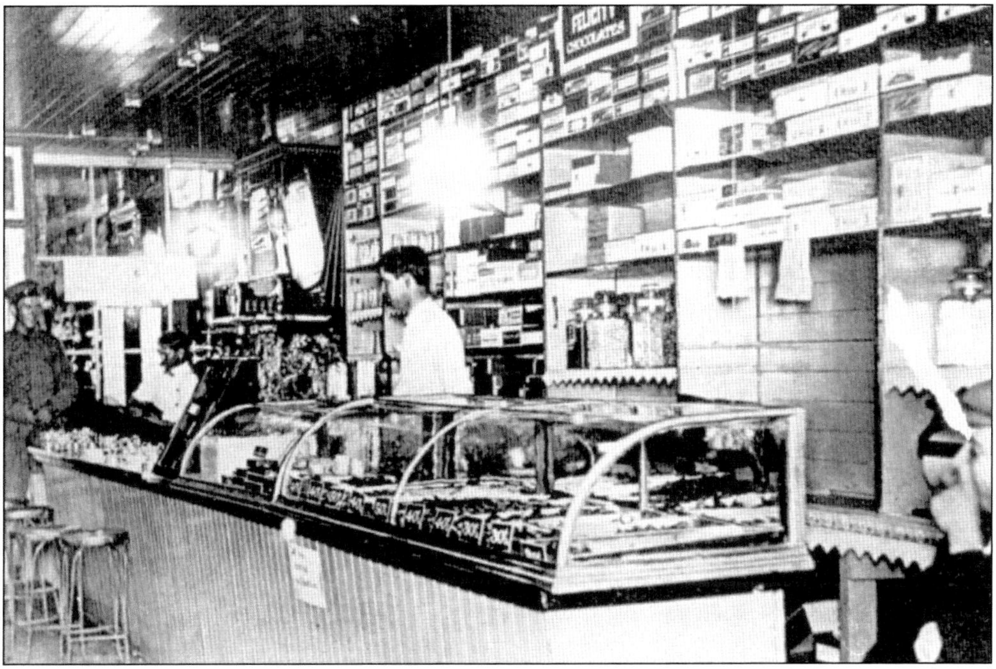

This is the confectionery counter at Charles E. Tompkins's store. On the shelves are packaged sweets and jars of hard candy, and in the glass-topped cases on the counter is bulk candy, sold by weight or by the piece.

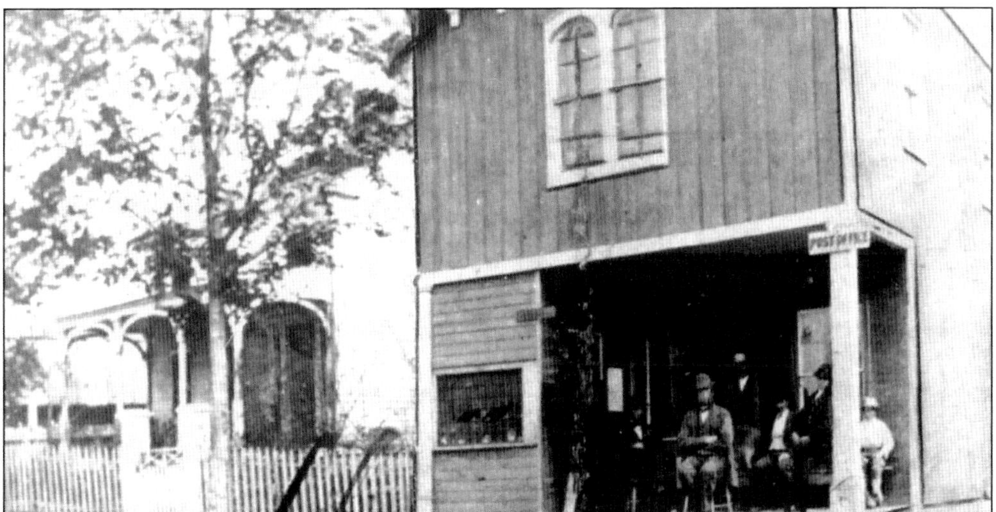

Chappaqua business proprietors and their families often lived above or very close to their establishments. In 1888, Amos Tompkins (1822–1908) owned a grain and feed store known familiarly as Feedbag Hall, located on the north side of Main Street. At this time, part of the store also served as the local post office, with mailboxes built into the outside wall, to the left of the entrance. The office of postmaster was a political patronage appointment, so postmasters changed as administrations changed, and the post offices moved with them. The upper floor contained an open room used for meetings and other functions, including some annual town meetings. But the property also contained a house (left), where the Tompkins family lived.

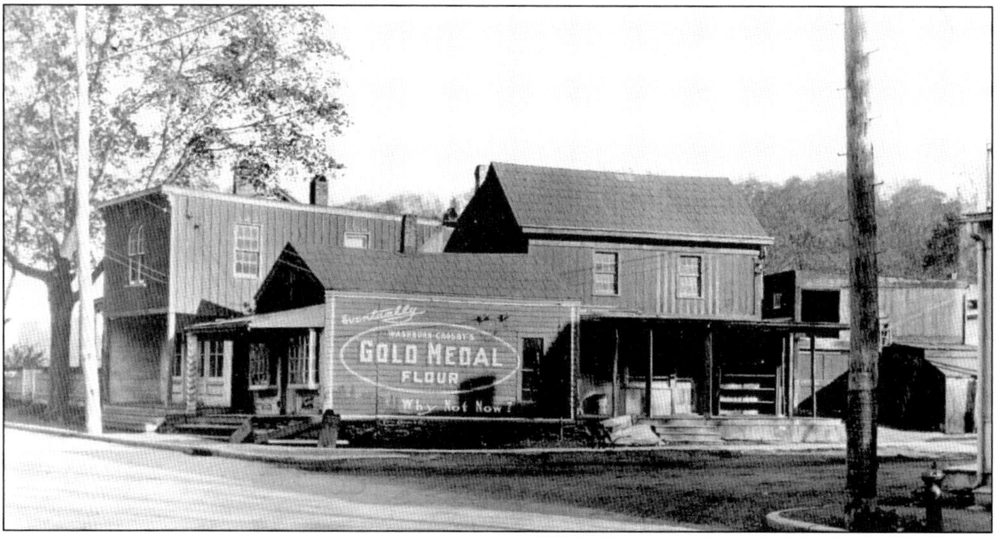

Amos Tompkins expanded his business in the early 1900s, adding further buildings at the northwest corner of Main Street and North Greeley Avenue. He leased a small connecting building next to Feedbag Hall to a barbershop. A large sign on the corner building advertised "Washburn-Crosby's Gold Medal Flour—Eventually, Why Not Now?"

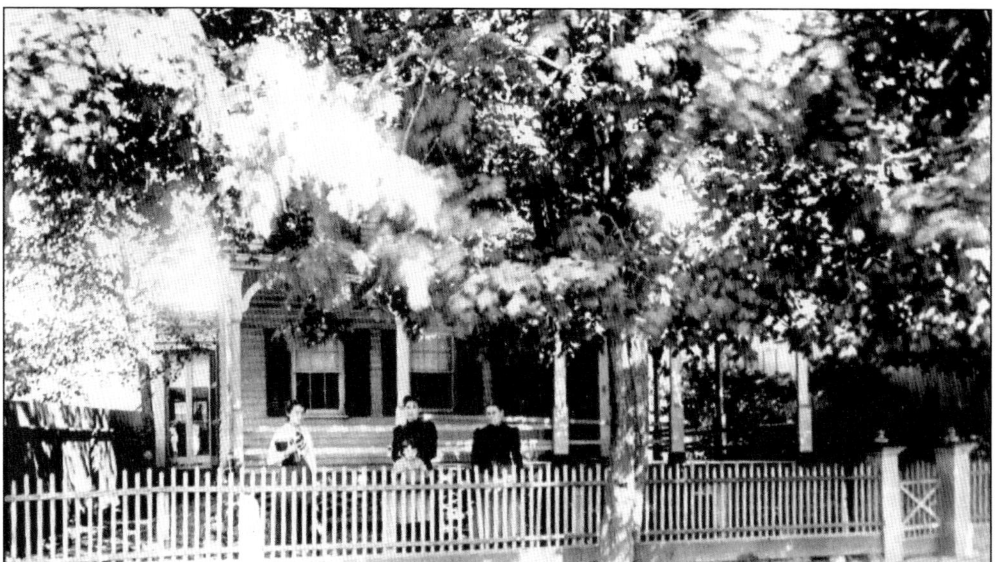

Generations of the Tompkins family continued to occupy the house west of the feed store well into the 1900s. They included Amos Tompkins's son Oscar (1850–1910), Oscar's wife, Mary Emma (1860–1928), and their seven children. The last family member to live there was their daughter Amelia.

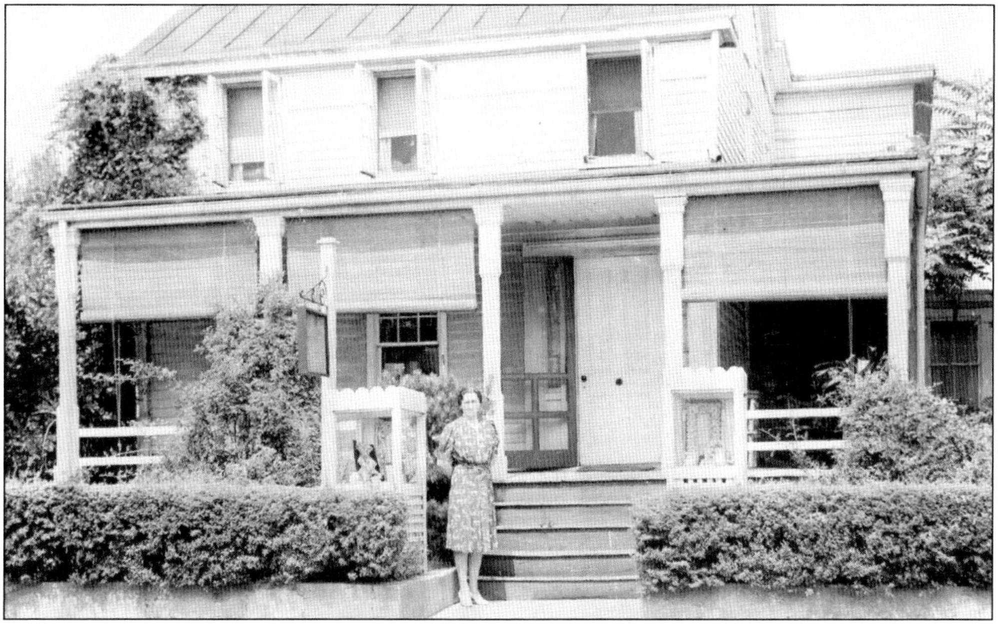

Amelia Tompkins was born in 1893. She married Rolando Caiani of Florence and, after World War I, established the Florentine Linen Shop in her family's home. She operated this business until her retirement in 1961 and died in 1985 at the age of 93. The house still exists, but its front facade has since been extensively altered, with large display windows replacing the old front porch.

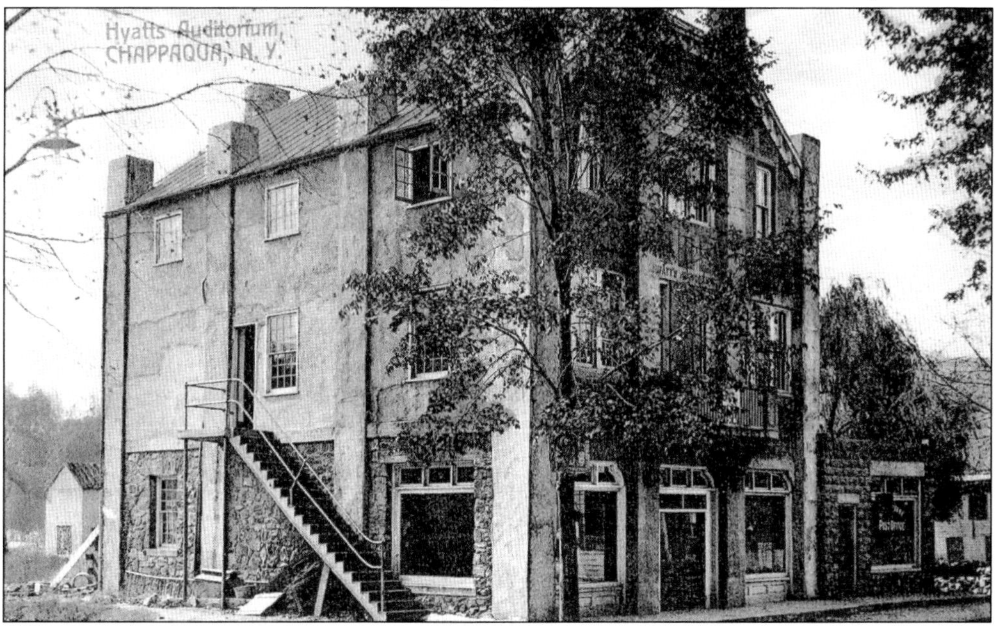

In 1910, a multipurpose commercial building was completed on King Street, a short distance east of the intersection with Greeley Avenue. It was known as the Hyatt Auditorium because it contained a public room on the second floor, where activities ranging from dances and lectures to the showing of silent movies took place. But it also housed a store on the ground floor and offices above, including the telephone exchange. In the 1930s, the upper stories were sheared off, leaving only the ground floor, which today is divided into two commercial spaces.

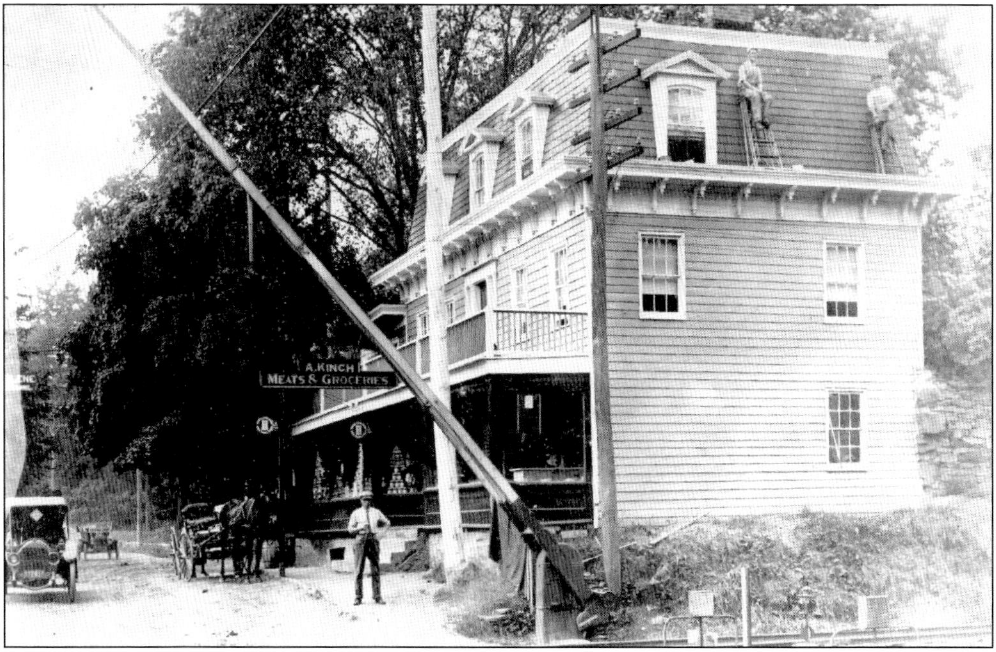

Before the completion of the railroad overpass bridge in 1930, Main Street continued across the tracks, with several stores and other businesses on the west side. One of these was the general store of Levi Hunt, housed in this Mansard-roofed building across the tracks from the Chappaqua Hotel. Part of the store served as the post office until that office was taken over by Amos Tompkins in the 1880s. Hunt's establishment was not only a major local business but also a popular gathering place for the men of the community. In the early 1900s, the proprietor was Ambrose B. Kinch (front), who installed the newfangled plate glass windows.

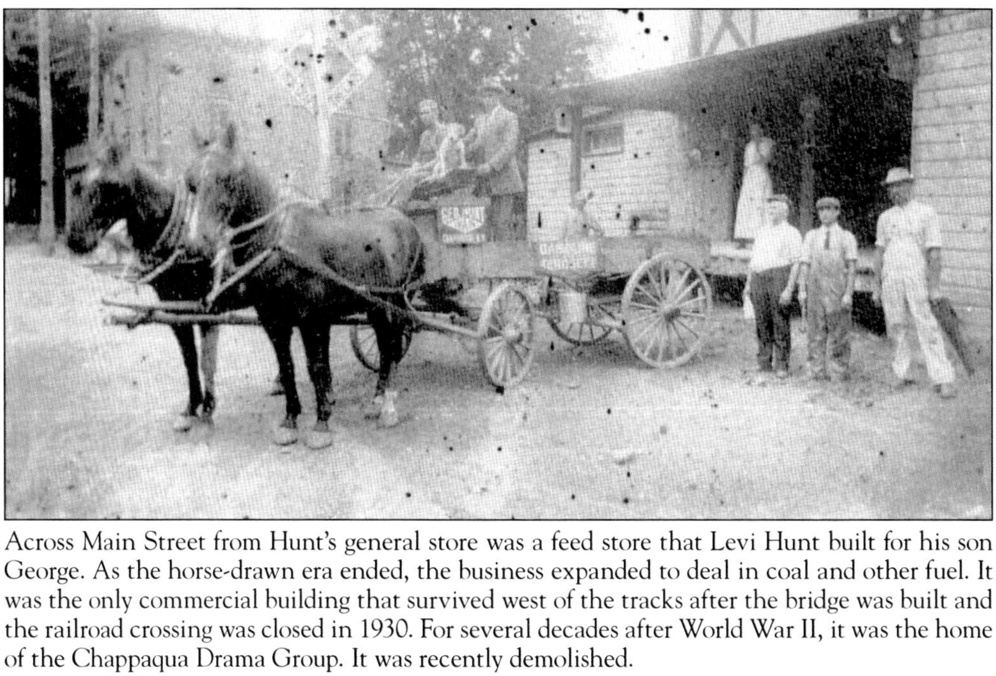

Across Main Street from Hunt's general store was a feed store that Levi Hunt built for his son George. As the horse-drawn era ended, the business expanded to deal in coal and other fuel. It was the only commercial building that survived west of the tracks after the bridge was built and the railroad crossing was closed in 1930. For several decades after World War II, it was the home of the Chappaqua Drama Group. It was recently demolished.

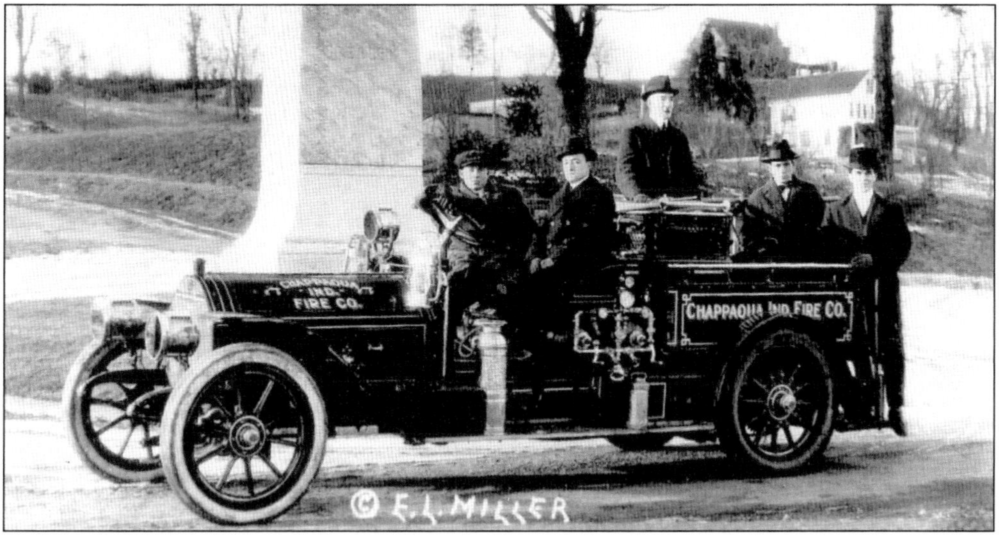

As the village of Chappaqua grew, so did its need for public services. Since the mid-1800s, loose groups of volunteers had formed to fight fires in the community. By about 1910, two of these had organized into volunteer fire companies. One, sponsored by local estate owner John I. D. Bristol, had its headquarters on Bedford Road (Route 117) near the intersection with King Street (Route 120). The other, the Chappaqua Independent Fire Company, was in the downtown business district. The companies adopted the most advanced technology available. Leo Ivey, John Cornell, James Redmond, William Moran, and William Ferrick pose with their recently acquired engine at the base of the Horace Greeley statue.

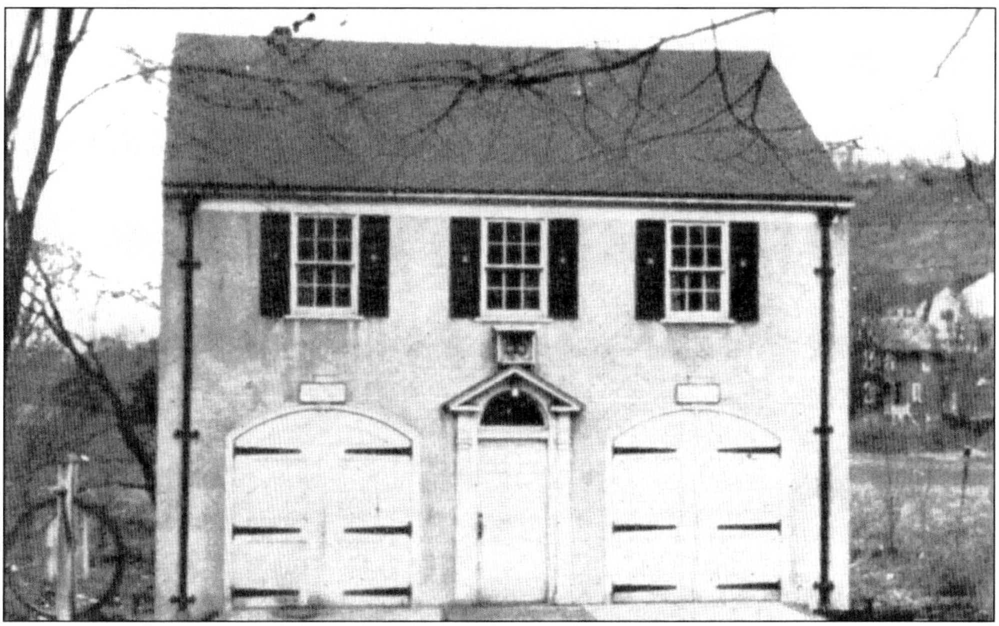

One of the basic needs of a volunteer fire company was a firehouse, not only to house its equipment but also to provide a place for meetings, training, and social activities. The Chappaqua Independent Fire Company firehouse stood on the extension of Main Street west of the railroad crossing. It was demolished in the early 1930s, during the construction of the Saw Mill River Parkway, and replaced by a new firehouse on Senter Street.

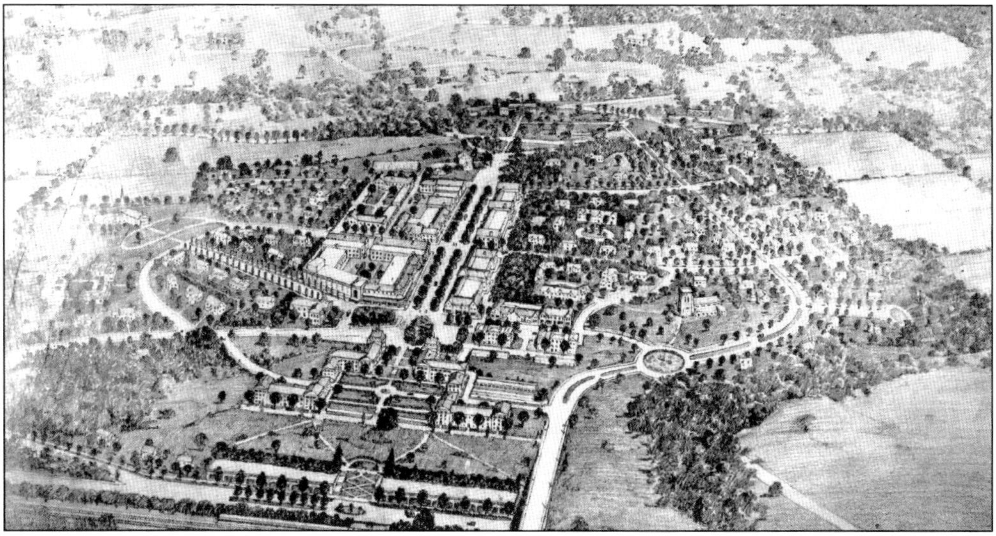

In the 1920s, the Lawrence Real Estate Company was engaged in an extensive development called Lawrence Farms in the northeast part of New Castle. Many homes were built, together with a country club and golf course, but the Lawrences had even more ambitious plans. They commissioned a design for a whole new suburban community on Roaring Brook Road, complete with its own railroad station and commercial district. The design was completed in early 1929, but the stock market crash and subsequent Depression put an end to this vision.

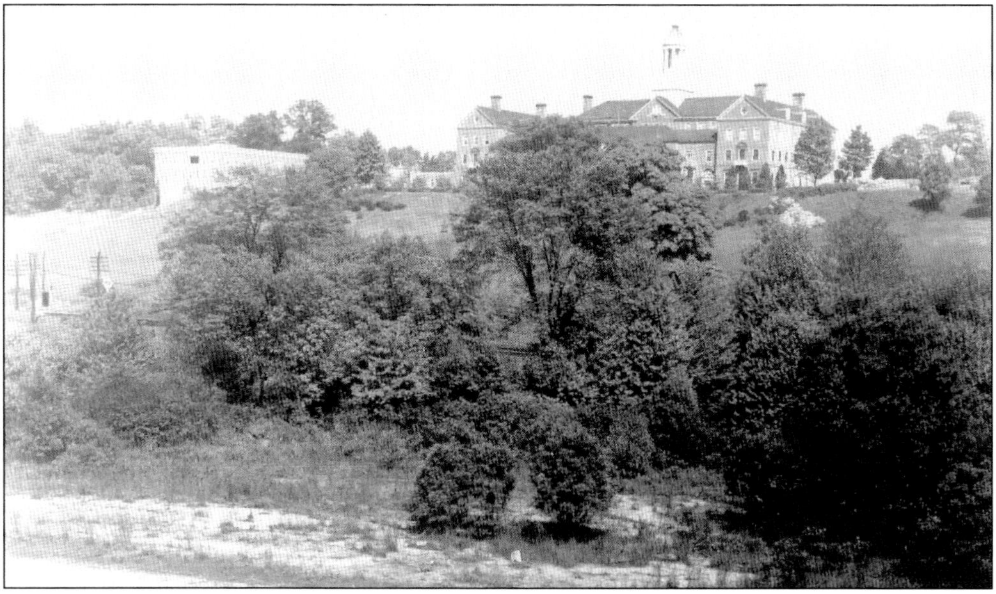

In 1938, the land was sold to a company that had successfully weathered the Depression, the *Reader's Digest*, headed by DeWitt and Lila Acheson Wallace. In 1939, the company, which had outgrown its offices in nearby Pleasantville, erected an elegant Georgian Revival headquarters on a conspicuous site between two ancient white oak trees, overlooking the railroad and the Saw Mill River Parkway. It was the largest business to be centered in New Castle. Although located in Chappaqua, the company kept its Pleasantville mailing address. In the mid-1900s, the company enlarged its building complex. In recent decades it reduced operations there and finally sold the property for redevelopment, leasing back the area occupied by its headquarters offices.

Three

The Railroads

The New York State legislature in 1831 granted a charter to the New York and Harlem Railroad Company to lay tracks and provide service over the seven miles between lower Manhattan and the village of Harlem. With many extensions and changes in ownership, the New York and Harlem Railroad still survives, as the Harlem Division of the Metro-North Railroad.

By the early 1840s, the railroad had crossed the Harlem River, and in late 1846, it reached Chappaqua. In anticipation, New Castle had realigned the roads near the railroad right-of-way. King Street descended from Haight's Corners (the intersection with Bedford Road), plunged precipitously down what is now Maple Avenue to the narrow valley at the foot of Chappaqua Mountain, veered left on Hunt's Lane, and bore right on Hunt's Place to Quaker Street. In the spring of 1846, Maple Avenue and Hunt's Lane were temporarily closed, and a new, less steep section of King Street was opened to the broader valley at the foot of the hill, where it turned west to meet Hunt's Place. The New Road (as it was called) became the main street of Chappaqua, and the railroad crossing became the core of the rapidly growing hamlet.

In 1881, the New York and Northern Railroad, later the Putnam Division of the New York Central, began operations through the West End. A station was built at Merritt's Corners, which was later renamed Millwood.

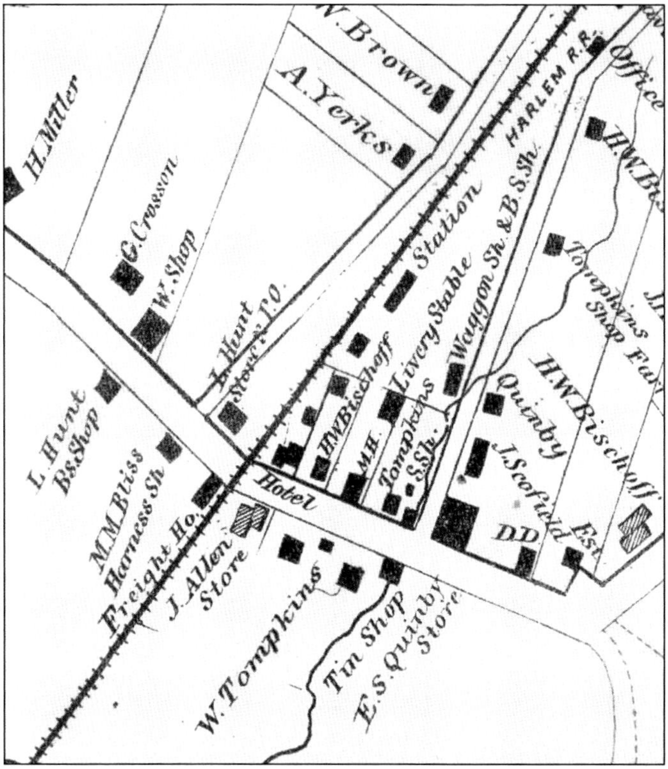

When the railroad arrived in 1846, the first passenger station was in the Chappaqua Hotel, where the new street crossed the tracks. The freight depot was on the other side of the street. But about 1870, North Greeley Avenue was opened up, Maple Avenue was reopened, and a new, separate station was built. It was mainly intended for passenger traffic—the freight house on Main Street remained in use. Freight was, in fact, the most important part of the railroad's business. The railroad transformed the agricultural economy of the area: self-sufficient farms became market farms, shipping dairy and apple products to the city.

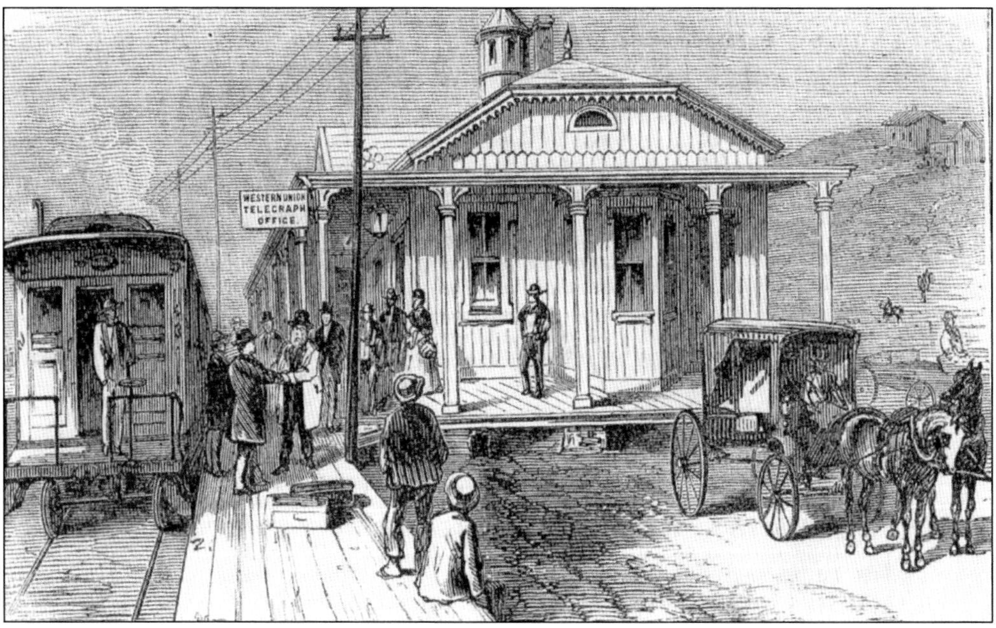

This wood engraving from a June 1872 edition of *Leslie's Illustrated Newspaper* shows Horace Greeley disembarking from the train at the new station. As in other stations on the line, the interior was divided into two main spaces: a passenger waiting room with a ticket office and telegraph terminal, and a baggage room. Outside, a covered veranda protected passengers from rain, snow, and sooty steam from the locomotives.

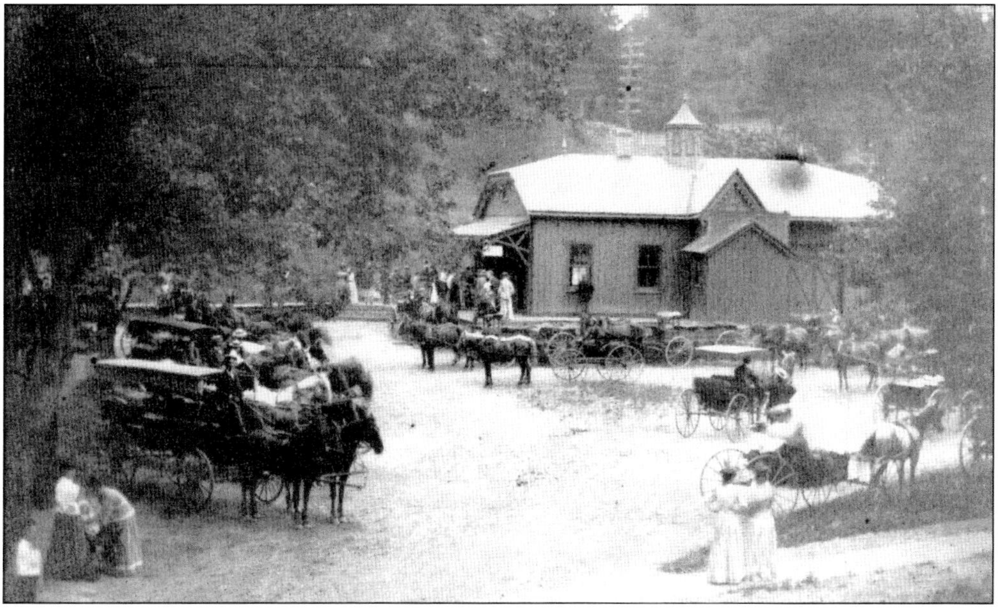

The 1870 passenger station remained in service until the end of the 1800s. This August 1894 photograph shows the wagons and buggies of local Quakers gathered at the station to carry attendees to a major conference at the Chappaqua Mountain Institute, a Quaker private school.

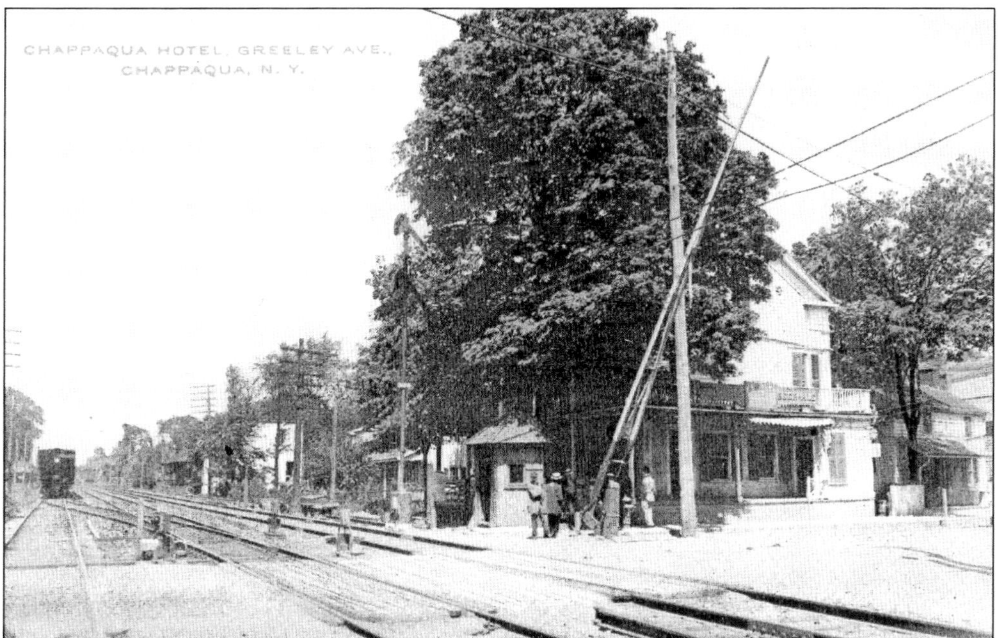

Around 1900, when the number of commuters to New York City was beginning to multiply and the hamlet center was expanding, Chappaqua outgrew its passenger station. Despite some resistance, particularly from neighborhood business proprietors, there was increasing popular support for building a new station on a larger site.

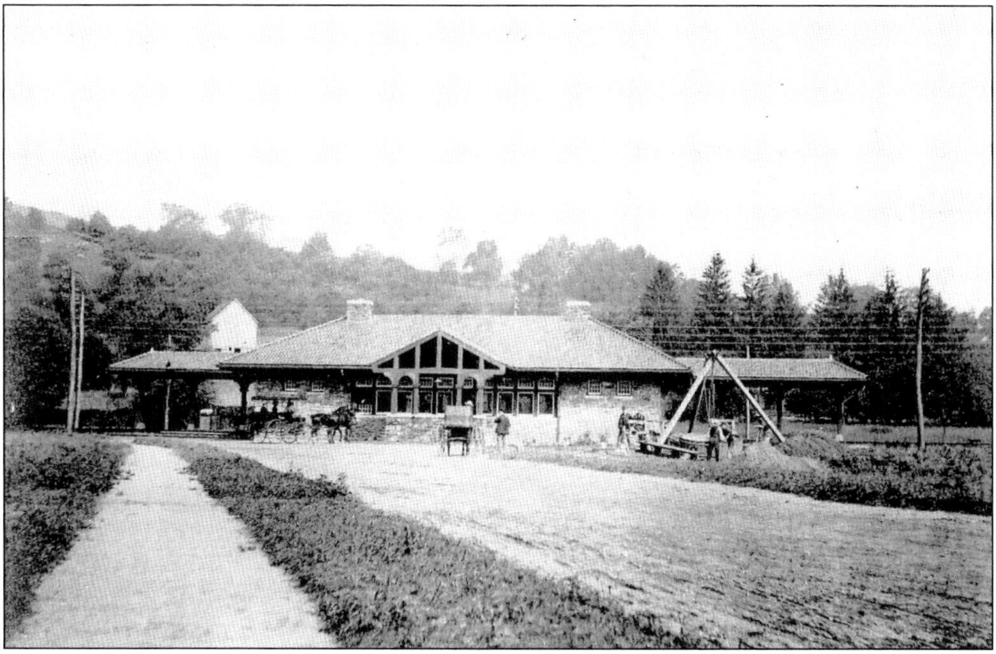

Popular sentiment became a consensus in 1901, when Horace Greeley's daughter Gabrielle Greeley Clendenin and her husband, Frank Montrose Clendenin, donated a site for the station on land from the former Greeley farm, south of Main Street. The new station was dedicated in June 1902 and has remained in operation ever since.

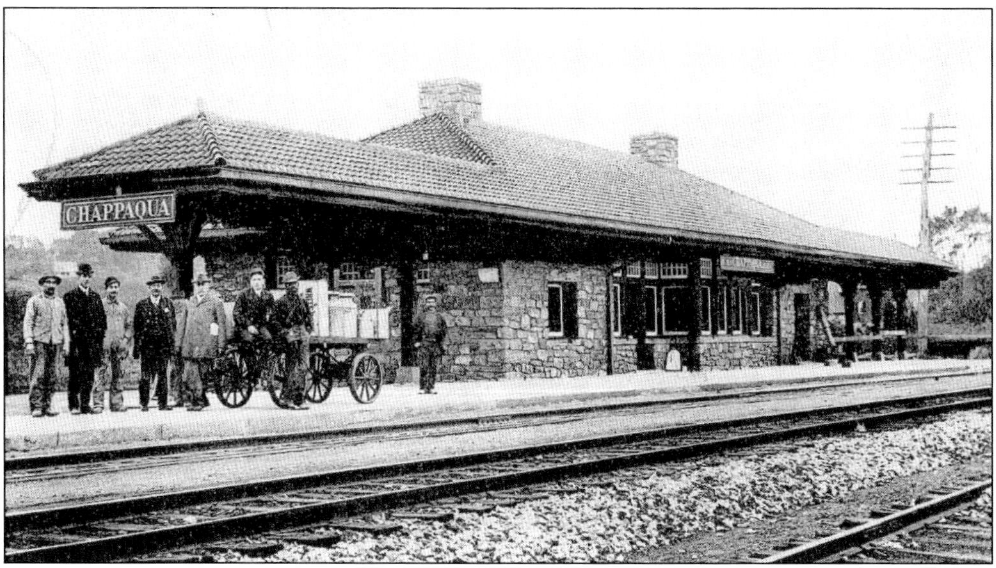

The station resembled several other New York Central commuter stations of the period. It was designed to be fire resistant, with masonry walls and a tile roof. Its eaves were broader than the old station's veranda, and an extended canopy sheltered the area next to the tracks.

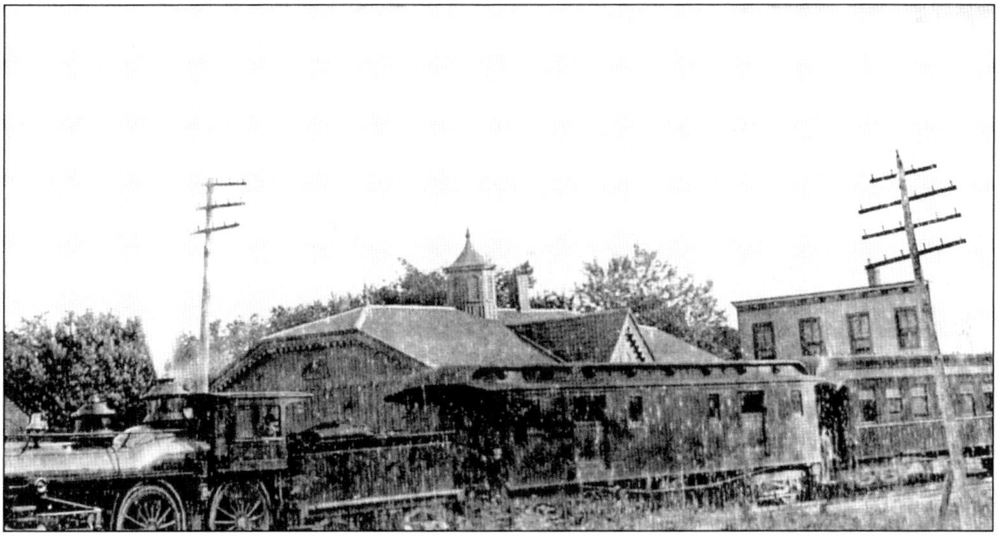

The former station was not abandoned but remained in use as a freight depot for several decades. Its roof is visible behind the passing train in this early-1900s photograph.

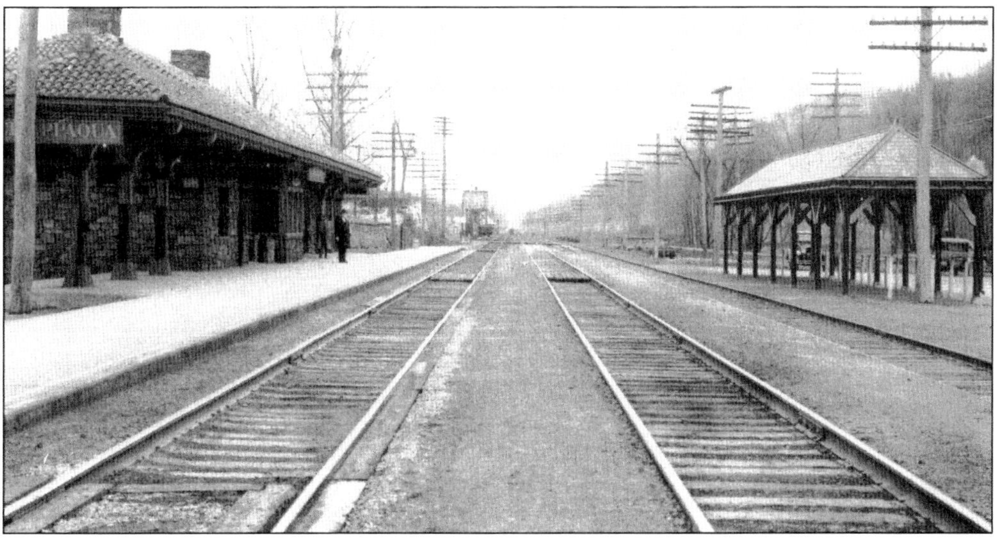

In the 1900s, as agriculture declined, the Harlem Division gradually ceased hauling farm products to the city, and its main focus shifted to passenger service. Pictured in the mid-1920s, the railroad station on the east side of the tracks was supplemented by another covered walkway on the west side, and passengers boarded and exited the trains on both sides. Down the tracks appears a water tower. The boilers of the early steam locomotives required frequent refilling, and there were many such water towers along the tracks.

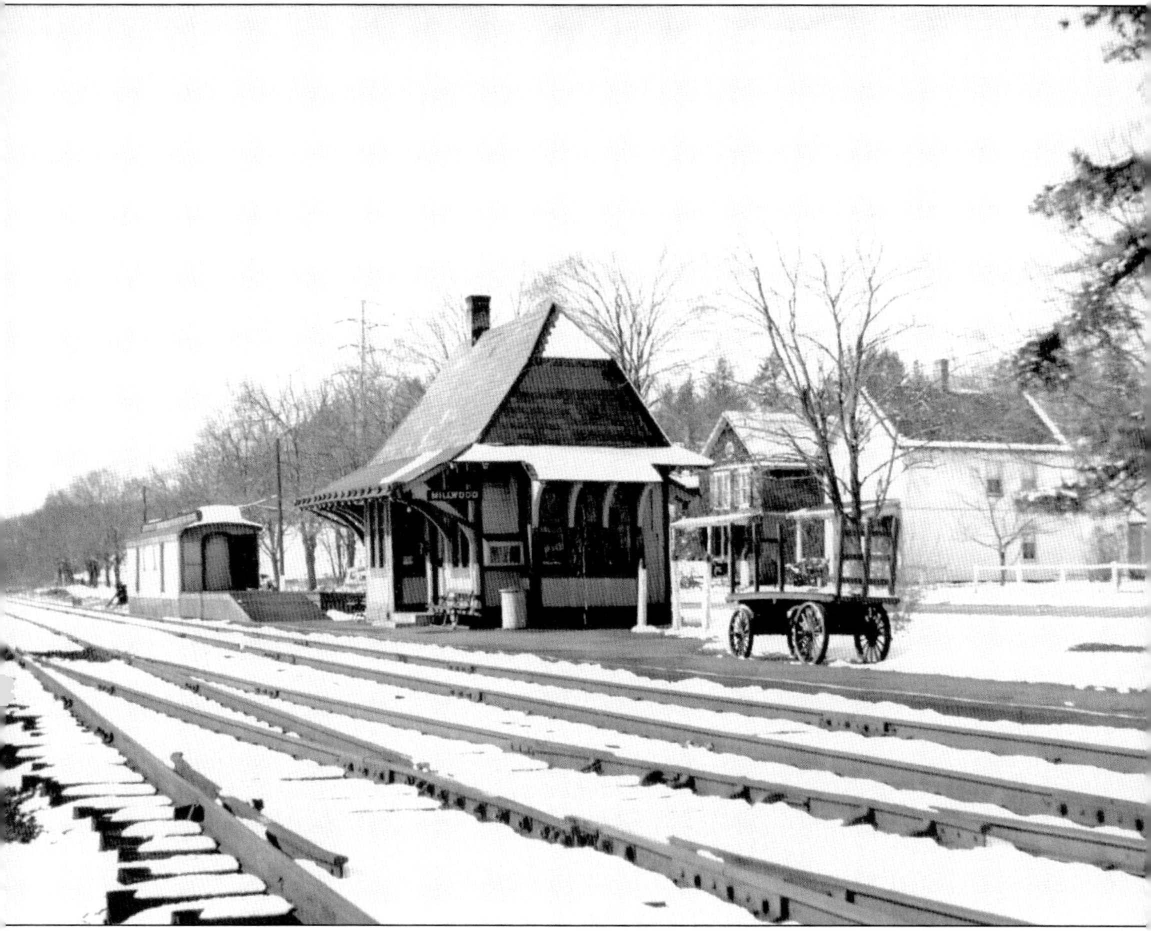

In 1881, a second railroad arrived in New Castle. The New York and Northern Railroad, later the Putnam Division of the New York Central Railroad, began operations through the West End. Shortly afterward, a station was installed where the railroad crossed the road to Chappaqua and Bedford (now a combination of Routes 120 and 133). First called Merritt's Corners, it was later renamed Millwood. The original Millwood station burned and was temporarily replaced by a converted railroad freight car. In 1909, when a new and more elaborate station was built in Briarcliff Manor (it is now the Briarcliff Library), the former station was moved one stop up the line for passenger service. It is pictured around 1945. The converted railroad car continued to be used but only as a freight depot.

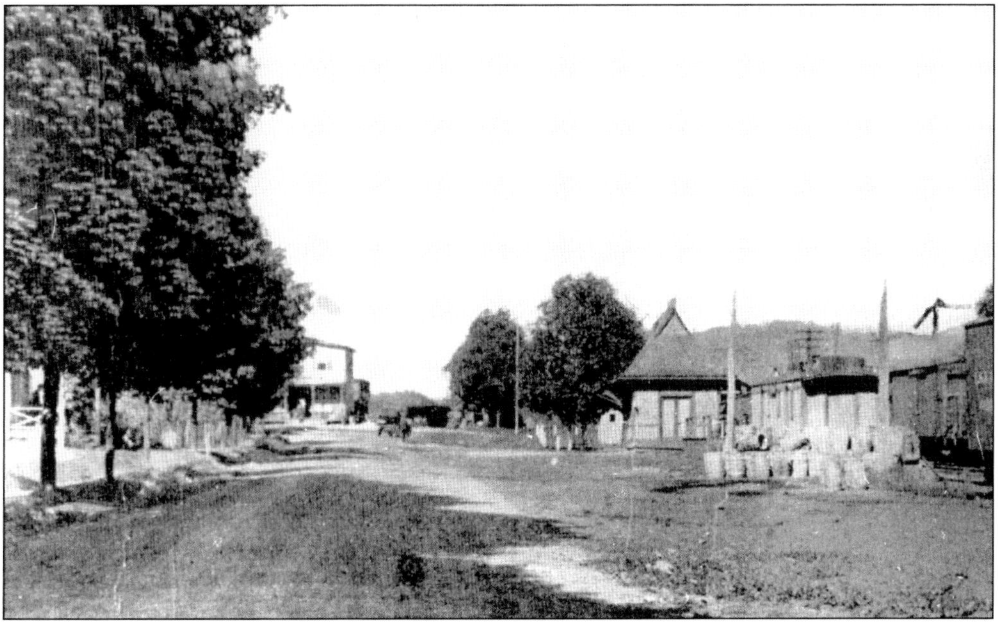

Familiarly called "the Put," the Putnam Division was never as busy as the Harlem line. It too carried dairy and apple products to New York City during the late 1800s and early 1900s. This photograph shows apple barrels piled up on Main Street in Millwood, near the freight depot.

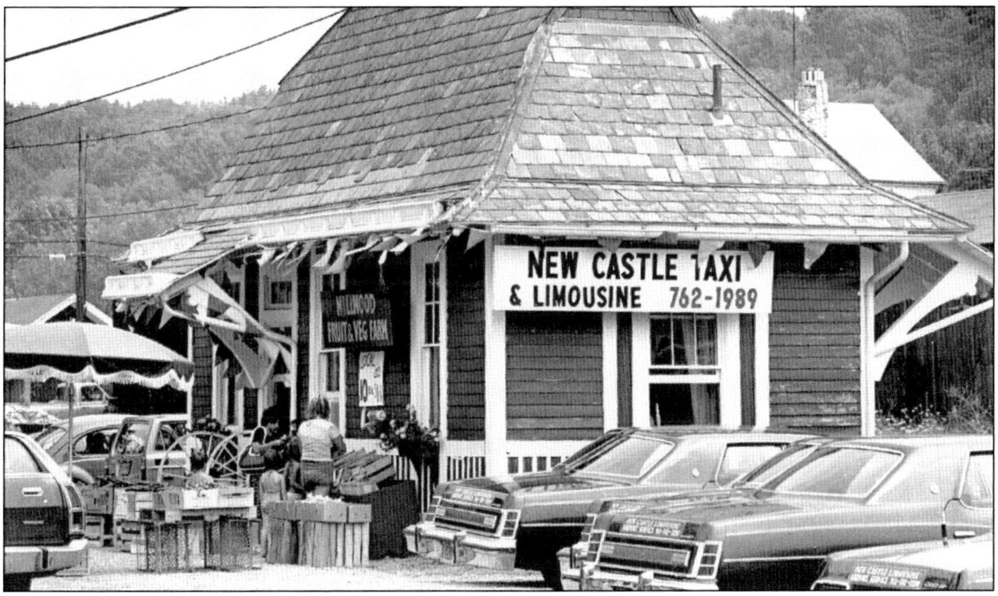

The Put also carried passengers but far fewer than those in the burgeoning suburb of Chappaqua. One big reason was that the Put did not extend to midtown Manhattan. Passengers either had to switch to a Hudson Division train in the Bronx or cross the Harlem River and take elevated trains downtown. Ridership dwindled after World War II, and the line was shut down in 1958. The former Millwood passenger station was then used for a variety of commercial enterprises, including a farmers' market and a taxi and limousine business. It is currently unoccupied. The railroad right-of-way through Westchester was acquired by the county and is now a popular trail way for bikers, runners, and bicycle riders. (Courtesy of the Westchester County Historical Society.)

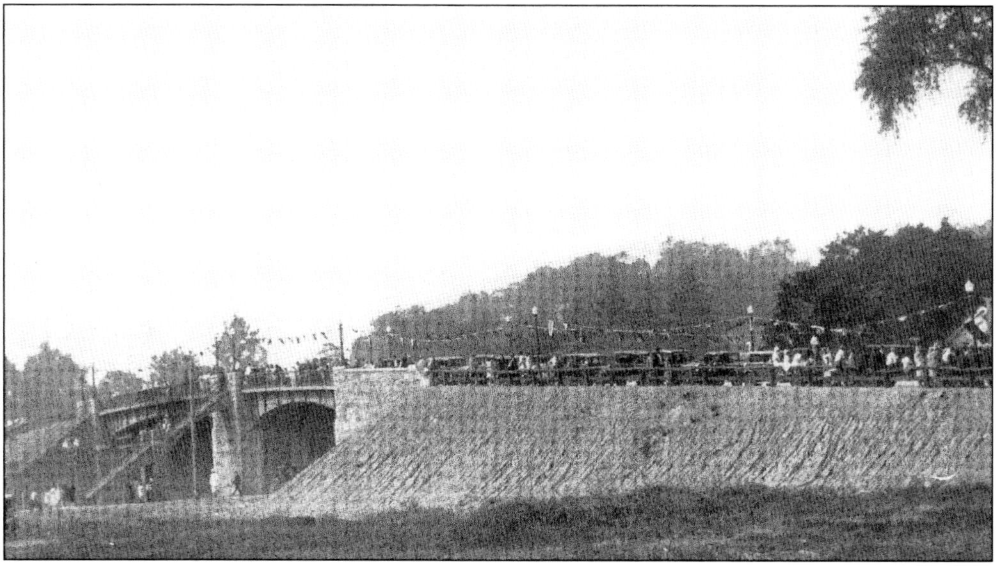

As motor vehicles supplanted those drawn by horses, traffic at the Main Street railroad crossing in Chappaqua became heavier, faster, and more potentially dangerous. Although no serious accident occurred at the crossing, Chappaqua in 1930 became one of the first communities in northern Westchester to build a highway overpass. The bridge was dedicated with much ceremony on September 6, 1930, in connection with the celebration of the 200th anniversary of Chappaqua's founding. The grade-level crossing was then closed, and Main Street was eventually renamed Lower King Street.

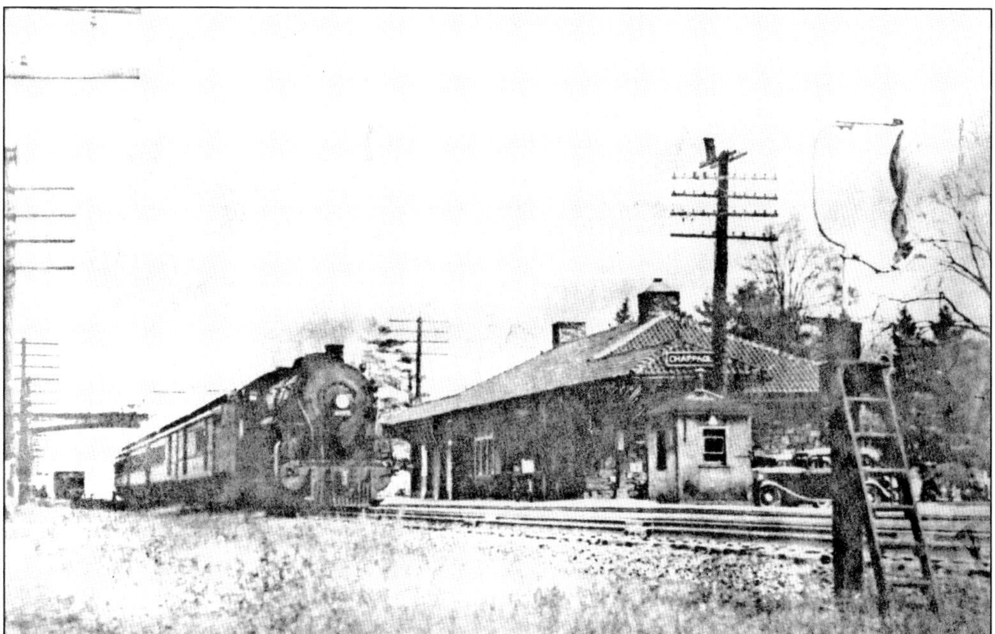

Through the first half of the 1900s, the Harlem Division north of White Plains continued to be powered by steam. At North White Plains, trains in each direction had to stop and switch locomotives, a process that added at least four minutes to the schedule.

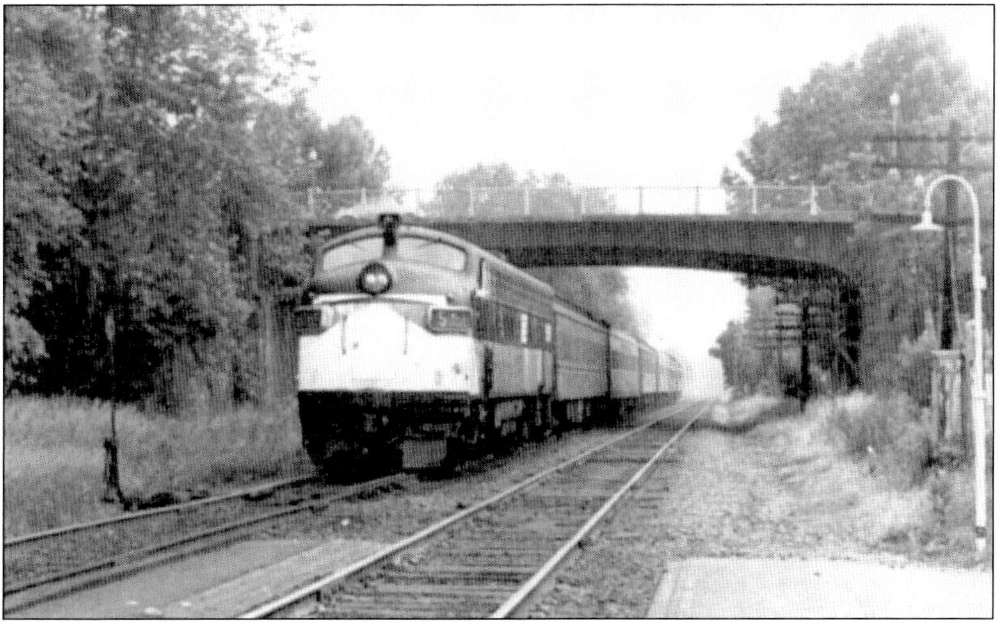

In 1952, the division switched to locomotives that could run on both electricity and diesel fuel. These diesel-electric trains eliminated the engine change at North White Plains and for a while shaved minutes from the schedule. But by the 1970s, the locomotives were wearing out and the quality of service was suffering a severe decline. (From *The Coming of the New York and Harlem Railroad*, by Louis V. Grogan, New York, 1989.)

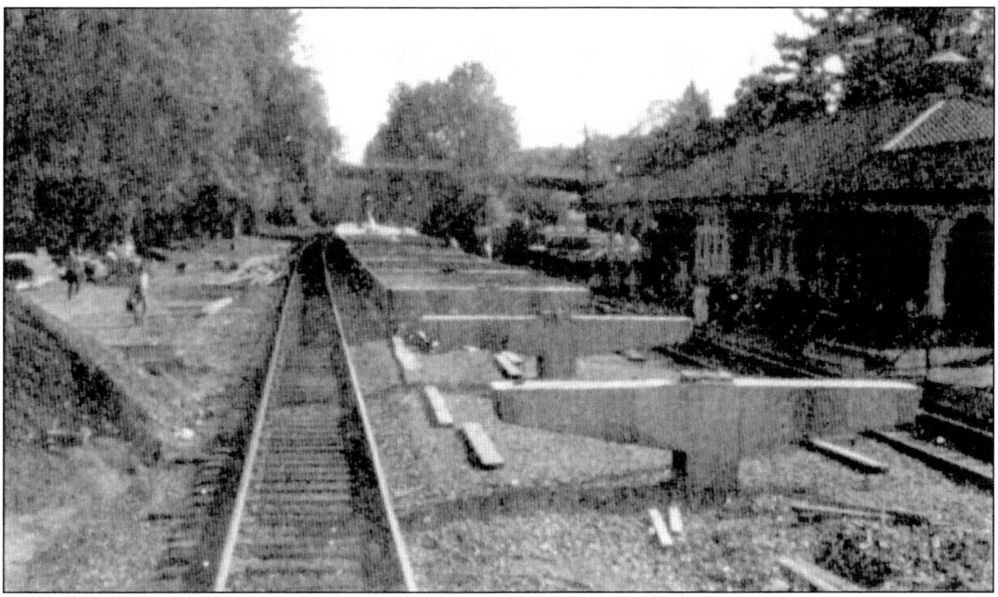

Service was not improved until 1984, when a major reconstruction of the Harlem line, now the Harlem Division of the Metro-North Railroad, was completed. The system was completely electrified, passenger platforms were raised and overpasses built, and old locomotives and passenger cars were replaced. The result was an immense improvement in service and a sharp increase in the number of riders. (From *The Coming of the New York and Harlem Railroad* by Louis V. Grogan, New York, 1989.)

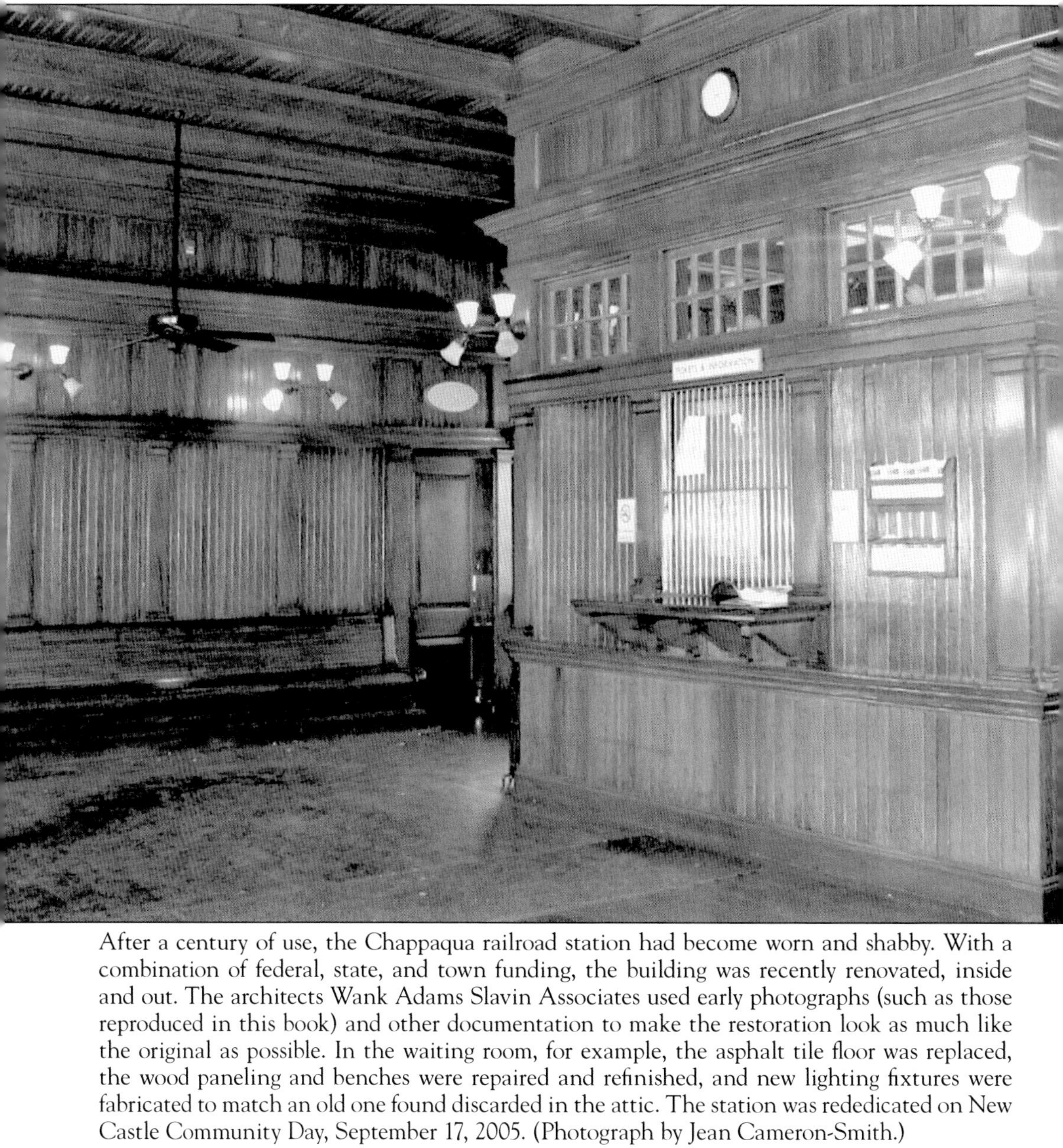

After a century of use, the Chappaqua railroad station had become worn and shabby. With a combination of federal, state, and town funding, the building was recently renovated, inside and out. The architects Wank Adams Slavin Associates used early photographs (such as those reproduced in this book) and other documentation to make the restoration look as much like the original as possible. In the waiting room, for example, the asphalt tile floor was replaced, the wood paneling and benches were repaired and refinished, and new lighting fixtures were fabricated to match an old one found discarded in the attic. The station was rededicated on New Castle Community Day, September 17, 2005. (Photograph by Jean Cameron-Smith.)

Four

Religious Institutions

Although most of the early settlers in New Castle were Quakers, a number of them belonged to other denominations, particularly the Church of England. St. George's Episcopal Church was built at North Castle Corners (now Mount Kisco) less than a decade after the Friends Meeting House in Chappaqua. Although St. George's no longer exists, its memory is preserved in the gravestones of its parishioners in the churchyard, including that of Charles Haight, who donated the land and built the original church.

After the Revolution, many other religious organizations came to New Castle, among them Methodists, Presbyterians, Baptists, Congregationalists, Lutherans, Roman Catholics, and Jews. By the end of the 1800s, the Quakers were a relatively small minority, although they continued to play a significant role in community life.

Quaker tolerance and respect for other beliefs may help account for the ecumenical spirit that has long been a feature of religious activity in New Castle. As early as the 1860s, for example, Quaker Robert Haviland built a union church on King Street in Chappaqua for congregations that did not have a building of their own. The building later became a Baptist church and is now the home of the Lutheran Church of Our Redeemer.. Quaker Richard F. Carr was the founder in 1887 of the local chapter of Christian Endeavor, a nondenominational youth organization that was active for several decades. Today, the Church of the Crossroads, in the process of looking for a home, worships at the Chappaqua Friends Meeting House.

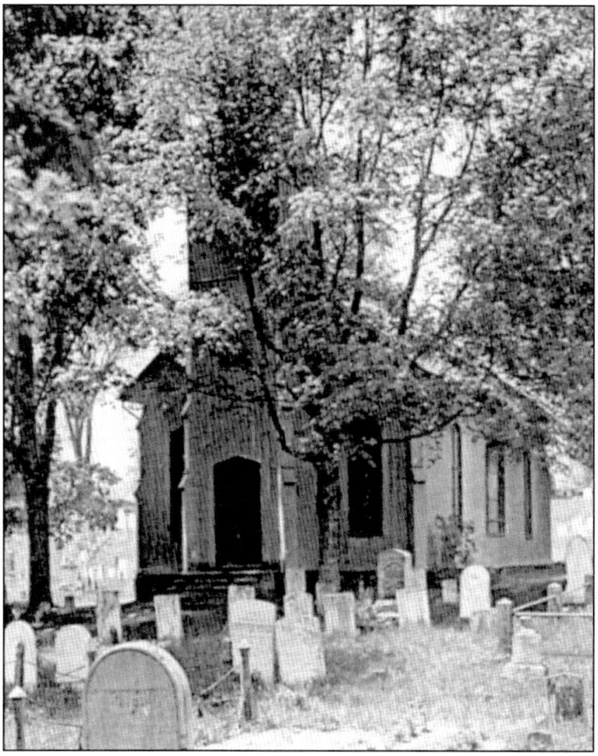

In 1761, Charles Haight donated the land and erected the building of St. George's Episcopal Church on Bedford Road in North Castle Corners (now southern Main Street, Mount Kisco). During the Revolution, the church was used as a military hospital, and soldiers who died there were buried in unmarked graves at the southeast corner of the churchyard. St. George's held services until 1810, and the building was demolished in 1819. In 1850, the congregation was revived as St. Mark's Episcopal Church. A small wooden church was erected in approximately the same location as St. George's. It remained in use until 1911, when the congregation moved to its current church in the center of Mount Kisco. The footprint of the old building is outlined in stone in the former churchyard.

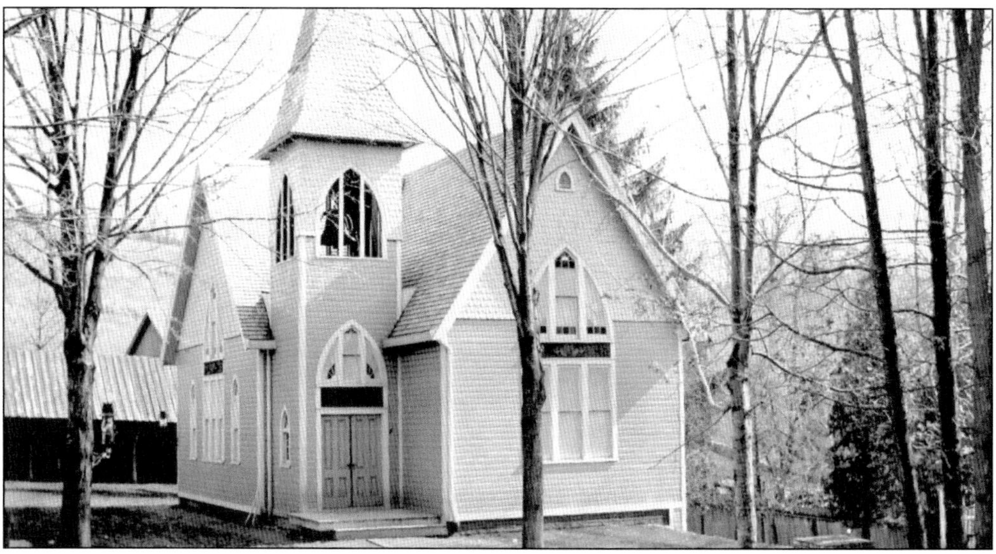

Robert S. Haviland was an active Quaker who had extensive land holdings near the center of Chappaqua. He sold Horace Greeley much of Greeley's farm, and at some time prior to 1867, he constructed a union church next to Greeley's home on King Street for use by congregations that lacked a church of their own. It became the exclusive home of a Baptist congregation in 1881. The original church burned in 1897 and was replaced by the one shown here, a yellow clapboard Carpenter Gothic structure with a tall steeple. During the 1930s, the congregation dwindled, and the church was vacated in 1938. It was reopened as the Lutheran Church of Our Redeemer on Easter Sunday in April 1946, and was extensively remodeled and modernized in 1948.

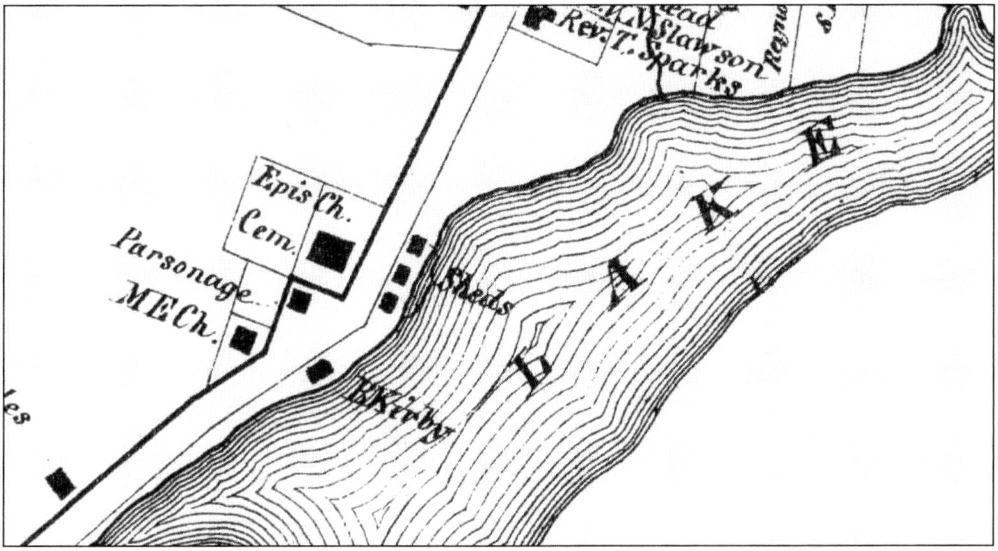

In 1791, New Castle was separated from North Castle, and the hamlet of North Castle Corners became New Castle Corners. In 1825, local Methodists, who had been meeting in private homes since the 1780s, built a church in New Castle Corners, next to the Episcopal church on what is now Main Street in Mount Kisco. A Methodist cemetery was established behind the Episcopal churchyard. In 1843, a larger Methodist Episcopal church ("M. E. Ch." on this 1867 map detail) was constructed on an adjacent lot to the south, and the original church became the parsonage. Within a couple of decades, the congregation had outgrown the new church, and the population center had shifted toward the Mount Kisco railroad station.

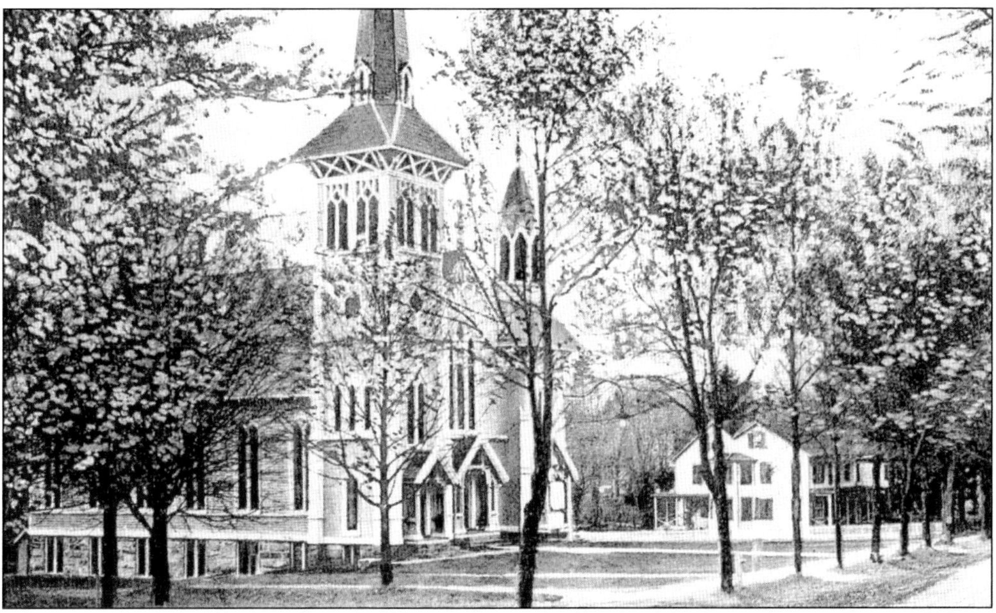

In 1866, the Methodists acquired a site halfway between New Castle Corners and the railroad station and, in 1868, completed construction of a new church. Its style was Carpenter Gothic, translating the stone decorations of Medieval architecture into wood. This church is still in use. No trace remains of the original Methodist church and parsonage, but the Methodist cemetery still exists behind the old Episcopal churchyard.

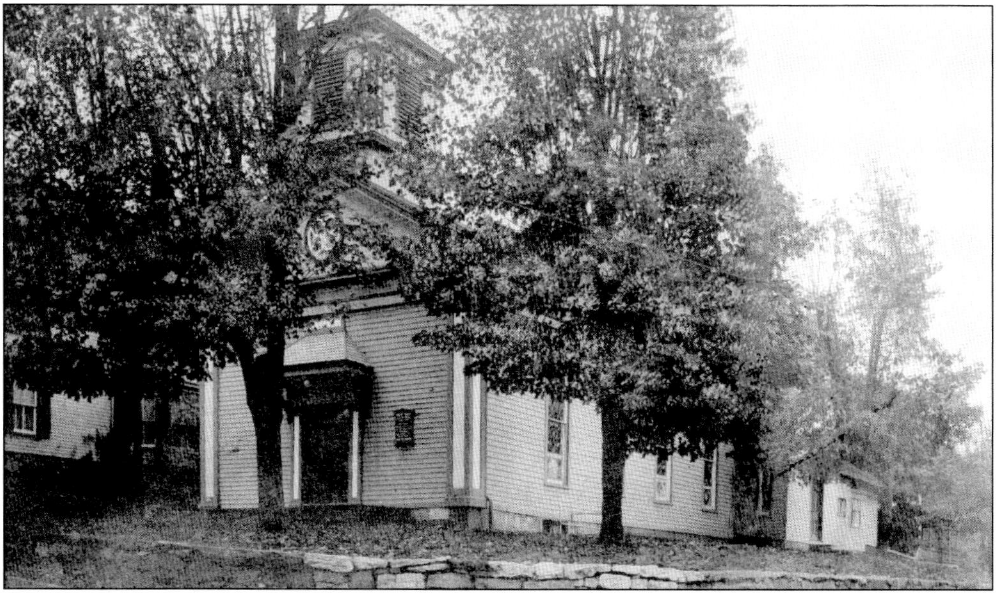

In 1851, Joseph M. Merritt donated a site for a church to a congregation of Presbyterians who had been meeting in private homes. The Greek Revival church was built in 1852 and became the Presbyterian Church of Mount Kisco when New Castle Corners was renamed in the 1860s. The congregation expanded over the next century and completely outgrew the church after World War II. The building is now the home of the St. Francis African Methodist Episcopal Zion Church. (Courtesy of the Mount Kisco Historical Society.)

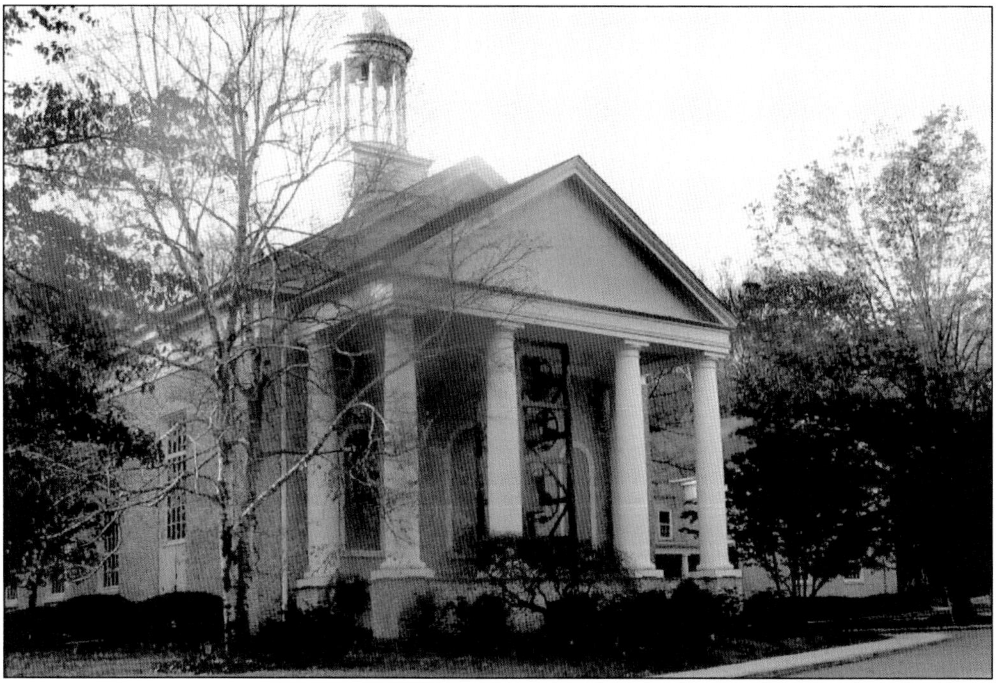

In the 1960s, members of the Joseph Choate family donated a site for a new and larger Presbyterian church across Millwood Road from their home at the corner of Crow Hill Road. Services in the new building began in 1969, and the carillon was added in 1976. (Photograph by Jean Cameron-Smith.)

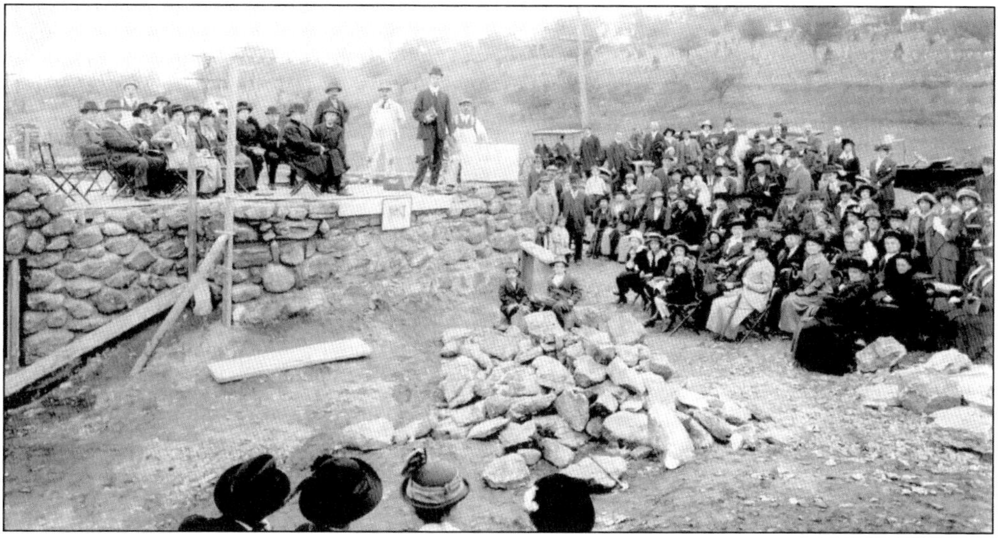

The congregation of the First Congregational Church in Chappaqua was formed in 1911 under the leadership of Emilee Barnes Turner. Services were initially held at Hyatt's Auditorium in the center of the village. A site for the church was purchased in 1913 at the corner of King Street and Orchard Ridge Road. Pictured is the laying of the cornerstone in October 1914. Constructed of rugged cobblestone, the building at first had only one story and a temporary roof. Completed in 1926, it served the congregation until 1952. The property was then successively occupied by Temple Beth El and the Westchester Baptist Church.

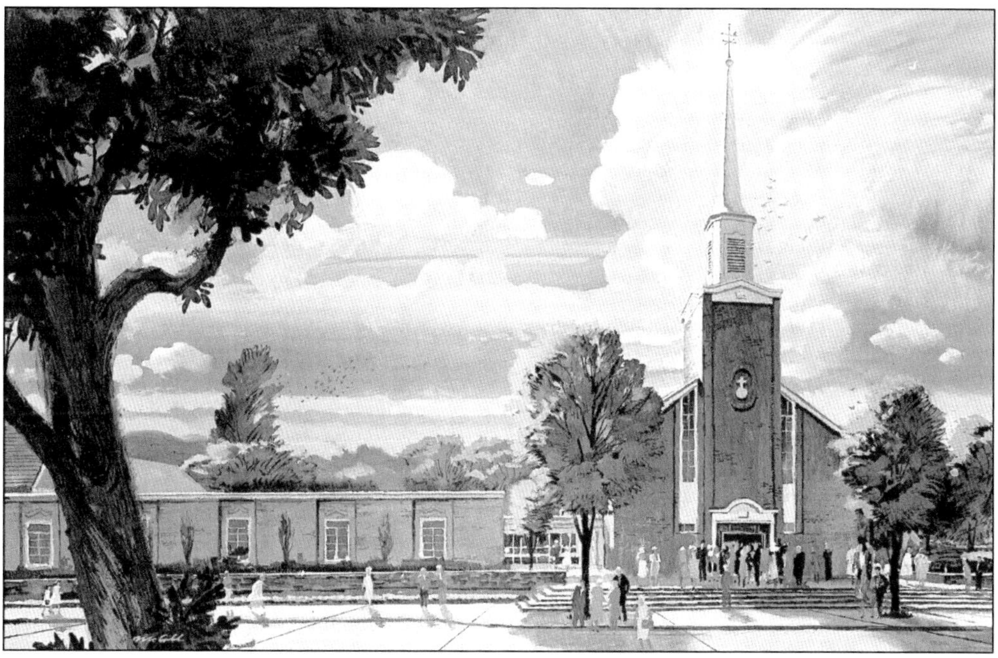

By the end of World War II, the Congregationalists needed a much larger facility. A building fund was established in 1945, a six-acre site at the corner of Orchard Ridge and Bedford roads was purchased in 1948, and the first part of the church was completed in 1952. As the membership grew, substantial additions were made to both the church and its service wings. (Courtesy of the First Congregational Church.)

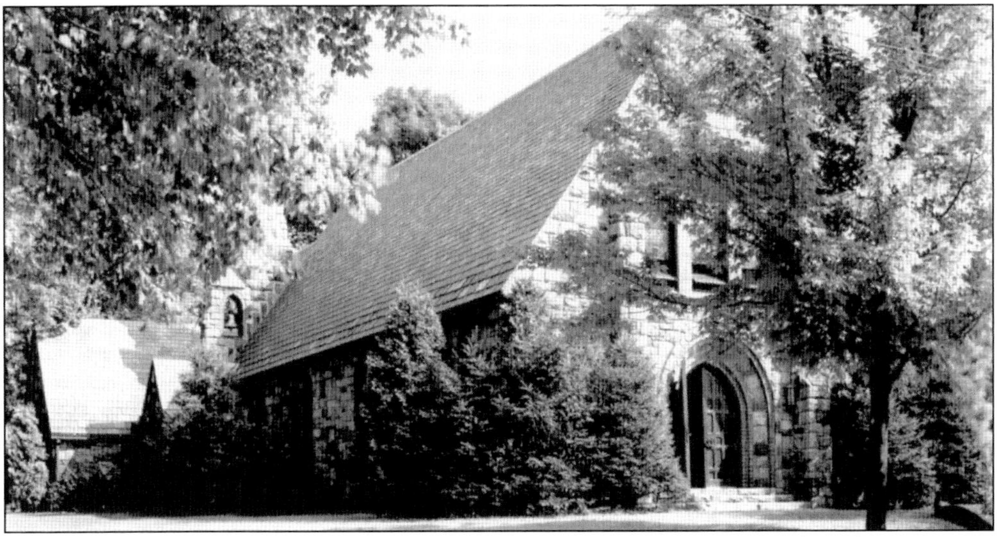

In 1922, the Roman Catholic Church of St. John and St. Mary was built of local stone across King Street from the Congregational church, at the corner of St. John's Place. Catherine Manning McKeon donated the site and the building in memory of her parents. The restrained Gothic style was reminiscent of English and Irish country churches. The rectory next door, built in 1929, was the gift of Catherine McKeon's son, Daniel Manning McKeon. The congregation eventually outgrew the building, and in 1974, the church's former parochial school auditorium was renovated for worship. Mass is now held in both buildings.

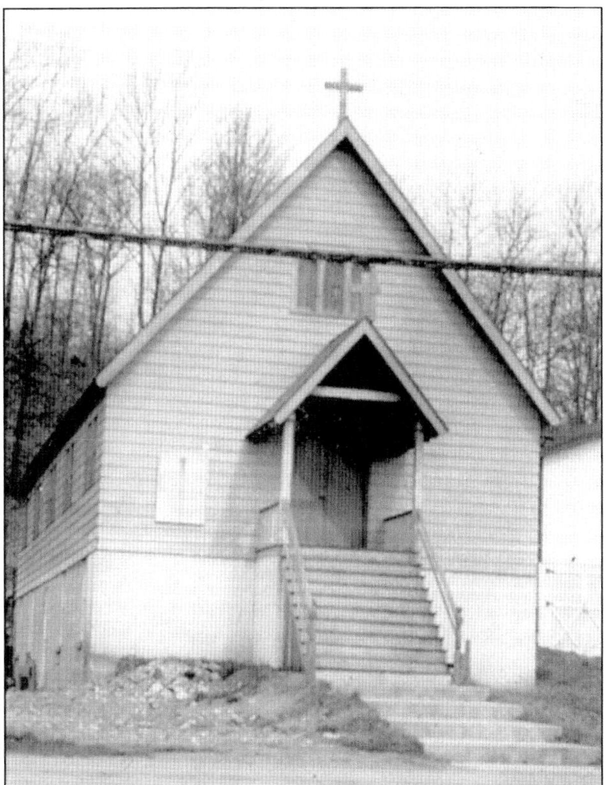

From the end of the 1800s, Catholics in the Millwood area began worshiping in private homes, with priests from nearby parishes offering mass. In 1924, Henry H. Law of Briarcliff Manor donated a site for a Catholic church on Route 100, and Our Lady of the Wayside was completed and dedicated on June 21, 1925. The building was raised to create a basement meeting room and kitchen after World War II. It is now a mission church of the parish of St. Teresa in Briarcliff Manor. (Courtesy of Richard Pogact.)

In 1923, the Society of the Helpers of the Holy Souls purchased the 40-acre estate of Percy Kent, east of Bedford Road and south of Overlook Drive. Over the next four years, the society erected the Novitiate of Our Lady of Providence, a training school and convent for nuns. In this 1927 photograph, construction workers pose on the heavy framing of the chapel roof. Identified here are Elmer Greenwood, unidentified, Joe Brown, Eddie Johansmeyer, Joe Brody, and Gus Allen.

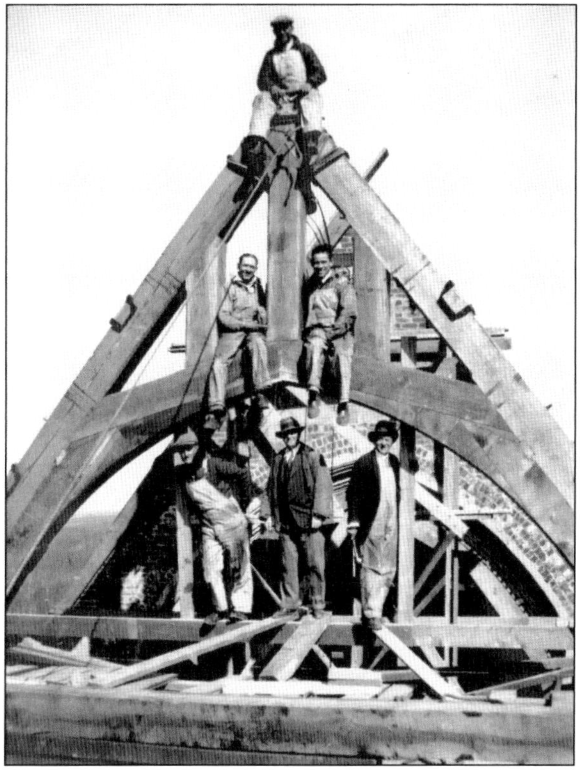

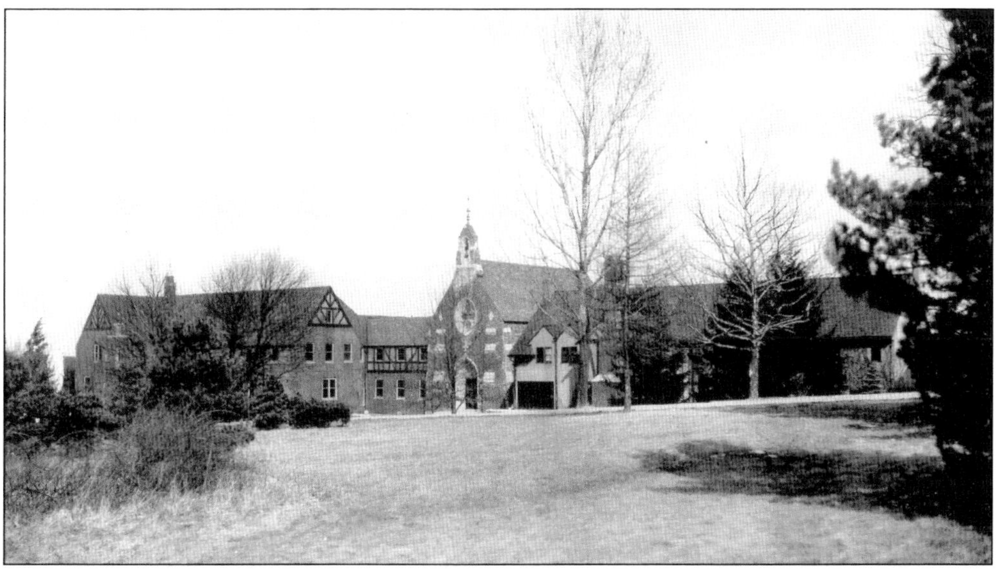

The Novitiate of Our Lady of Providence had largely ceased operations in 1973, when the property was purchased by the Christian Herald Ministries, an interdenominational evangelical organization with extensive relief and publishing programs. The former novitiate was the Christian Herald headquarters until 1993, when the organization centered its activities in New York City. Most of the buildings were thereafter demolished, and the land was subdivided for residential development.

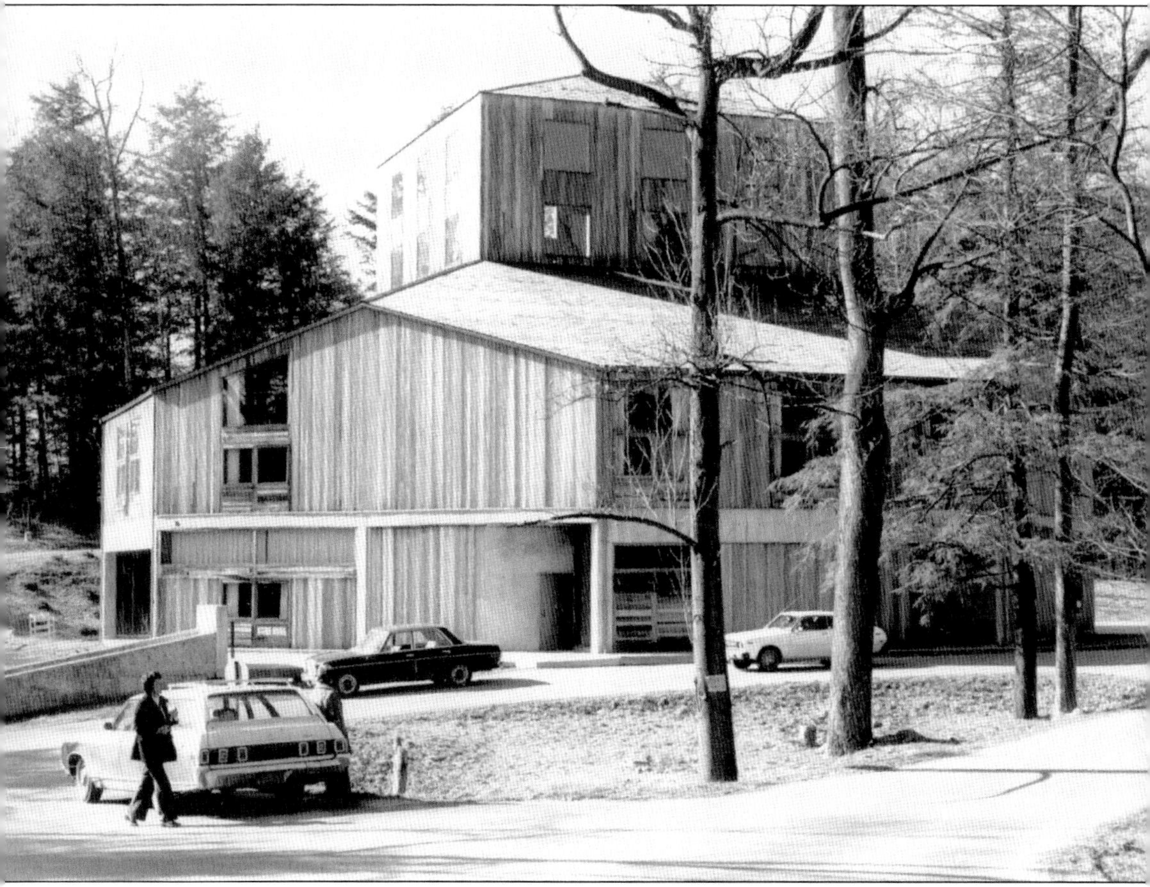

Founded in 1949, the Reform Jewish congregation of Temple Beth El first held services in the former Congregational church on King Street, then in the Mount Kisco Presbyterian Church on Kisco Avenue, and in 1954, back in the Congregational church, which had been remodeled as a synagogue with a travertine marble ark for the sanctuary. The congregation outgrew the building within a decade and, in 1965, bought nine acres of land on Bedford Road, once part of the woods on Horace Greeley's farm, for a new synagogue with room for a religious school. The purchase was financed largely by the Sisterhood of the Temple through proceeds from its Opportunity Shop thrift store. The dramatic synagogue and school, with a high central clerestory, was designed by architect Louis I. Kahn and was dedicated in 1972. (Courtesy of the Westchester County Historical Society.)

Five

THE PUBLIC SCHOOLS

New York State pioneered in public education, principally through a law passed in 1812 that required every town to be divided into school districts governed by elected school boards with the power to finance their schools by local taxes. With some adjustments and exceptions, this system has endured to this day.

At one time New Castle was divided into as many as a dozen public school districts. Throughout the 19th century, however, these districts had only "common" schools. The common schools were typically small and plain, with only one or two classrooms. They provided education only up to the present eighth-grade level.

More advanced, college-preparatory courses were available at private academies, for which tuition had to be paid. Not until the late 1920s was there a public high school in New Castle.

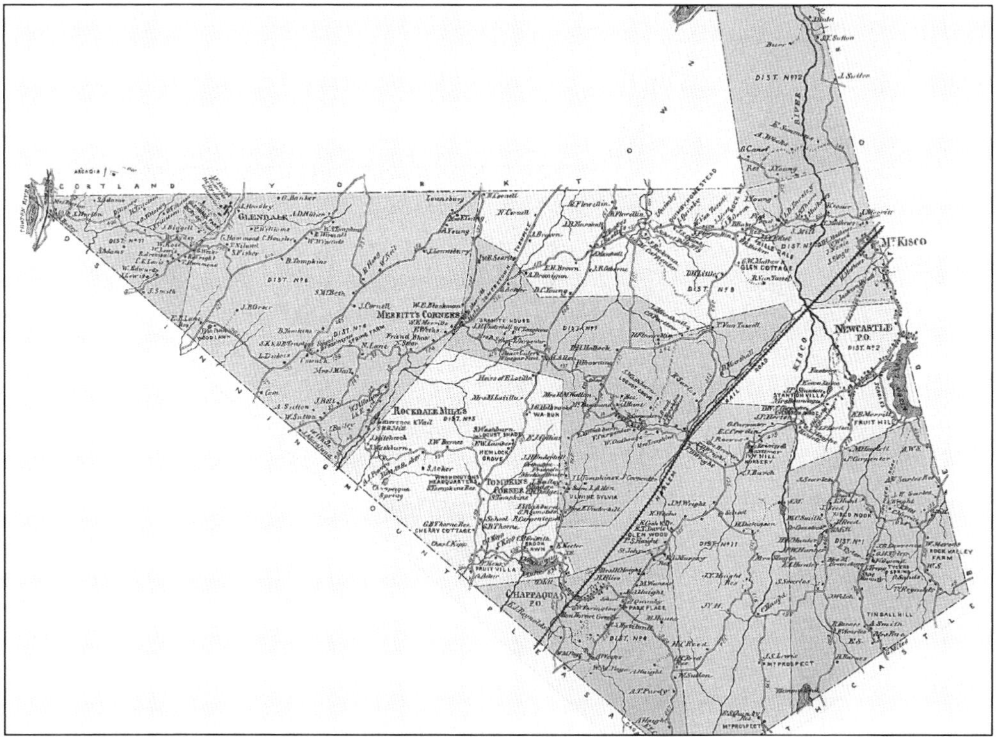

On this map from 1867, New Castle is divided into several sections. Each section represents a public school district, of which there were up to a dozen in the town.

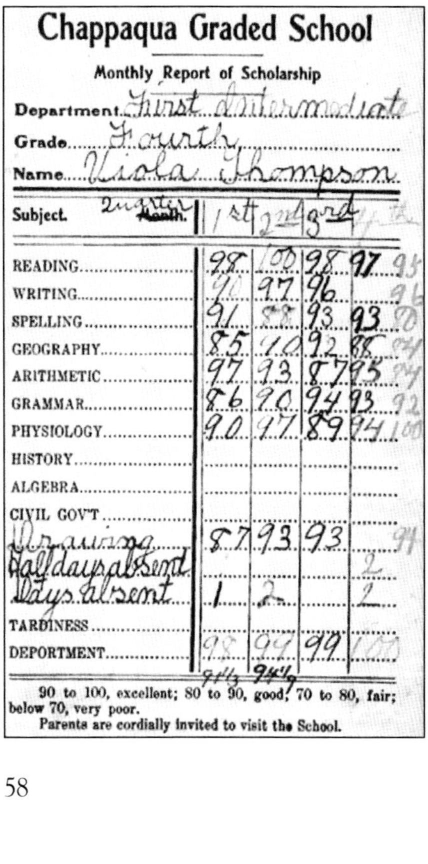

Chappaqua Graded School

Monthly Report of Scholarship

Department. First Intermediate

Grade. Fourth

Name. Viola Thompson

Subject. Quarter ~~Month.~~	1st	2nd	3rd	4th	
READING	98	100	98	97	95
WRITING	90	97	96		96
SPELLING	91	88	93	93	90
GEOGRAPHY	85	100	92	88	84
ARITHMETIC	97	93	87	95	84
GRAMMAR	86	90	94	93	92
PHYSIOLOGY	90	97	89	94	100
HISTORY					
ALGEBRA					
CIVIL GOV'T					
Drawing	87	93	93		94
Half days absent					2
Days absent	1	2		2	
TARDINESS					
DEPORTMENT	98	94	99	100	
	91 1/3	94 4/9			

90 to 100, excellent; 80 to 90, good; 70 to 80, fair; below 70, very poor.

Parents are cordially invited to visit the School.

Viola Thomson's fourth-grade report card shows the subjects typically taught in the common schools. The fourth-grade curriculum was composed of reading, writing, spelling, geography, arithmetic, grammar, physiology, and drawing. In the higher grades, history, algebra, and civil government would be added. She was also graded on deportment, and her attendance was recorded.

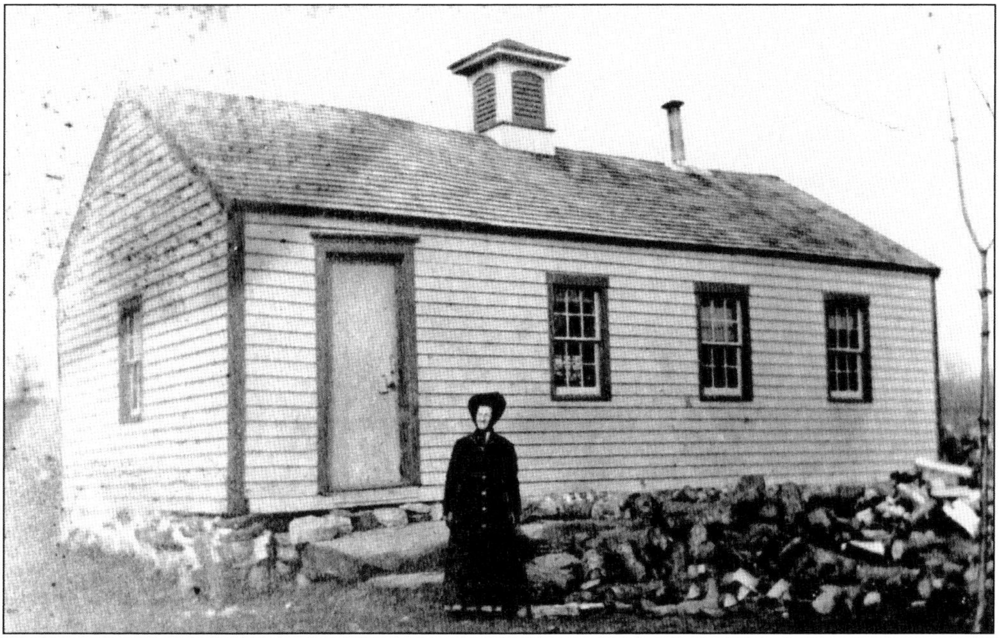

This 19th-century photograph shows the teacher and one-room building of the Pinesbridge-Inningwood School of District No. 6, located in the western triangle of New Castle, on Inningwood Road near its northern end at Pinesbridge Road. Although some common-school teachers were men, the great majority were unmarried or widowed women. Teaching was one of the few professions open to women until well into the 20th century, but it was not considered appropriate for married women and was quite unacceptable for women who were pregnant. (Courtesy of Phil Chadeayne.)

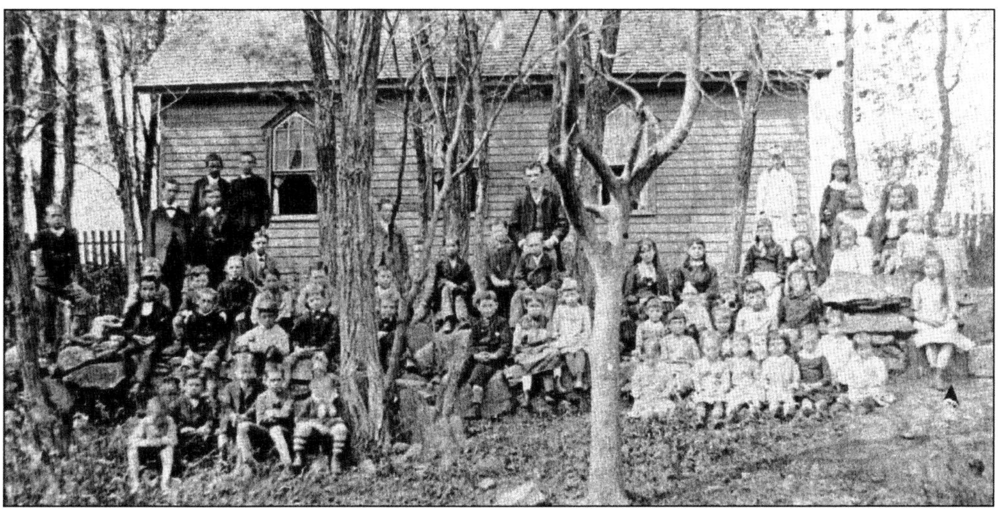

The King Street School of District No. 4, at the intersection of King Street (Route 120) and Bedford Road (Route 117), was until about 1885 a small, one-room facility. Because the district was in the fastest growing part of town, it rapidly expanded and eventually became the nucleus of the Chappaqua school system.

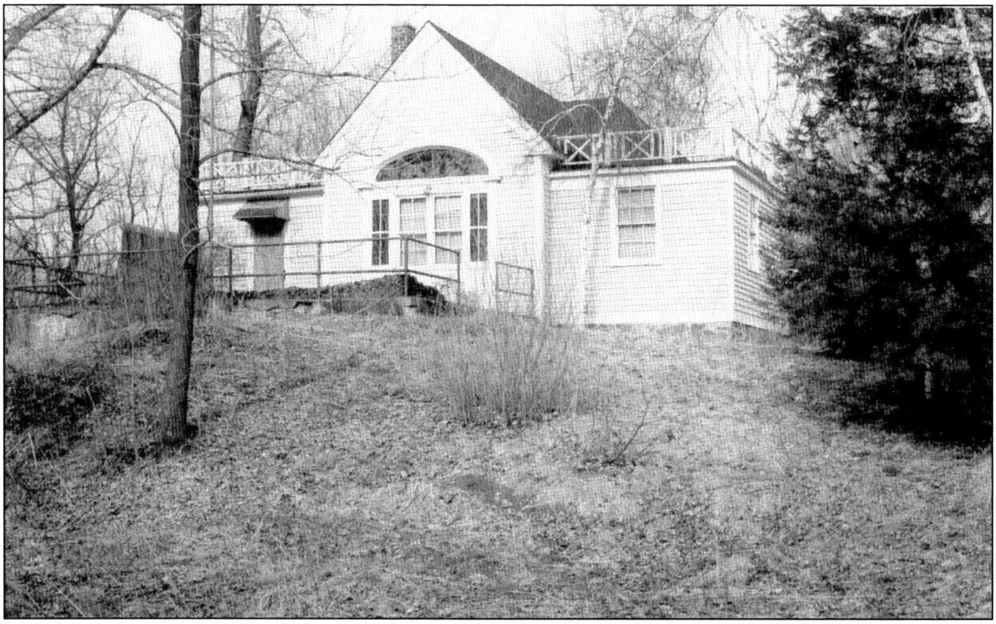

As New Castle's population increased toward the end of the 19th century, the common schools were enlarged. The Kipp Street School of District No. 5, erected in 1890, had two classrooms. Located on the edge of an extensive wetland, it was informally known as Swamp College. It served as a common school until about 1930 and continued to be used as a kindergarten until 1964. The building now houses a community center for art education.

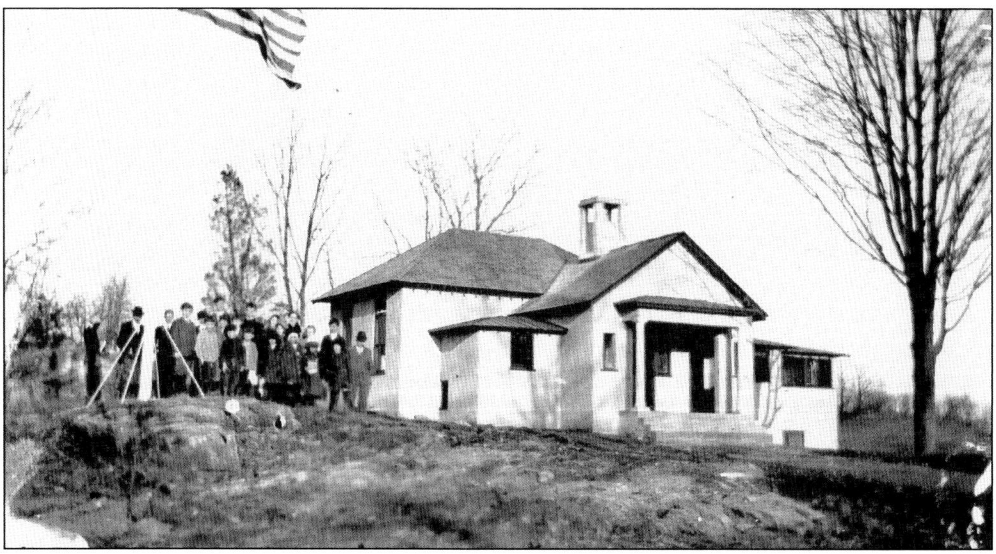

The "new" Roaring Brook School of District No. 7, completed in 1914, was the last of the common schools to be built in New Castle. In 1940, it was acquired by the Boy Scouts of America and for many years served as the scout hut for Troop 1. In the 1990s, it was demolished and replaced, on virtually the same footprint, by a private residence.

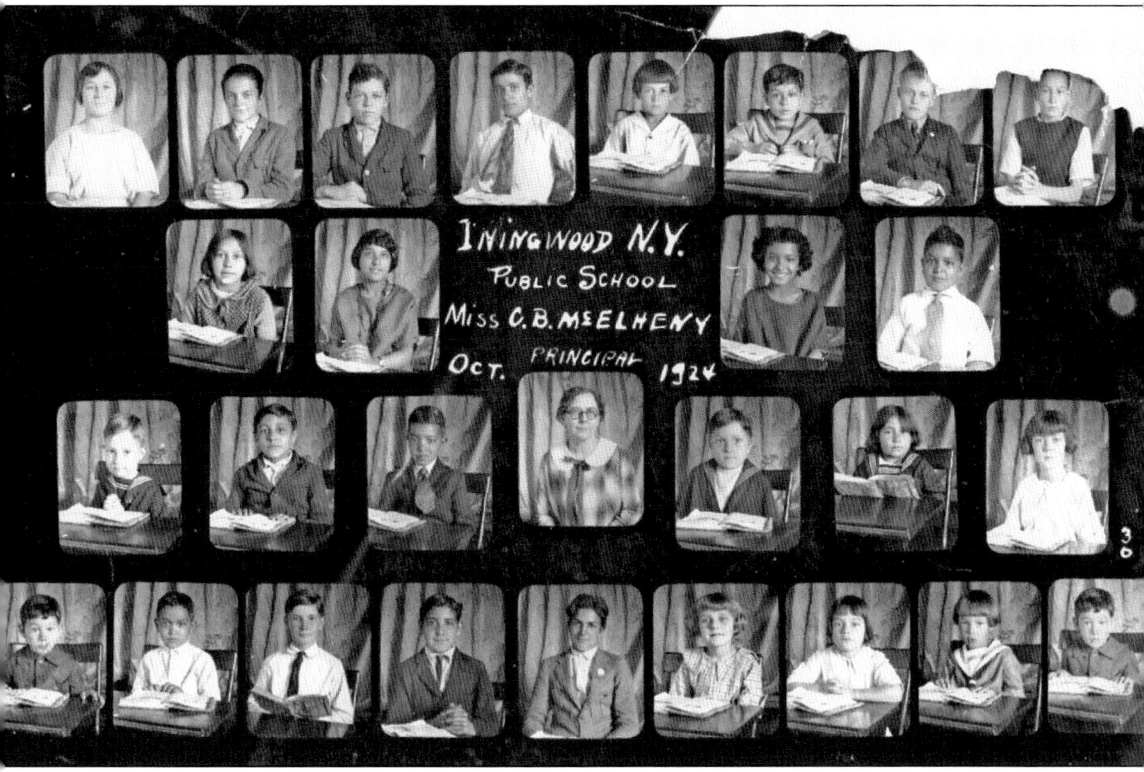

In the early, one-room common schools, all students from small children to early adolescents were taught together. As the population grew and the schools enlarged to two or more rooms, the primary grades might be separated from the more advanced grammar-school levels, but classrooms for individual grades did not become established until the end of the 1920s. This composite portrait of 27 students of the one-room Inningwood School shows a range from rather scared-looking first-graders, probably no more than six years old, to assured teenage eighth graders. The principal, Claire McElheny, was almost certainly the sole teacher.

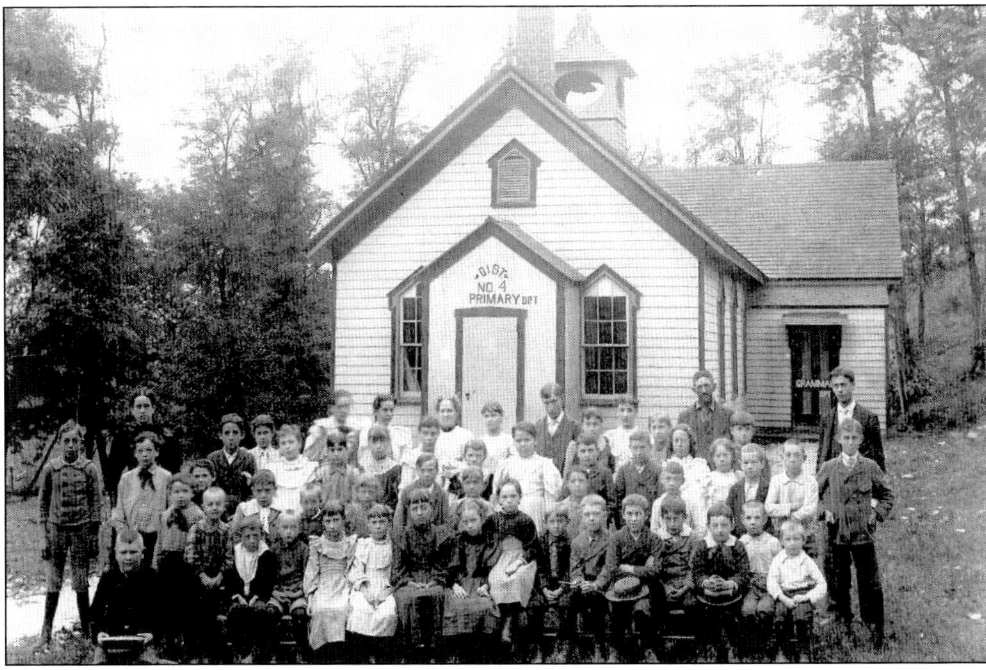

Photographs document the rapid growth and change in the King Street School of District No. 4, also known as the Village School. Up to about 1885, it was a one-room school, and it was then enlarged to contain two classrooms, one for the "primary department" and the other for the "grammar department."

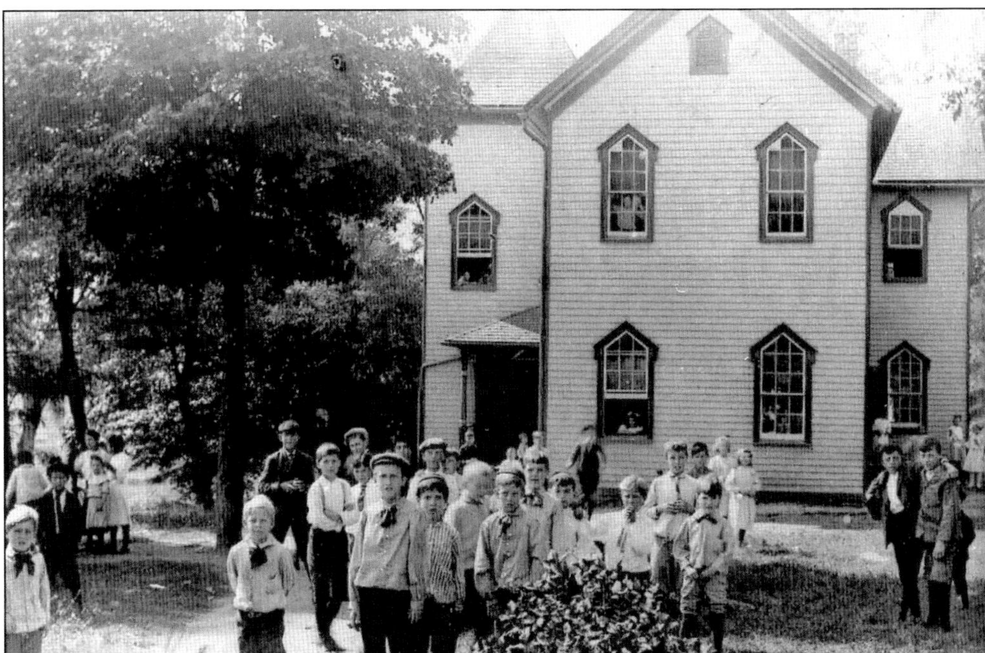

Toward the end of the 19th century, the school was enlarged to two stories. It continued to have one distinctive architectural feature: its pointed, vaguely Gothic windows.

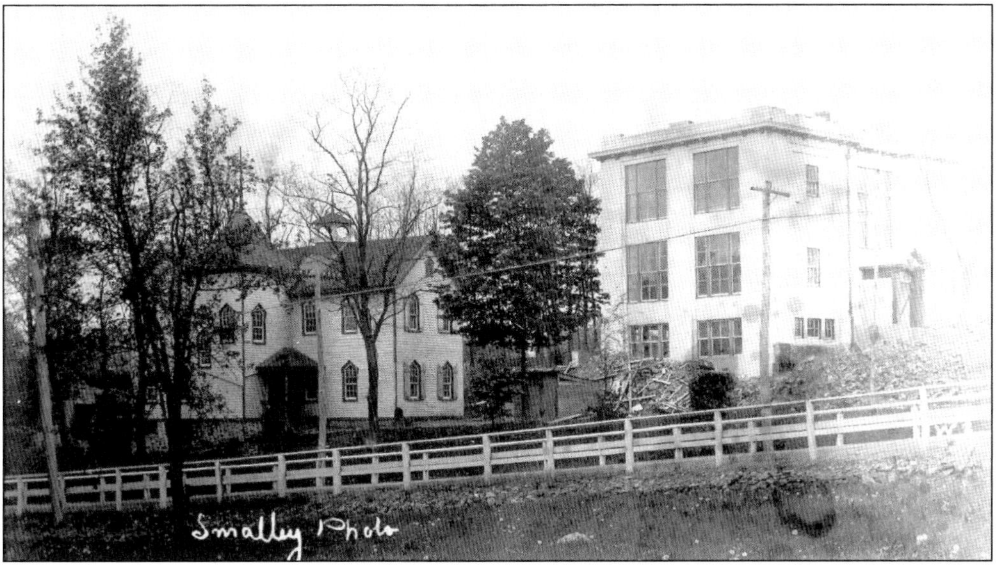

This August 1909 photograph shows the frame building of the King Street School (left), with a new and much more modern masonry building under construction next to it. It became the "new" King Street School, with several important innovations. First of all, it was constructed of fire-resistant steel and masonry rather than wood. Its classrooms were larger, with high ceilings and large windows for improved light and ventilation. It had central heating rather than individual stoves, and, last but not least, it provided indoor bathrooms.

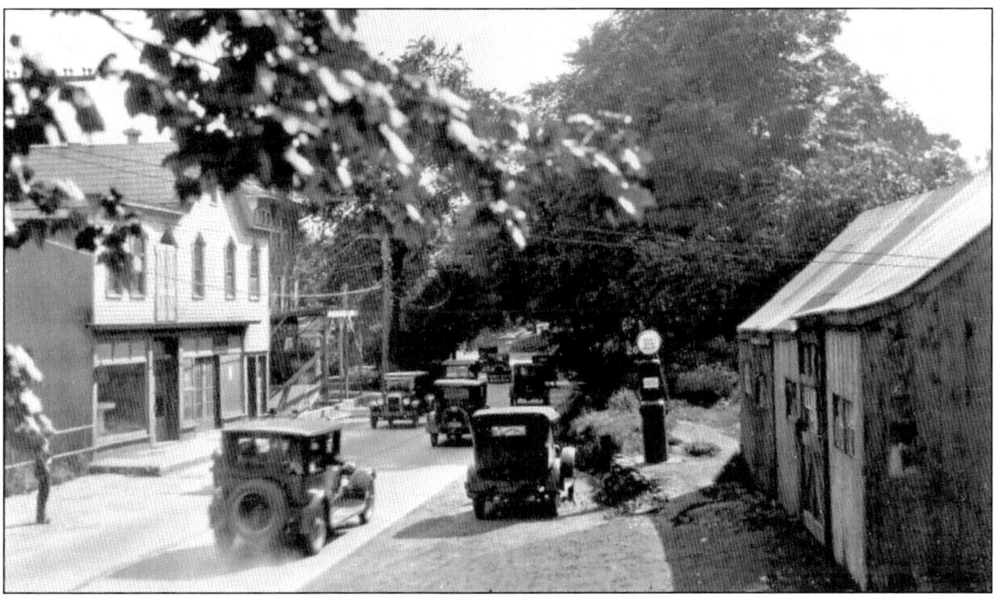

The old frame building was taken down, but elements from it were reassembled in a commercial building across the street. The distinctive pointed windows of the former school are evident at the left in this view down South Bedford Road in the 1920s. The building still survives, and its exterior has changed only slightly.

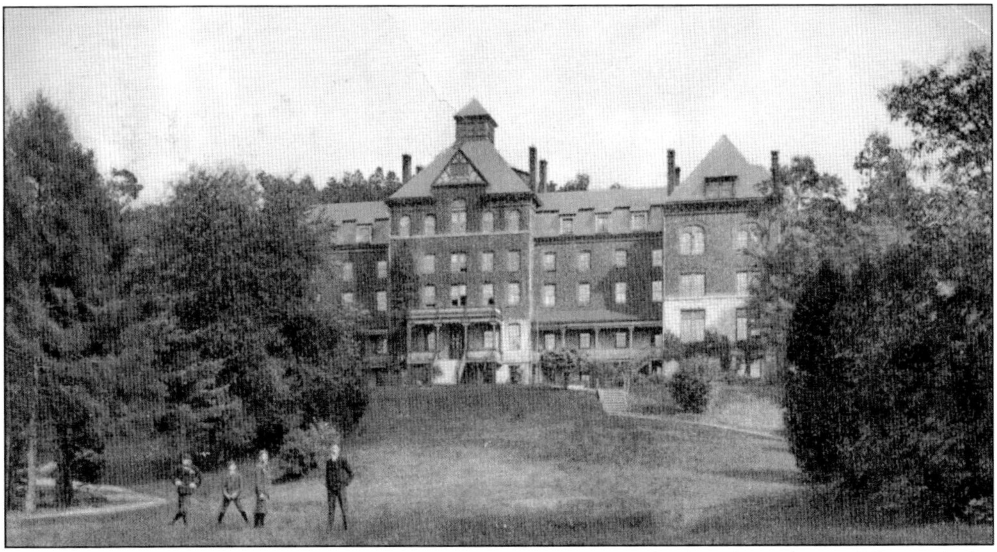

Until the early 20th century, New Castle students who wished to be educated beyond the common-school level had to attend private academies that charged tuition. One of the most highly regarded academies in this area was the Chappaqua Mountain Institute, operated by the Quakers. Its imposing four-story building and 40-acre campus were located on Quaker Street, across the road from the Friends' Meeting House. Founded in 1870, the school was nonsectarian and coeducational, and offered a four-year program roughly equivalent to high school. In later years, it provided elementary classes as well. Most of the students were boarders from elsewhere, but in each class there was always a substantial minority of local day students.

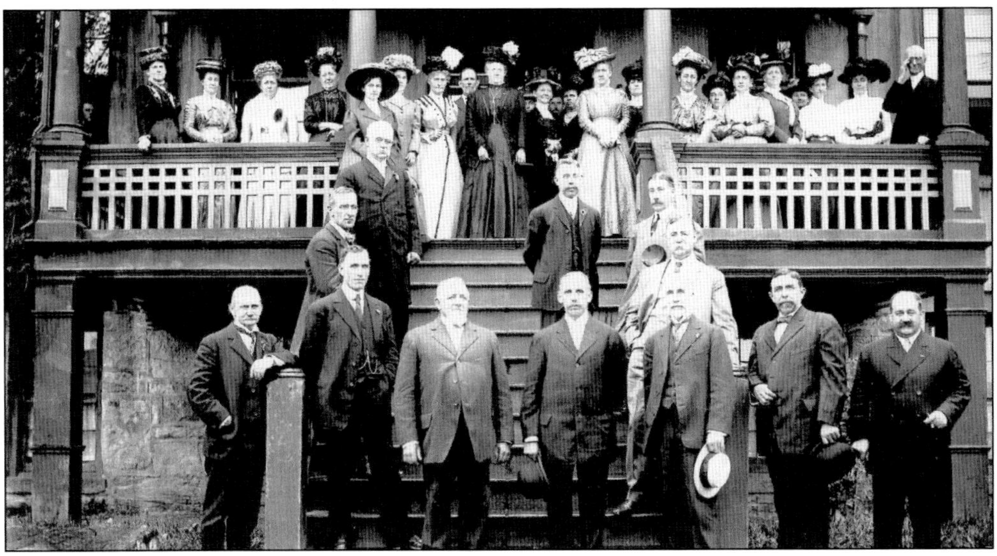

The Chappaqua Mountain Institute remained in operation until 1909. In this photograph, taken that year, the former administration and staff gather on the front steps for a group portrait. The school property was sold to the Children's Aid Society, and for several decades the building was used as a convalescent home, mainly for children from New York City. The home closed after World War II, and the building remained unoccupied until it burned. Starting in 1956, the grounds were occupied by Wagon Road Camp, a summer camp for children with illnesses and disabilities. It is now simply a day camp for area children.

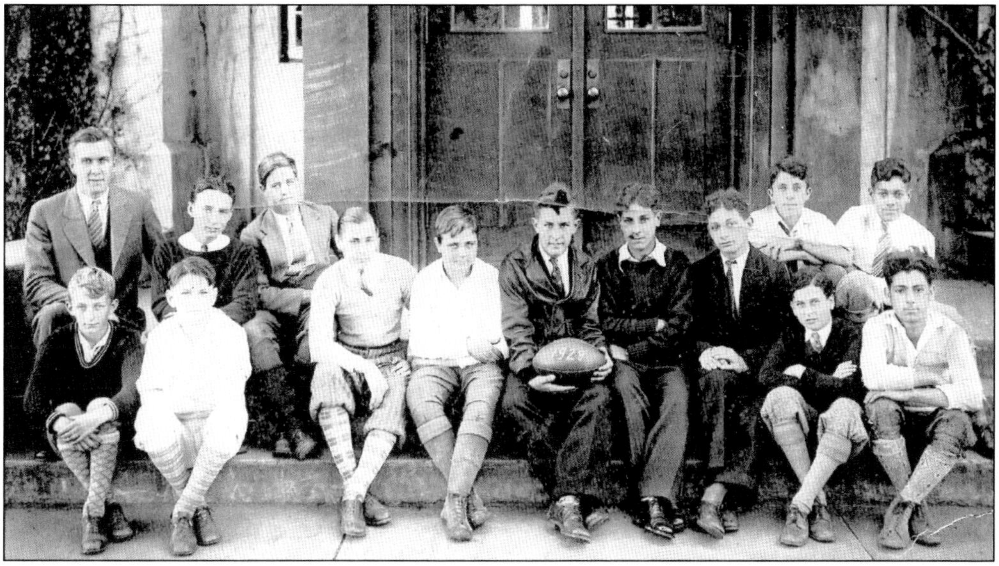

Through most of the 1920s, New Castle had only common schools, and education extended only to the eighth grade. Pictured in 1928 is the senior football team of the "new" King Street School on the steps at the building's back entrance.

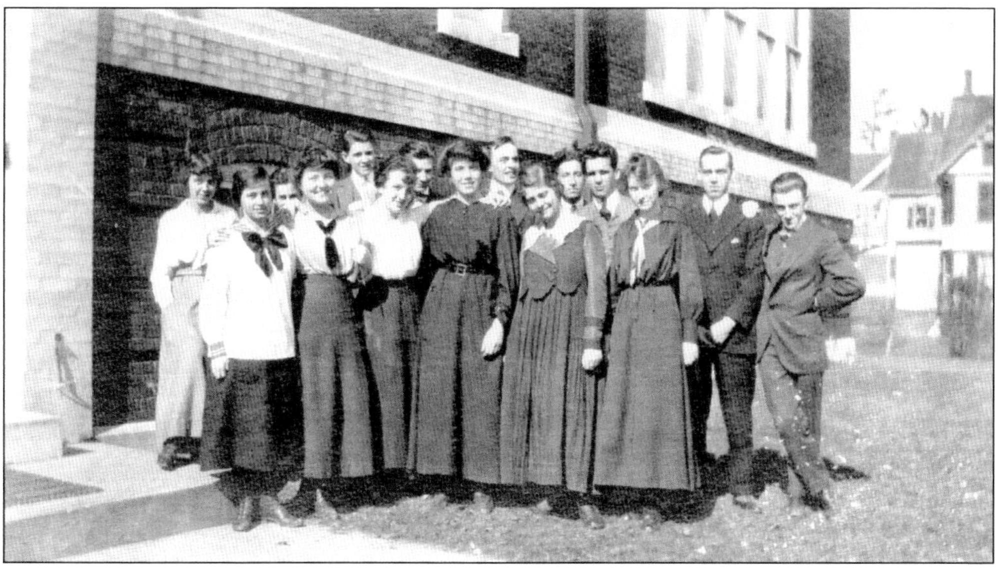

By the 1920s, some surrounding communities had public high schools that New Castle students could attend if their own districts were willing to pay the necessary fees. In the Chappaqua area, most high-school students traveled to Pleasantville. Several Chappaqua students are among those pictured next to Pleasantville High School. Names listed on the back are Rabe Burrage, Viola Thompson, Russell Jones, Alma Canavello, Harry Marshall, Anna Adrian, Milton Chamberlain, Mildred Mack, Robert Clark, George Mack, and Allen Wilkinson.

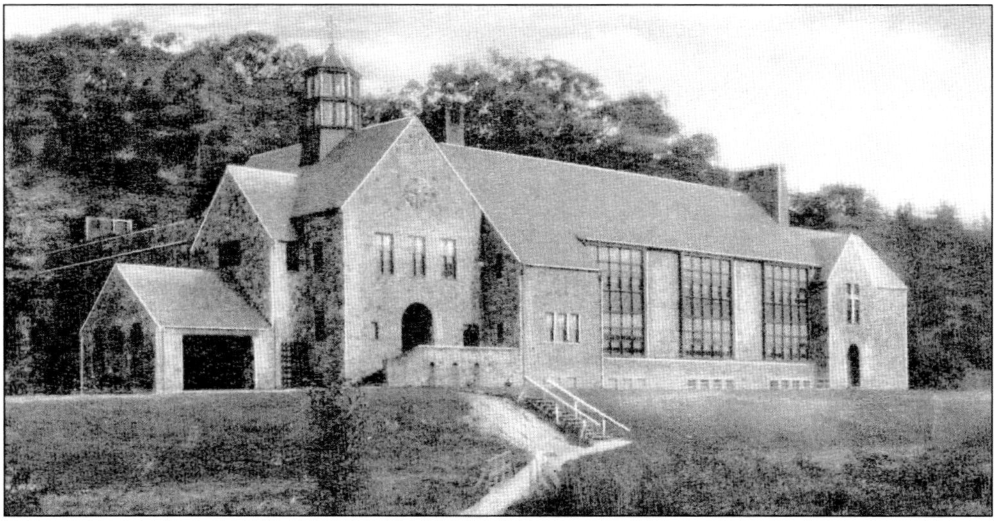

In 1926, School District No. 4 absorbed several other New Castle districts to form what was originally called Chappaqua Central School District No. 4 and eventually just the Chappaqua Central School District. The new district acquired about 10 acres of Horace Greeley's former farm in Chappaqua from his daughter Gabrielle Greeley Clendenin and proceeded to build a comprehensive school that would replace the old common schools. The Horace Greeley School, designed by local architect James Renwick Thomson, opened in early 1929. Like the common schools, it initially went only to the eighth grade, but high school classes were added, one at a time, until 1932.

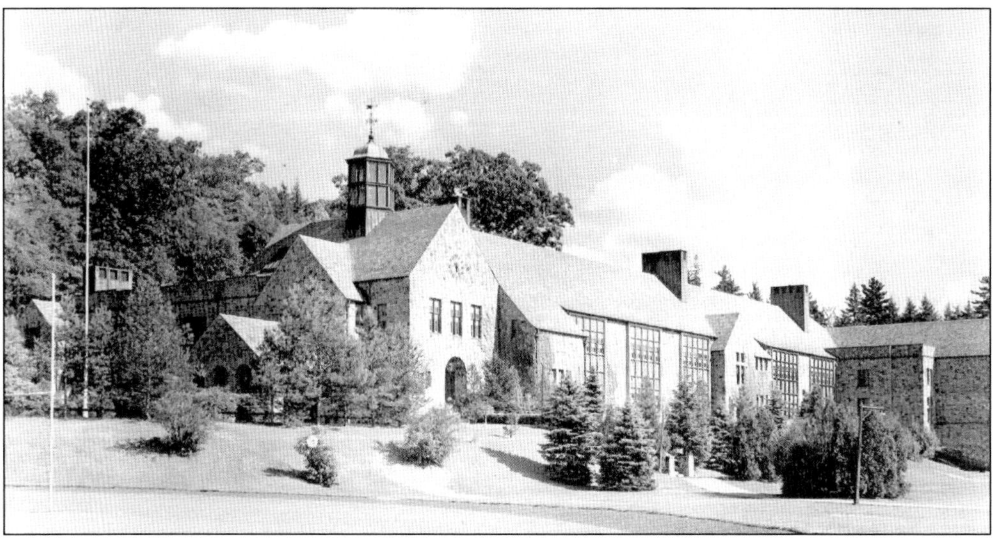

A matching addition was built in 1939. Unlike the small common schools, the new school contained not only classrooms but also facilities such as an auditorium, cafeteria, gymnasium, and library, not to mention extensive playing fields. The Horace Greeley School, highly visible on its downtown site, became a major community center.

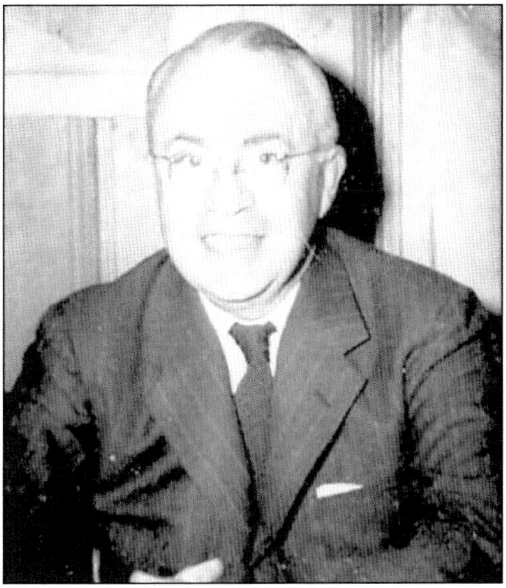

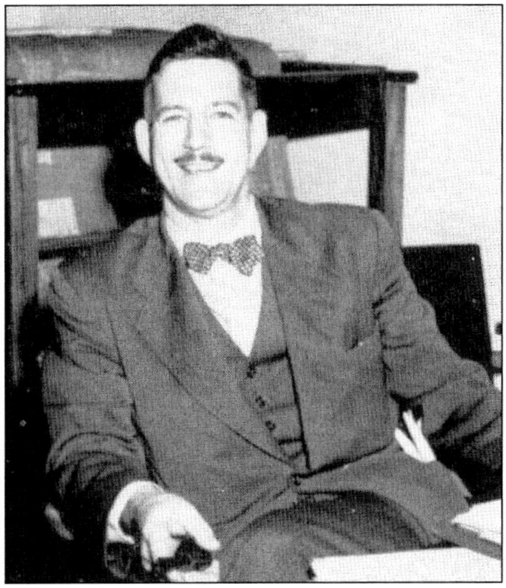

Chappaqua schools progressed not just because of new facilities but also because of the contributions of outstanding educators. The year that the new school opened, Robert E. Bell (upper left) was hired as district principal to manage the transition to a kindergarten-through-12th-grade system. An inspiring administrator, Bell attracted a staff of skilled teachers and quickly established Chappaqua as one of the leading school districts in the area. In 1942, he was promoted to superintendent of schools for northern Westchester, and Douglas G. Grafflin (upper right) succeeded him as district principal. Grafflin, an equally inspiring leader, oversaw the expansion of the curriculum in the junior- and senior-high grades. When the Horace Greeley High School opened in 1957, Donald W. Miles (lower left) became principal and oversaw its transformation to high-effort school, offering advanced-placement courses, and making it competitive with the region's leading private and public college-preparatory institutions. Miles's successor, Edward Hart (lower right), completed and consolidated that transformation when he became principal during the late 1960s.

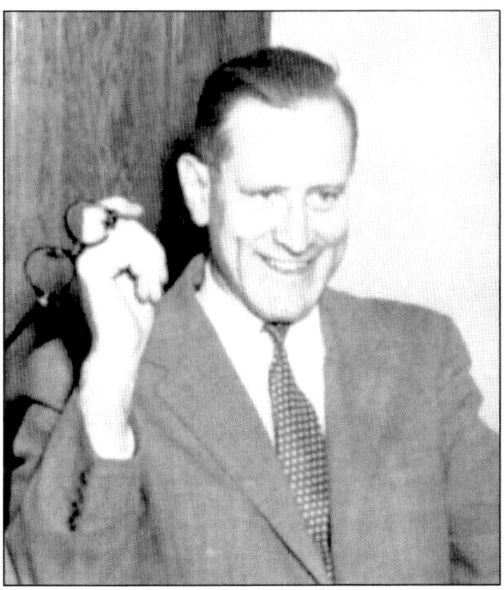

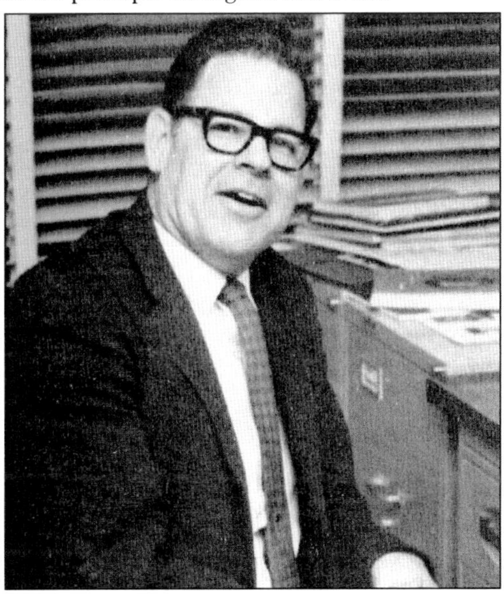

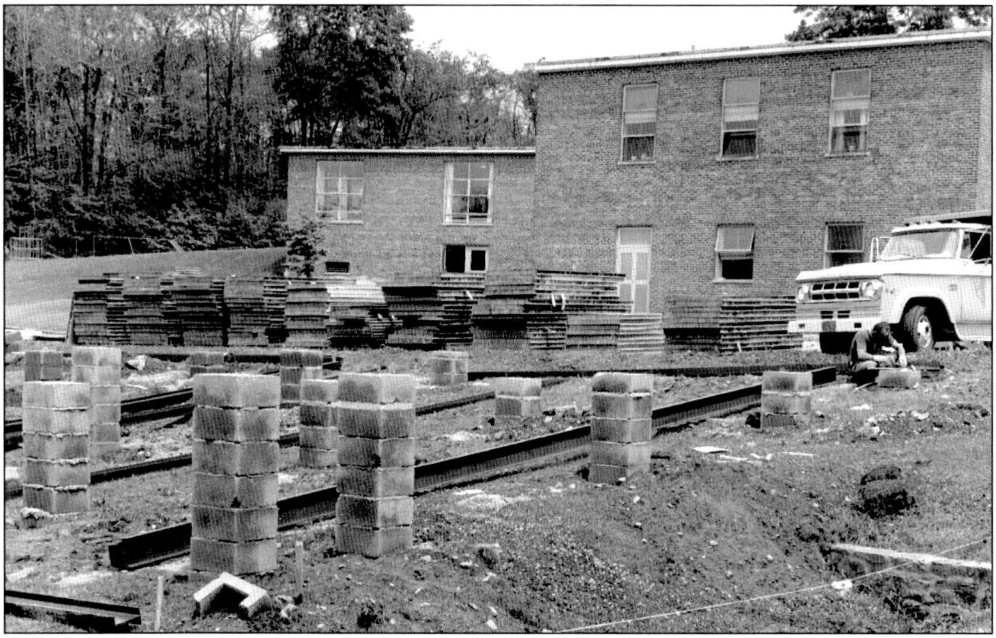

After World War II, the population in the Chappaqua school district exploded, due in great part to the recognized excellence of the schools. Through the 1950s and 1960s, the district struggled to keep up with the steadily growing number of students. Three new elementary schools and a high school were built, and the existing Horace Greeley School, renamed the Robert E. Bell Middle School, was greatly expanded. The first of the postwar schools was the Roaring Brook Elementary School on Quaker Street at the intersection with Roaring Brook Road. It took the name of the former common school for District No. 7, located across the street. In 1969 (as pictured), it required a substantial addition. (Courtesy of the Westchester County Historical Society.)

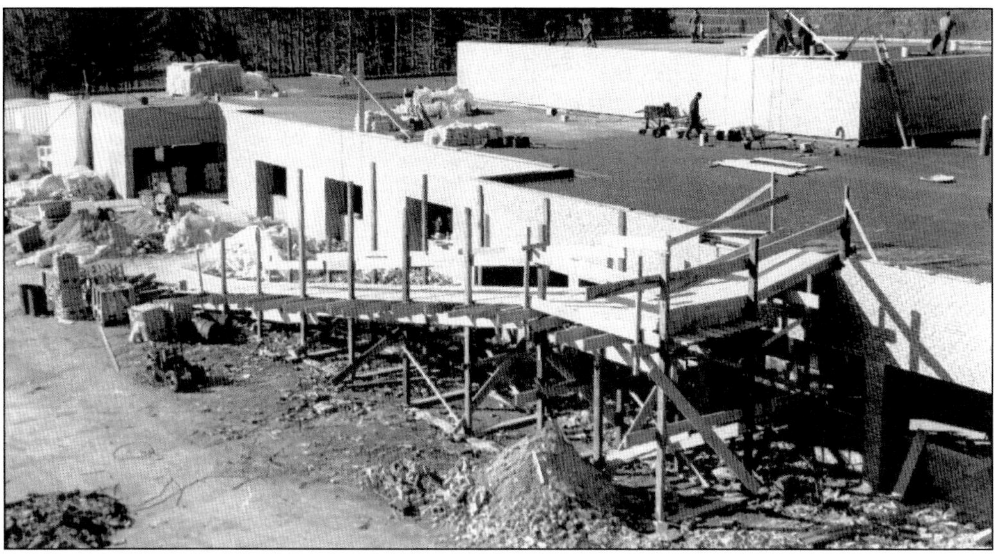

To soften the impact on taxpayers, the Westorchard Elementary School, on Granite Road near Millwood Road, was constructed in two stages, the first in 1971. But the student population rose so fast that the second stage had to be hastily built just six years later. (Courtesy of the Westchester County Historical Society.)

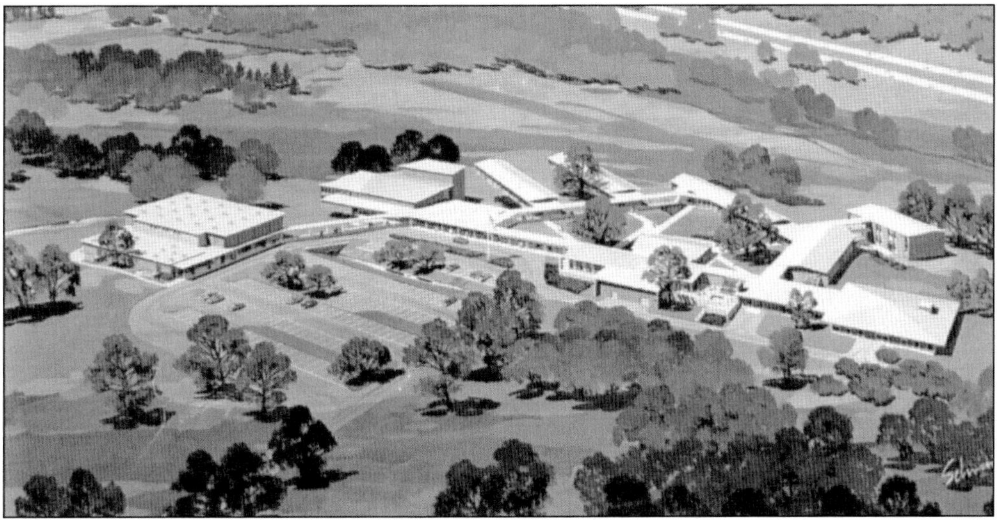

The most elaborate construction project in the district was the Horace Greeley High School, built in 1957 on a large site on Roaring Brook and Bedford Roads that had been the Wright-Barnum farm. Its design was quite innovative: instead of a large, single, multistory building, it was a campus of several separate buildings, most of which had a single story. (Courtesy of the Westchester County Historical Society.)

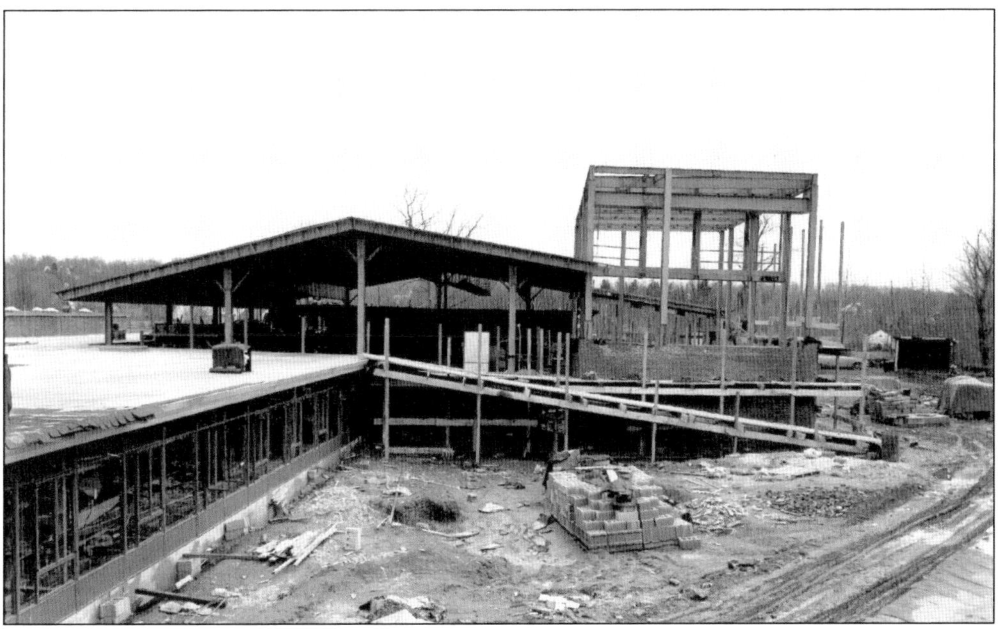

The individual buildings of the complex were connected by covered walkways. Shown is the construction of the large auditorium wing. The high school, like the other schools in the district, has required several additions and extensions over the years. (Courtesy of the Westchester County Historical Society.)

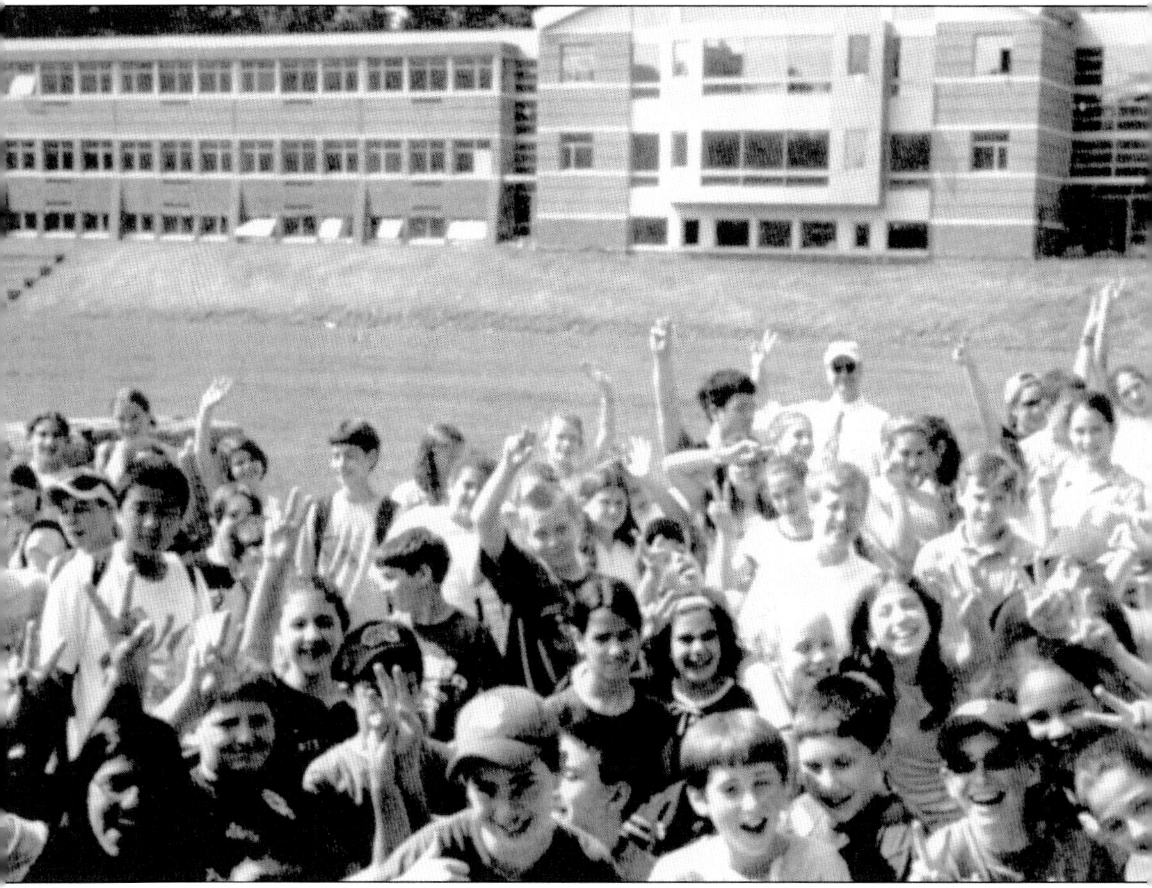

The most recent addition to the school district is the Seven Bridges Middle School, which opened in the fall of 2003 on a site between Seven Bridges and Hog Hill Roads. Although land available for new houses is diminishing, Chappaqua continues to attract more families, in large part because of the quality of its schools.

Six

Millwood and the West End

The western portion of New Castle, known familiarly as the West End, is the tip of a triangle of land that extends to the Croton River, not far from where it empties into the Hudson. The curious shape is the result of the two great land grants of the Colonial era: Cortlandt Manor to the north and Philipsburgh Manor to the south. The boundary of Cortlandt Manor ran east from the Croton River, but the boundary of Philipsburgh Manor diverged to the southeast, leaving the triangle of unclaimed land that became western New Castle.

The main settlement in the West End is the hamlet of Millwood. It originated along the Somerstown Road from Ossining—Route 133 from Ossining to Millwood and Route 100 from Millwood to Pines Bridge and Somers. Somerstown Road joins Route 100 at the home of W. H. Halsted.

At Merritt's Corners, Shingle House Road branches off toward Pinesbridge Road, and Millwood Road branches off toward Chappaqua and Mount Kisco. Here was located the hotel of William E. Merritt, known as the Granite House. To the southwest was Rockdale Mills, where a tributary of the Pocantico River was dammed to form Echo Lake, providing water for the sawmill and gristmill of Stephen B. Lawrence and Thomas L. Vail.

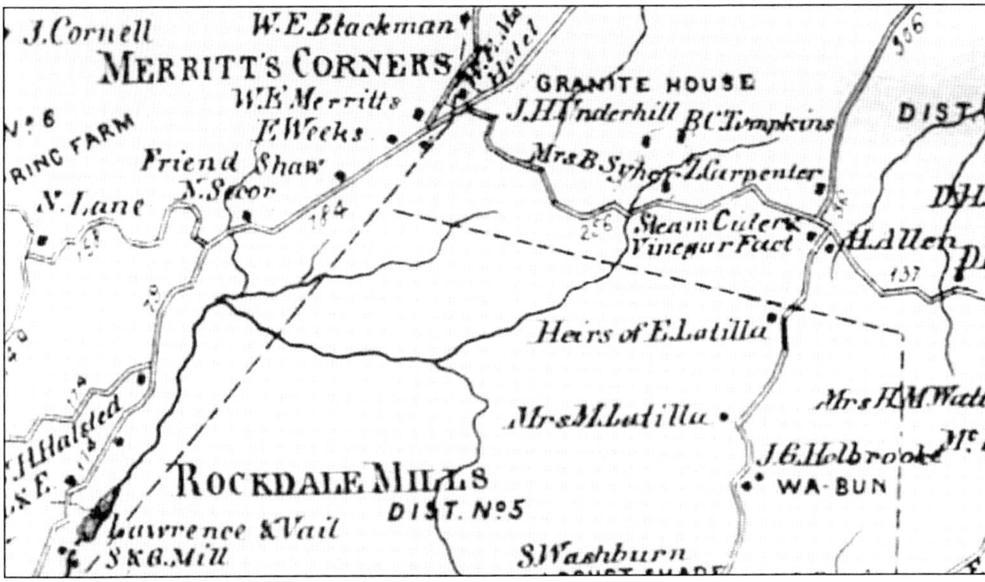

On this 1867 map, Somerstown Road runs diagonally from the lower left and joins Route 100 at the home of W. H. Halsted. At the upper center is Merritt's Corners, where Shingle House Road branches left from the highway toward Pinesbridge Road and Millwood Road branches right toward Chappaqua and Mount Kisco. William E. Merritt's hotel, the Granite House, was located here. Rockdale Mills, where a tributary of the Pocantico River was dammed to form Echo Lake, was to the southwest. Echo Lake provided water for Stephen B. Lawrence and Thomas L. Vail's sawmill and gristmill.

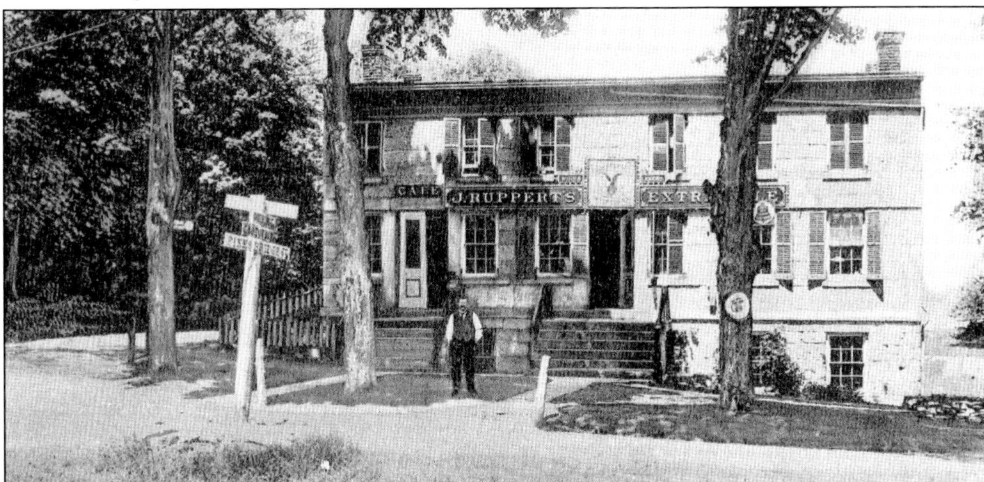

Town records suggest that Seymour Partelow may have operated a tavern here as early as 1801. The Granite House is believed to have been built between 1814 and 1817, when the property belonged to David Crasto. Constructed of locally quarried stone, with walls 18 inches thick, it was a major stop along the highway between Ossining and Somers. Like other inns and taverns, it was often used during the 1800s for town meetings, elections, and public auctions. It is pictured when George Ruckert and family owned it, from 1895 to 1927. It continued in business under a succession of owners and operators until 1976. Later, it became vacant and was demolished in 1993. (Courtesy of Richard Pogact.)

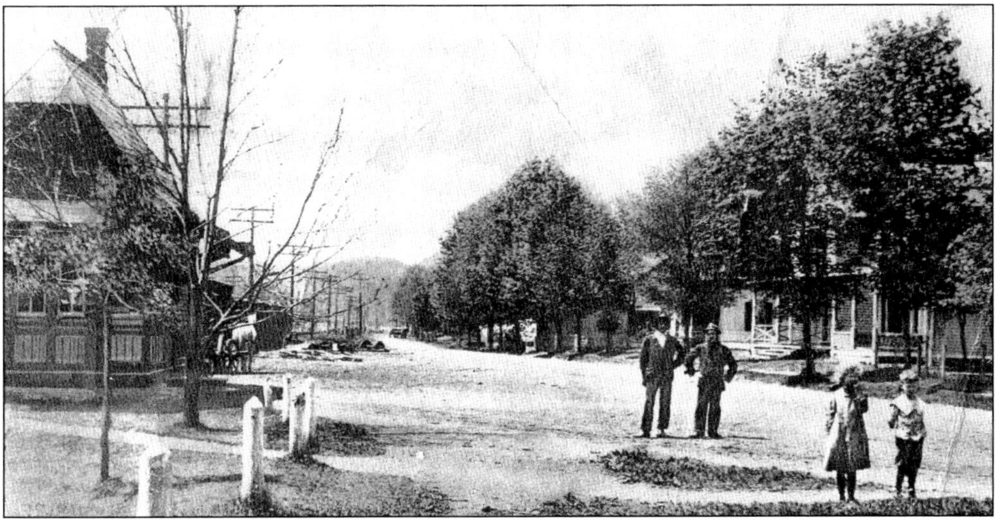

In 1881, the New York and Northern Railroad, later the Putnam Division of the New York Central Railroad, began operations through the West End. Within a few years, a station stop was established where the road to Chappaqua and Mount Kisco (the combined Routes 120 and 133) crossed the tracks. It was first called Merritt's Corners and later renamed Millwood. The village center gravitated toward the railroad, and its main street, Station Place, ran parallel to it. In this 1890s photograph, the railroad station is on the left and the recently constructed buildings along Station Place are on the right. (Courtesy of Richard Pogact.)

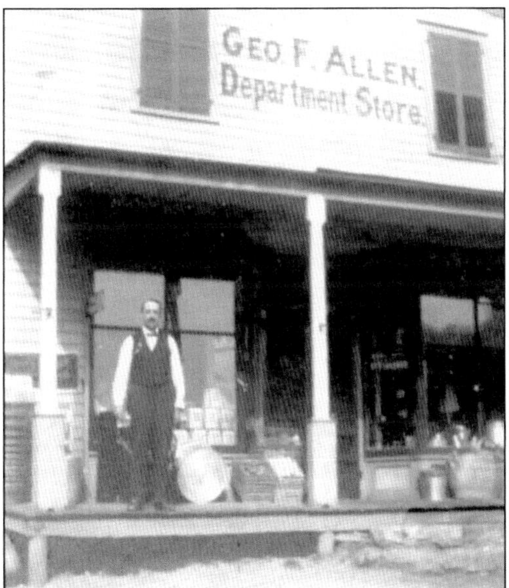

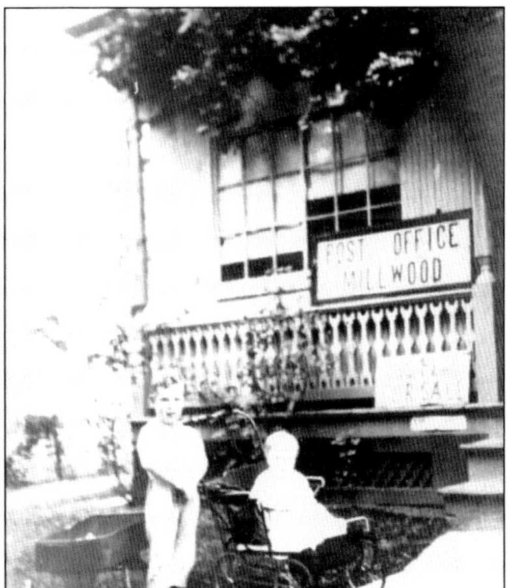

George F. Allen's general store (left) was in business at Millwood Road and Station Place from 1886 to 1933. George Allen was the brother of Henry Allen, the proprietor of a nearby cider mill and vinegar factory on Hardscrabble Road. The building now houses offices. Until the civil service reforms of the 1900s, the office of local postmaster was a political patronage appointment. In rural areas like Millwood, the post office might be moved to the business or home of the new appointee. Around 1900, the Millwood Post Office was located in the Orser house (right) on Station Place. The two children in front of the entrance are Peter Hope and Orville Orser.

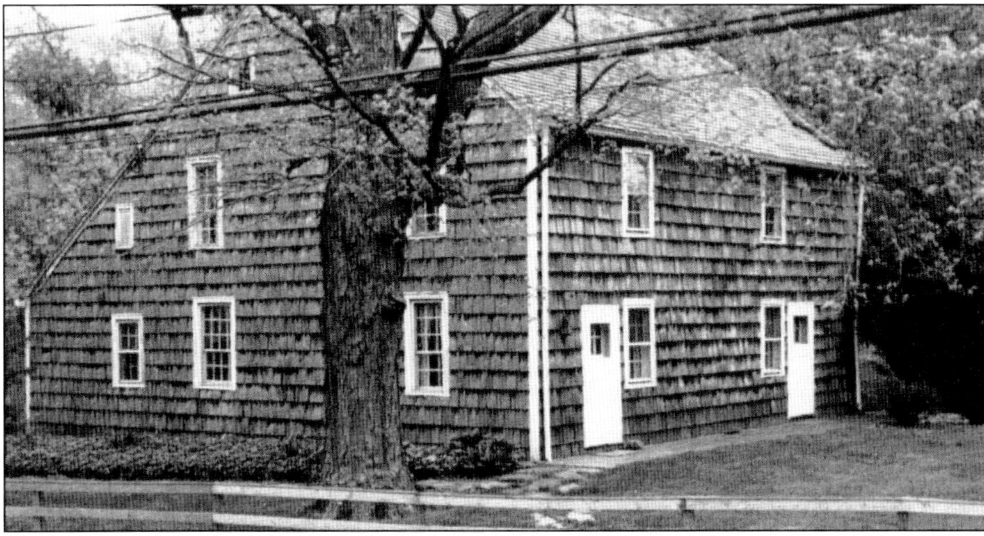

In the West End are several fine old houses that date from at least the early Federal era. The Shingle House was built about the time of the Revolution on Pinesbridge Road, near its intersection with a saddle path that later became Shinglehouse Road. The first known occupants were James and Elizabeth Chadeayne Cornell, who married in 1780. The front parlor of the house has two entrances and was once divided in half. The room nearest the road served as a store, where James Cornell is said to have sold tea, spices, and tobacco. The property remained in the Cornell family for several generations and then belonged to in-laws, the Flewellins, until the 1920s. With several additions, it remains a private home.

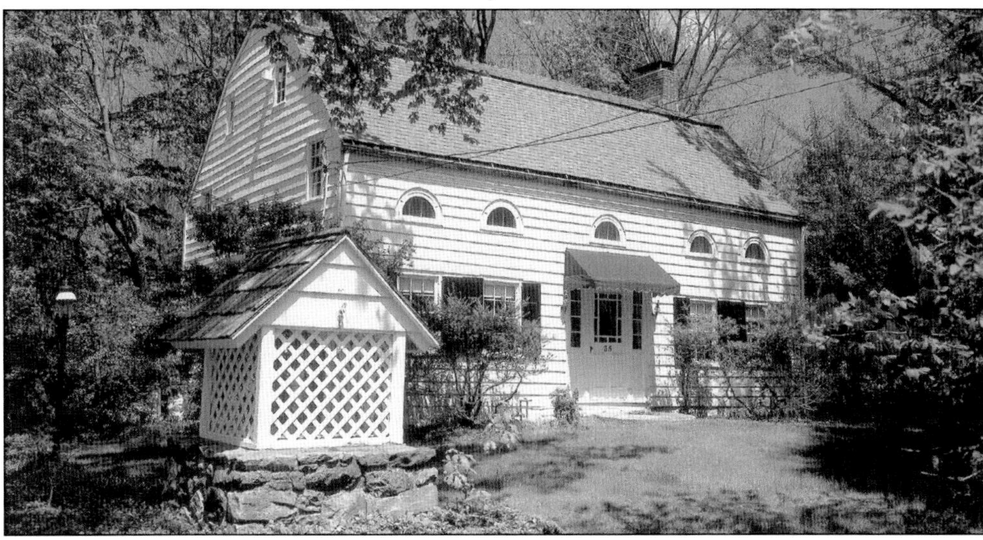

The Williams-DuBois house, on Pinesbridge Road at the corner of Grace Lane, was probably built just after the Revolutionary War by Arthur Williams. The five small "eyebrow" windows on the second floor were originally rectangular, but about 1820, when the house belonged to Arthur's son William, they were replaced with semicircular lunettes—now the most distinctive feature of the house. William Williams was a sea captain who drowned in 1826. The farm was inherited by his eldest daughter, Georgianna, who married Huguenot descendant Lawrence DuBois. The farm was subdivided in 1926, but the house remained in the DuBois family until 1940. It is still a private residence. (Photograph by Gray Williams.)

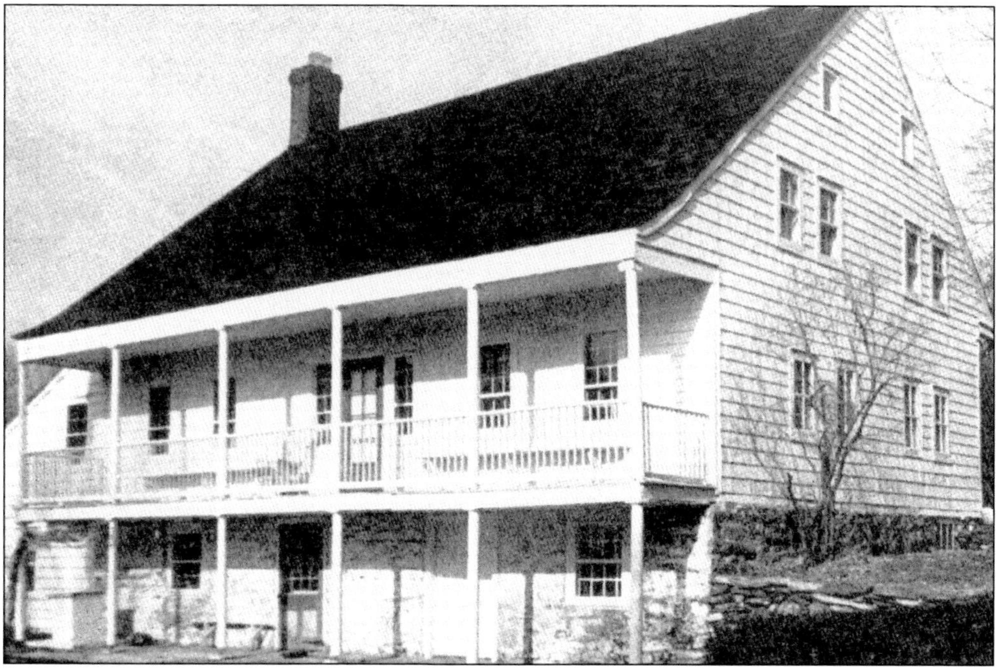

The double-galleried Conklin-Chadeayne farmhouse on Inningwood Road near Pinesbridge Road appears to be a genuine Colonial building. It was likely constructed around 1760 by Thomas Conklin and was later either bequeathed or sold to his daughter Anna and her husband, Jacob Chadeayne. The basement was the winter kitchen, the floor above held the main living areas, and the top floor contained the bedrooms. The small wing at the far left, originally a separate summer kitchen, was later connected to the house. (Courtesy of Phil Chadeayne)

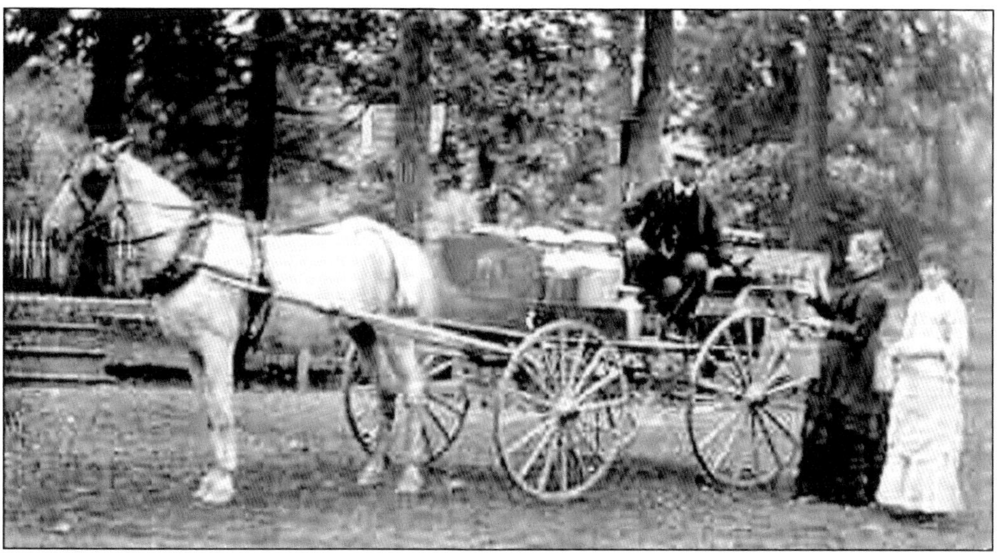

The Chadeayne homestead remained in the family for several generations. It was primarily a dairy farm. A brook was diverted through a trough in the basement of the house to keep milk and other dairy products cool during the summer. Many New Castle dairy farms primarily served the New York City market, but Wilbur Chadeayne also ran a local milk and dairy-products delivery service around 1900. (Courtesy of Phil Chaydeane.)

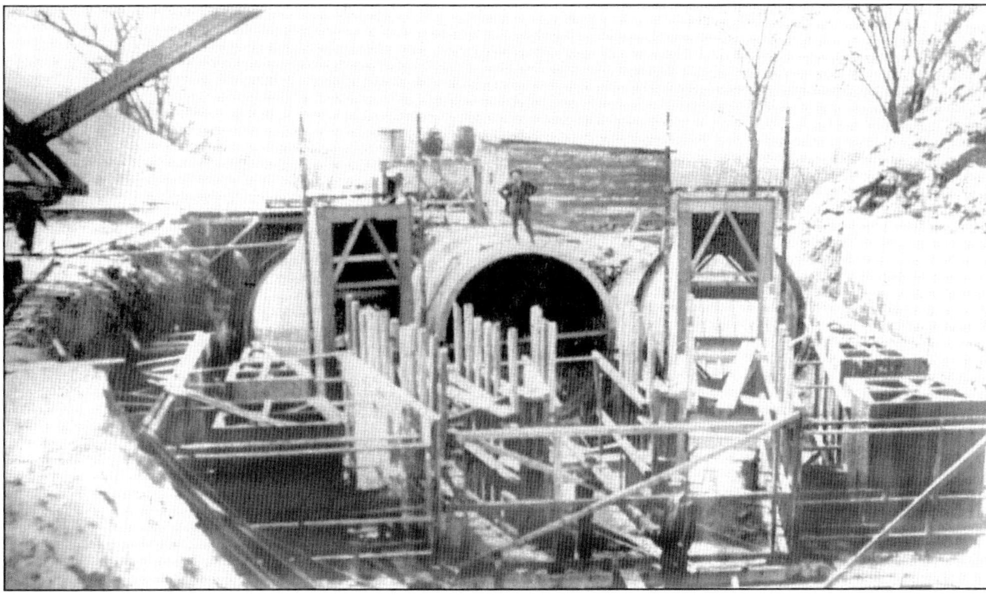

The biggest construction project in the history of the West End was the Catskill Aqueduct, built between 1907 and 1917. One segment passed through the middle of Millwood, but it was just a small part of a system that carried water from reservoirs in the Catskills, under the Hudson River, and through Westchester County to the Kensico Reservoir en route to New York City. The aqueduct channel, 17 feet in diameter, was constructed of reinforced concrete. (Courtesy of the Westchester County Historical Society.)

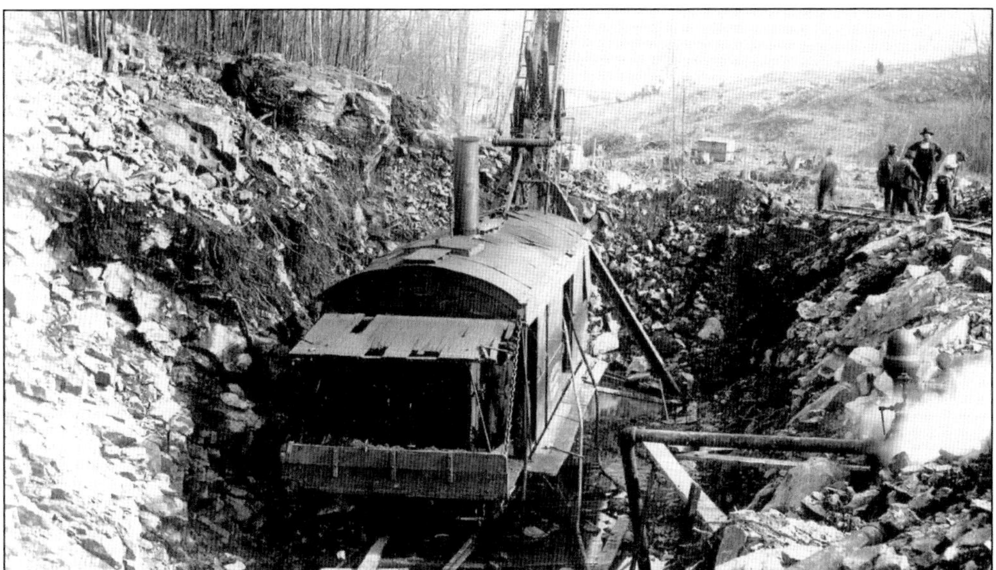

The construction of the aqueduct was a massive and complex project. Excavation of its deep trench required large steam shovels, like this one. (Courtesy of the Westchester County Historical Society.)

Most of the aqueduct laborers were immigrants from southern Europe, particularly southern Italy. They lived in temporary camps along the route of construction, but many of them settled permanently in the area after the aqueduct was completed. (Courtesy of the Westchester County Historical Society.)

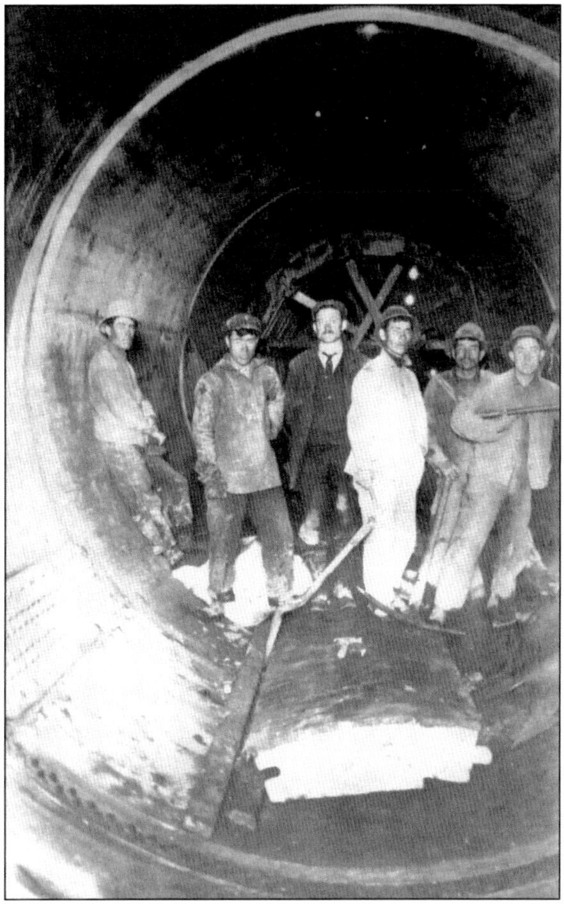

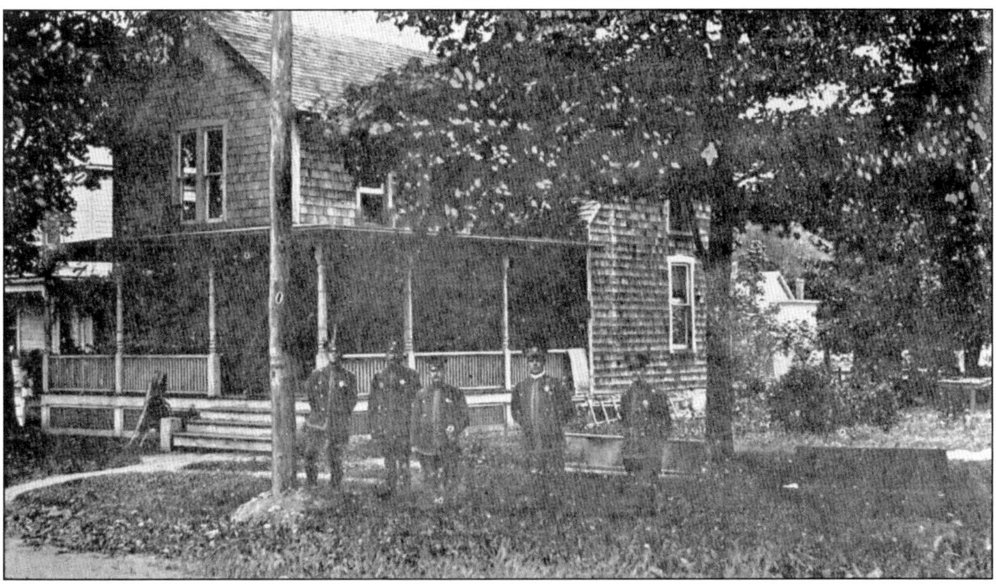

New York City, which owned and controlled the aqueduct, provided security police for it during World War I. A house in Millwood served as headquarters for a contingent of this force.

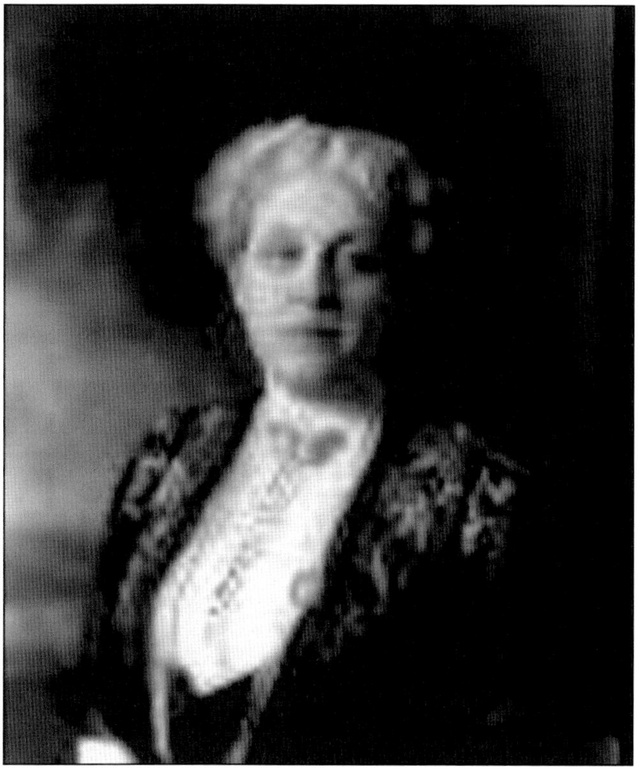

The most notable resident of the West End and, along with Horace Greeley, the most notable in all of New Castle was Carrie Chapman Catt, who lived in Millwood from 1919 to 1928. Catt was a major leader in the long struggle for woman's suffrage and was a founder of the New York League of Women Voters. After the ratification of the 19th Amendment in 1920, she continued to promote equal rights for women and also devoted herself to the cause of world peace.

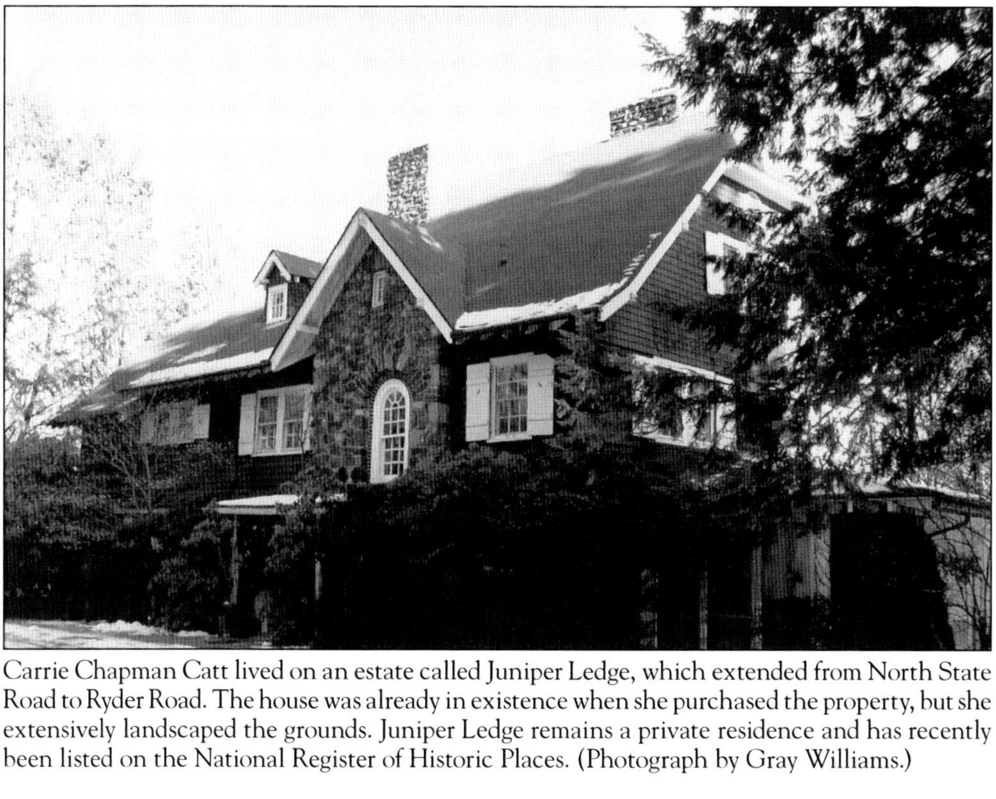

Carrie Chapman Catt lived on an estate called Juniper Ledge, which extended from North State Road to Ryder Road. The house was already in existence when she purchased the property, but she extensively landscaped the grounds. Juniper Ledge remains a private residence and has recently been listed on the National Register of Historic Places. (Photograph by Gray Williams.)

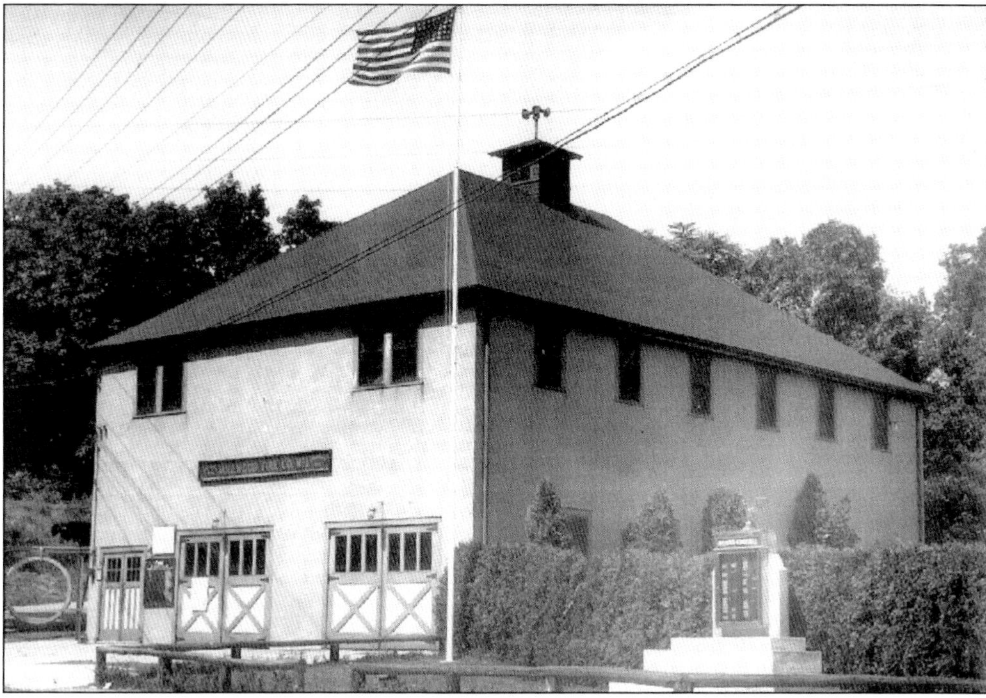

After World War I, the West End gradually became more suburban and faced the need for more public services, such as fire protection. The volunteer Millwood Fire Company was founded in 1924, and the firehouse shown here was built on Route 120 in 1926. An addition was constructed in 1950, but the building is no longer large enough to accommodate modern engines, and the department is seeking to enlarge or replace it. (Courtesy of the Millwood Fire Company.)

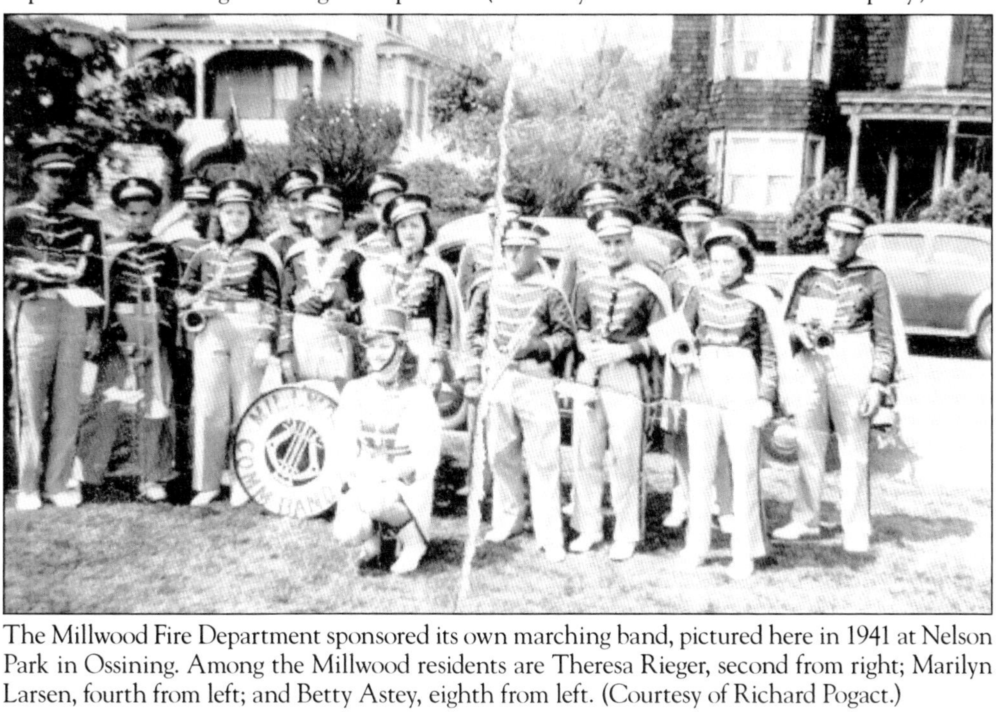

The Millwood Fire Department sponsored its own marching band, pictured here in 1941 at Nelson Park in Ossining. Among the Millwood residents are Theresa Rieger, second from right; Marilyn Larsen, fourth from left; and Betty Astey, eighth from left. (Courtesy of Richard Pogact.)

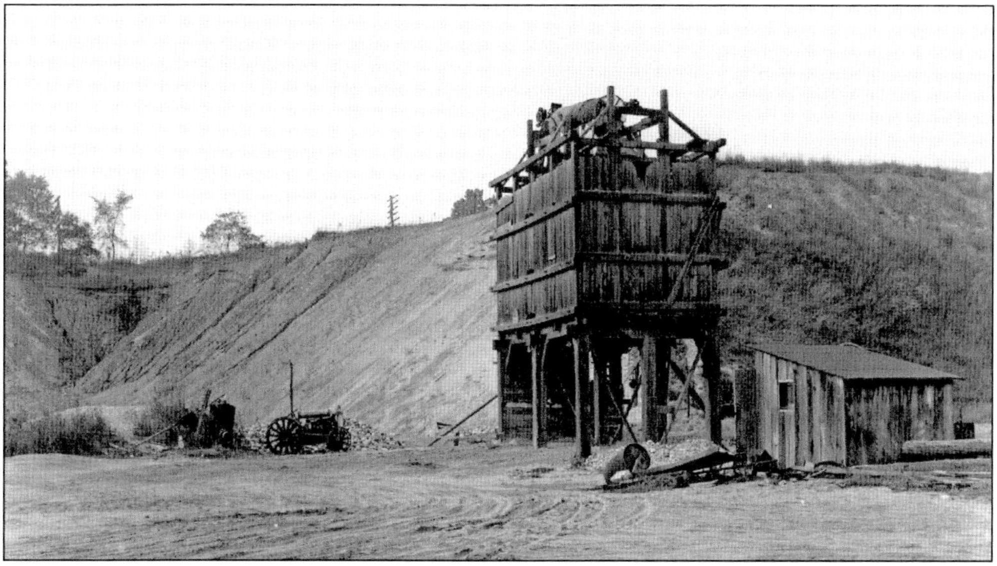

Sand Street, off Route 100 in Millwood, is the only reminder of what was an important local business in the early 1900s. At the end of Sand Street, conveniently located near the Putnam Division of the New York Central Railroad, were deposits of construction-grade sand on properties owned by Herbert Johnson and William Orser. The sand from Orser's sandpit was used locally on projects such as the construction of Maryknoll Seminary on Pinesbridge Road. Sand was also loaded on Putnam Division freight cars for shipment to New York City and elsewhere. (Courtesy of the Ossining Historical Society.)

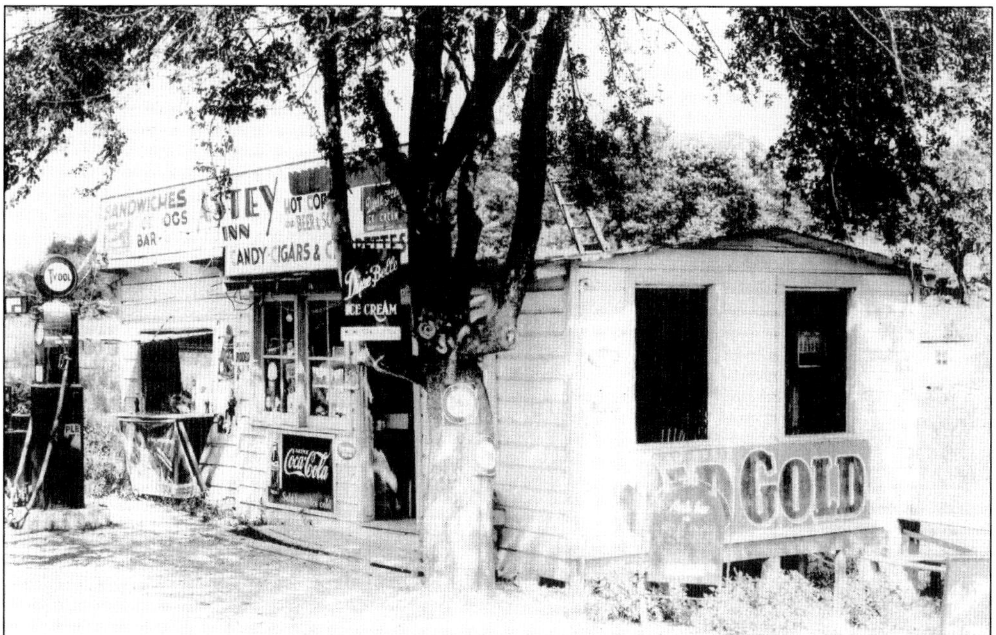

The construction of the Taconic State Parkway in 1931 and 1932 brought additional traffic and business to the part of Millwood where the parkway crossed over commercial Route 100. About this time, for example, Eugene Astey opened the Astey Inn, a luncheonette and gas station at the corner of Route 100 and Station Place. (Courtesy of Richard Pogact.)

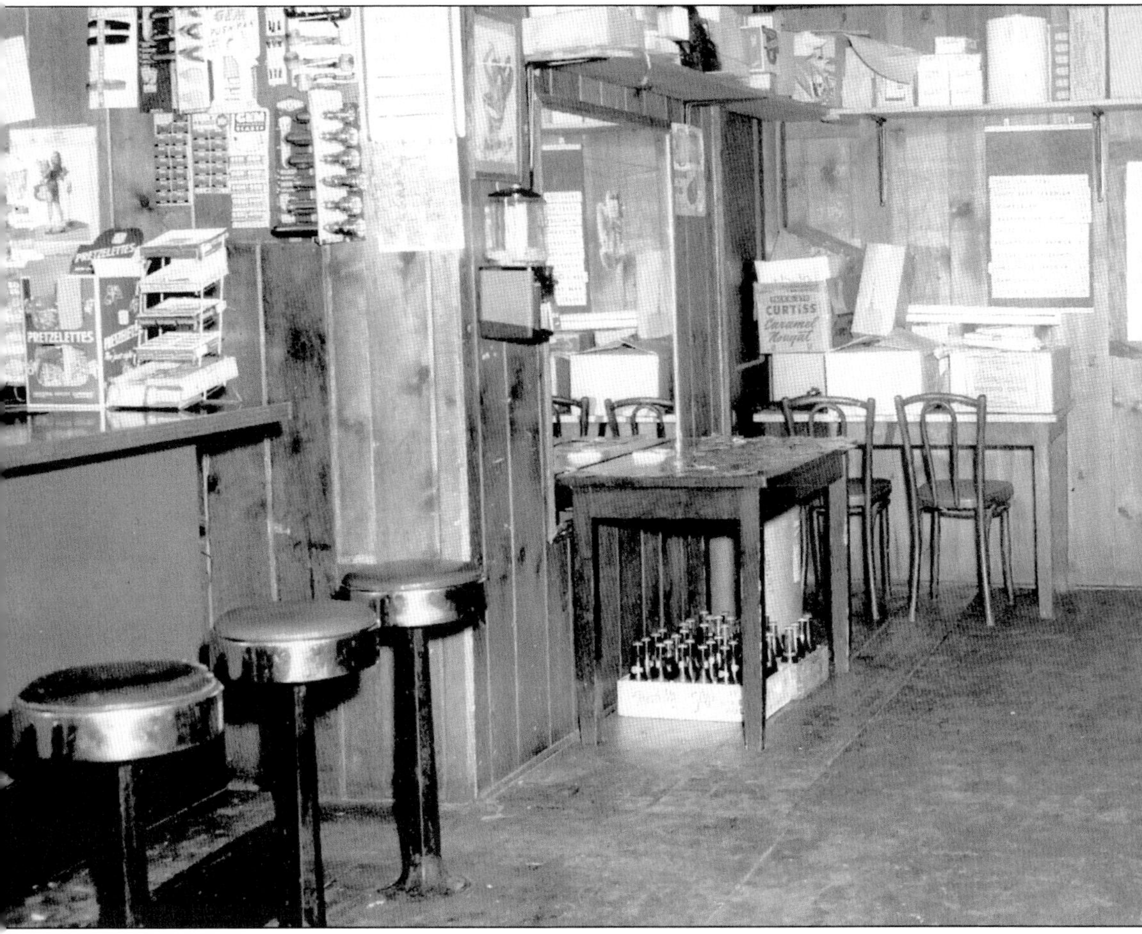

About 1937, Ralph and Evelyn Cassell built a restaurant behind the Astey Inn called the Babbling Brook. This photograph from the late 1940s shows its informal rustic interior. The lunch menu on the back wall features hamburgers for 25¢; coffee, milk, and Coca-Cola for 10¢; and chili con carne for 35¢. The sites of both the Astey Inn and the Babbling Brook Restaurant are now occupied by the A&P shopping center. (Courtesy of Richard Pogact.)

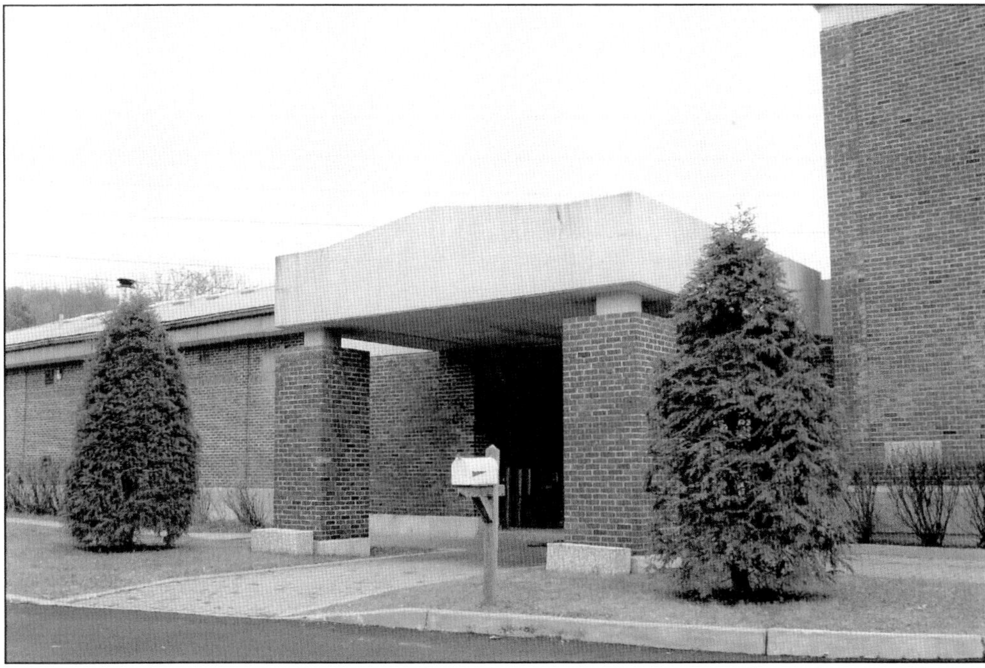

New Castle obtains its drinking water from the New York City aqueducts that pass through Millwood. Concerned about the amount of sediment entering the town water mains, the town built its own filtration and purification plant in 1993. It uses state-of-the-art technology to provide clean, good-tasting water to the community. The cost to New Castle water users, though, is relatively high. (Above, photograph by Gray Williams; below, town of New Castle.)

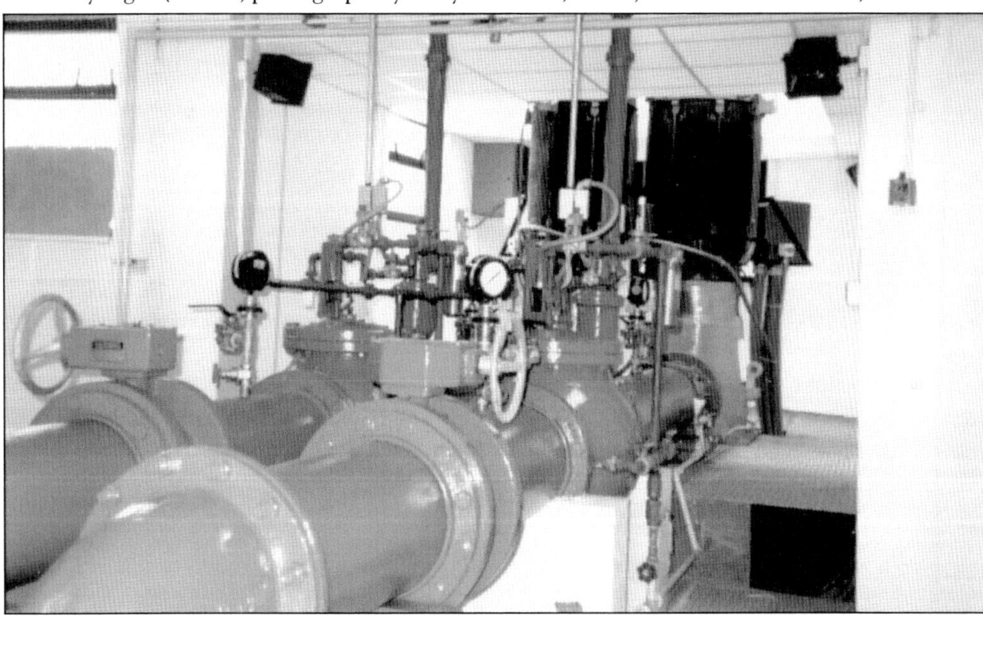

Seven

Horace Greeley and the Greeley Heritage

New Castle's most celebrated resident was Horace Greeley, who made his country home in Chappaqua from 1853 until his death in 1872. Greeley was the founder and editor of the *New York Tribune*, an enormously influential and well-respected newspaper in an era when most papers were either scandal sheets or political pamphlets. He was nicknamed "Old Honesty" for both his scrupulous reporting and his frankly expressed opinions.

Greeley was also deeply involved in the major issues and events of his day. He championed women's rights and labor unions and attacked slavery. He was a founder of the Republican party and played major roles in the nomination, election, and reelection of Abraham Lincoln as president. And in 1872, he himself ran for president against Ulysses S. Grant.

In 1852, Greeley started buying farmland near the village of Chappaqua to serve as his own vacation home and as the full-time home of his wife and children from spring to fall. He considered Chappaqua his main residence—the place where he voted, the place where the census recorded his household in 1860 and 1870.

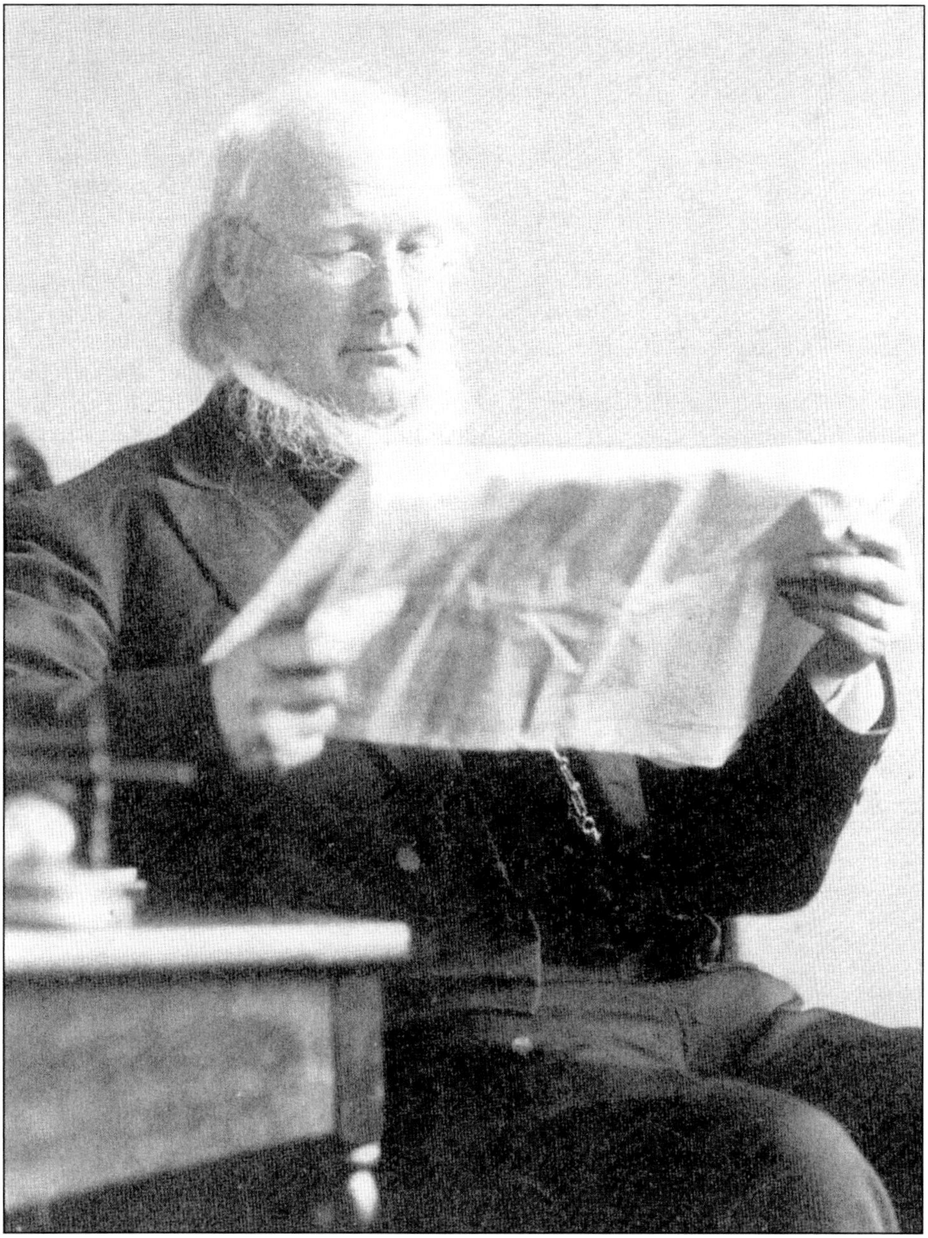

Horace Greeley founded the *New York Tribune* in 1841, and served as its editor for 30 years. In 1872, he ran for president and was defeated by Ulysses S. Grant.

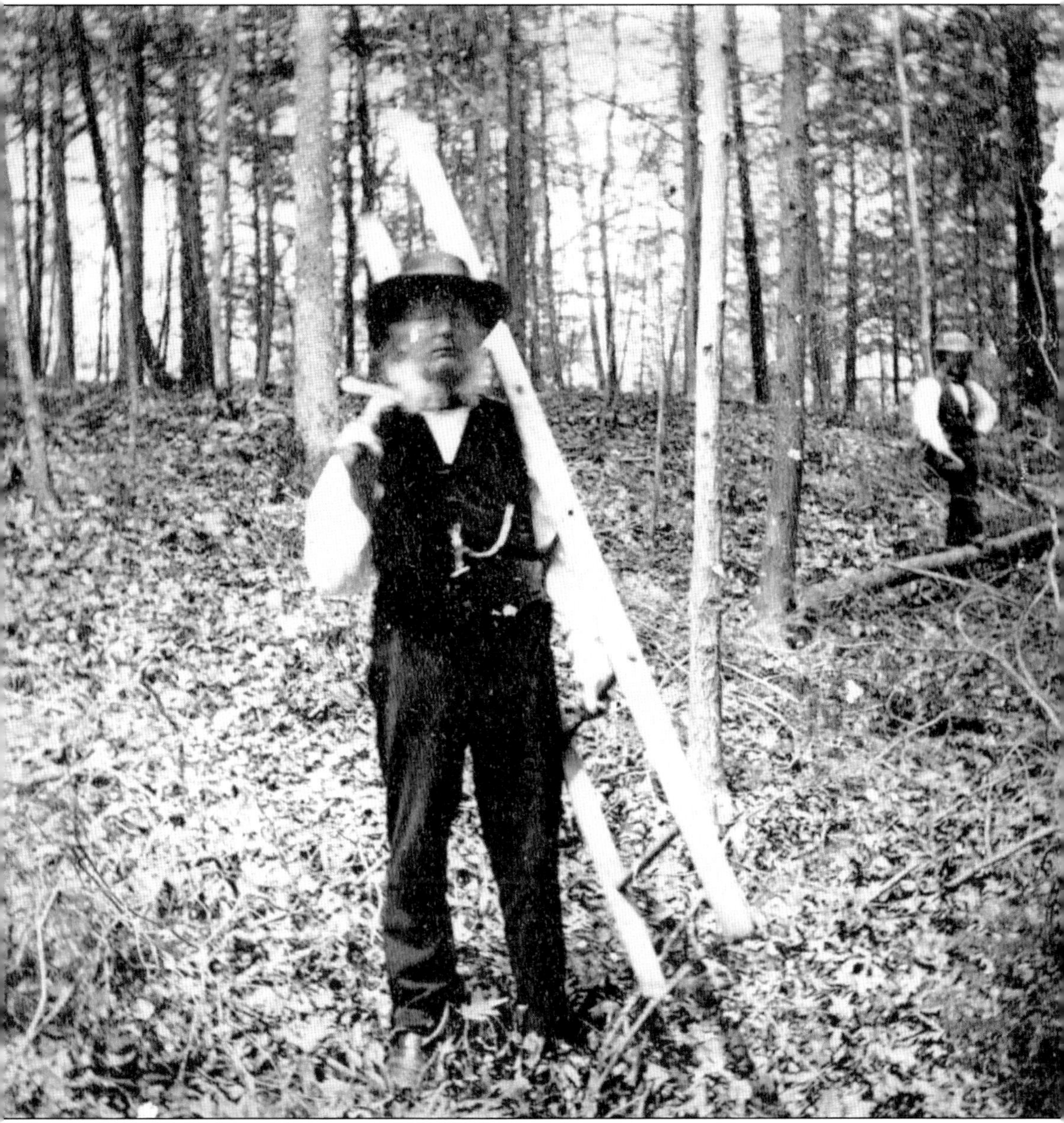

Horace Greeley could only manage to be a part-time farmer, mainly on weekends. He would usually come out from the city on Friday evening and return on Sunday. He particularly enjoyed pruning trees and chopping wood. "The ax," he wrote in his autobiography, "is the healthiest implement that man ever handled. And it is especially so for habitual writers and other sedentary workers. I am a poor chopper, yet the ax is my doctor and delight."

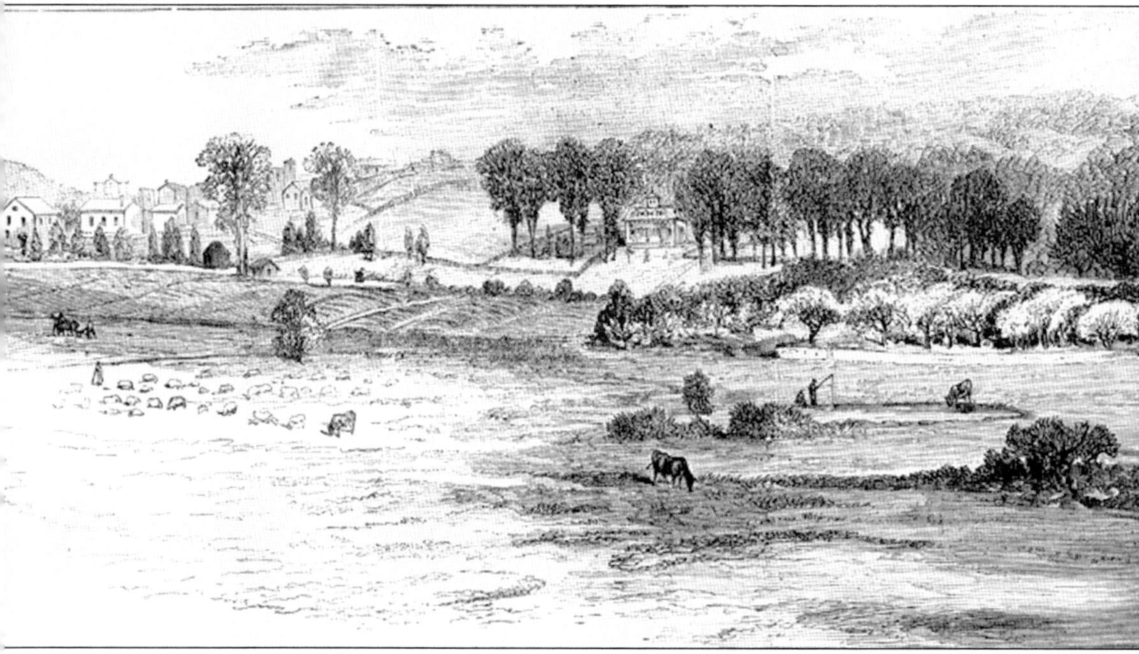

Horace Greeley assembled a 78-acre farm that extended over much of what is now downtown Chappaqua. The village was then clustered along King Street, as shown at the far left of this panoramic wood engraving. In the foreground is the wet meadow that Greeley tried vainly to drain, and that is now occupied by South Greeley Avenue, the playing fields of the

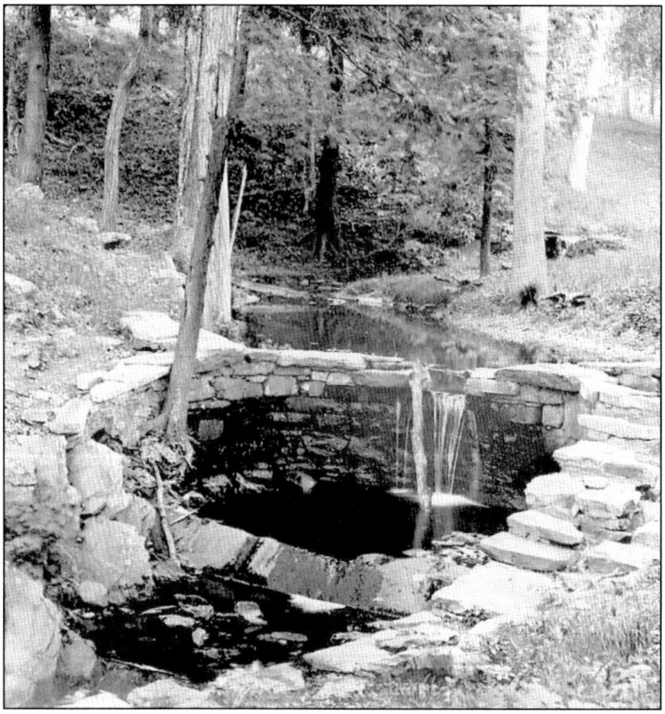

The House in the Woods was located near the cascading stream of Tercia Brook. Horace Greeley dammed part of it to create a pond to water his livestock and irrigate his garden. Much of the stone dam still remains.

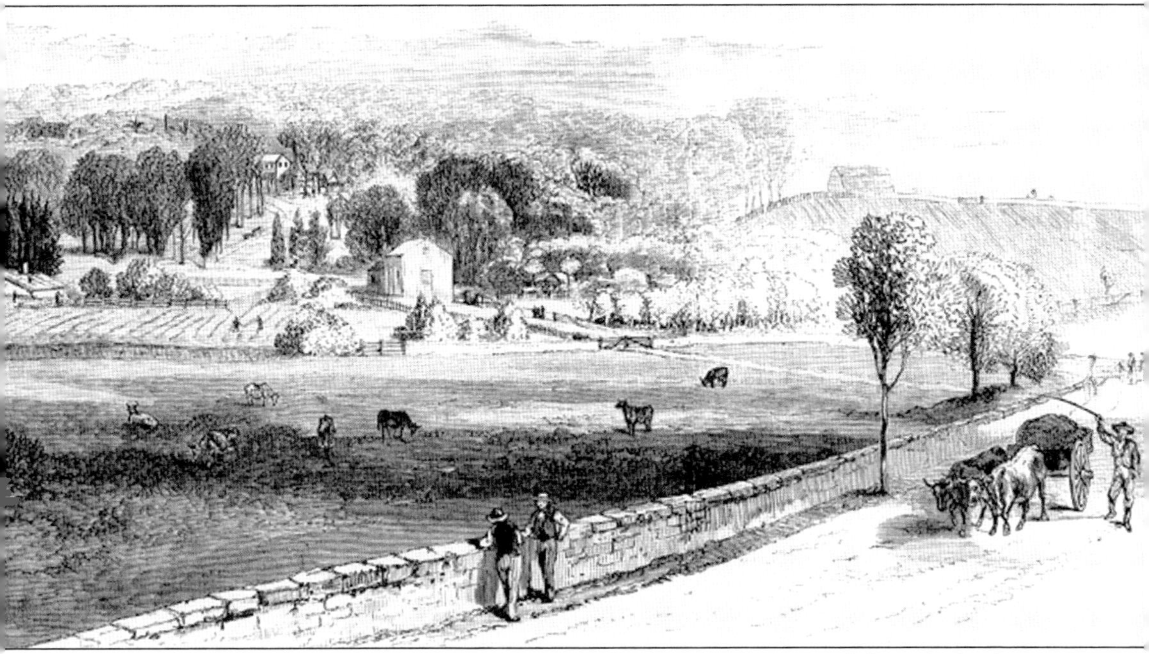

Robert E. Bell School, and the parking plaza of the railroad station. The road through the farm, now Senter Street, ran from King Street south to the main buildings of the farm. Partway up the hillside, as shown in the upper center, Greeley built his first home, the House in the Woods, where the family spent their first 10 years.

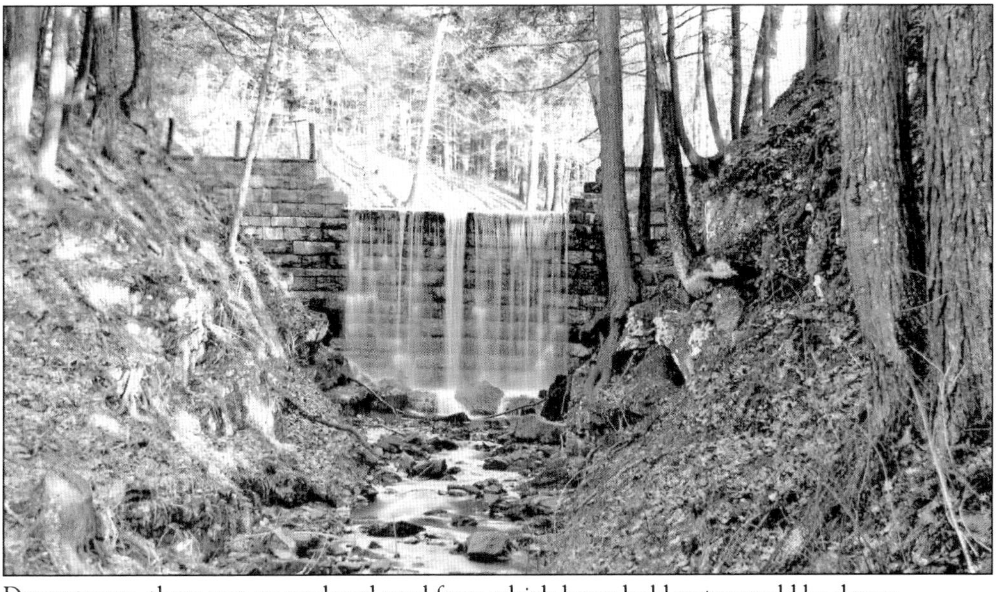

Downstream, there was an enclosed pool from which household water could be drawn.

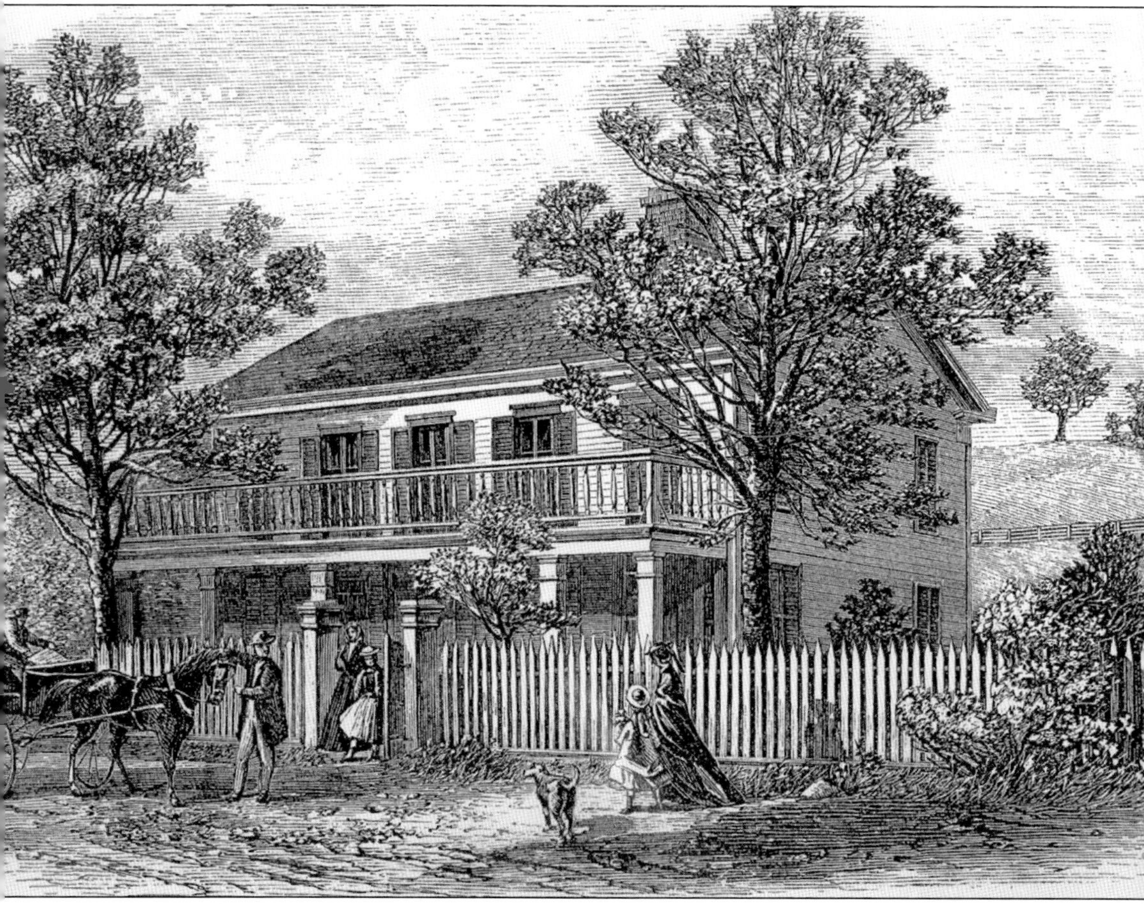

Mary Greeley was never completely satisfied with the House in the Woods, which she found dank and remote. So, in 1864, Horace Greeley bought a house in the middle of the village at the entrance from King Street to the farm. Depicted in an 1868 wood engraving, the house became the family home until the end of Horace and Mary Greeleys' lives in 1872. It is now the museum and headquarters of the New Castle Historical Society.

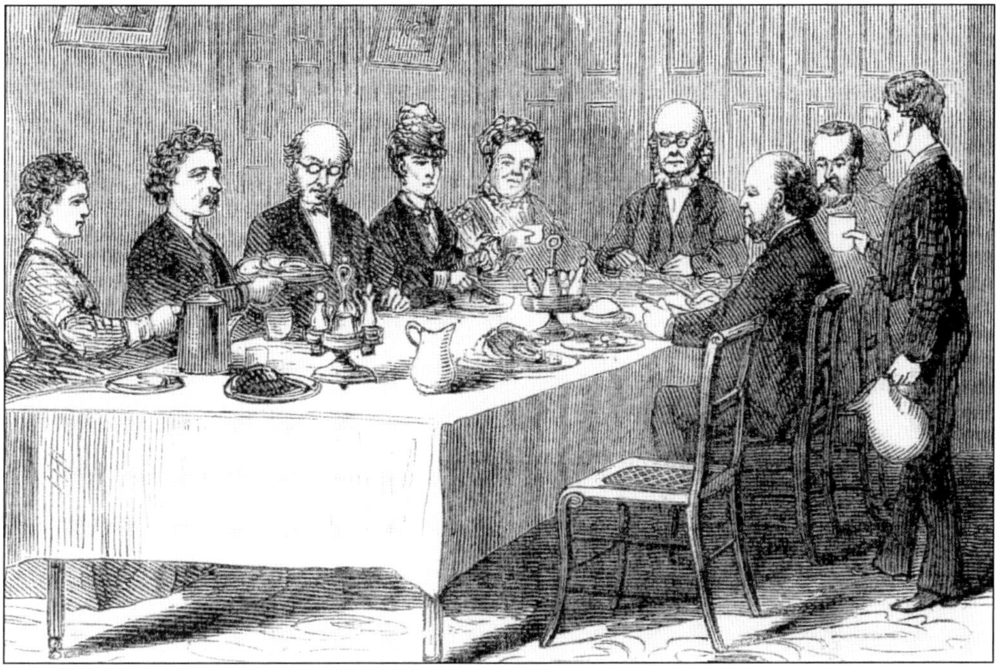

Although Horace Greeley could never spend as much time in Chappaqua as he would have liked, he became a familiar figure in the village, collecting his mail at the post office in Amos Tompkins's feed store or dining with family and friends at the Chappaqua Hotel. He made many friends and became involved in community improvements, such as the planting of street trees and the establishment of Fair Ridge Cemetery. His admirers called him the Sage of Chappaqua; his critics, mindful of his often unorthodox ideas, nicknamed him Old Chappaquack.

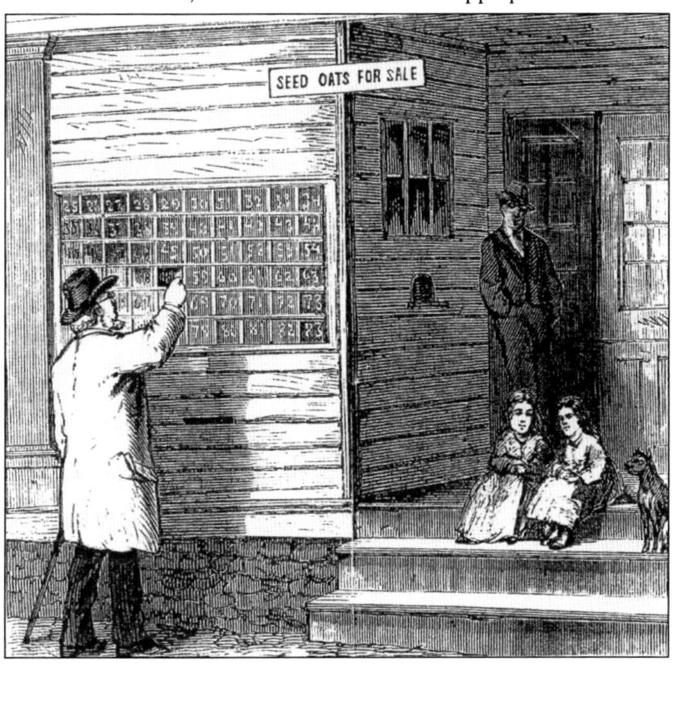

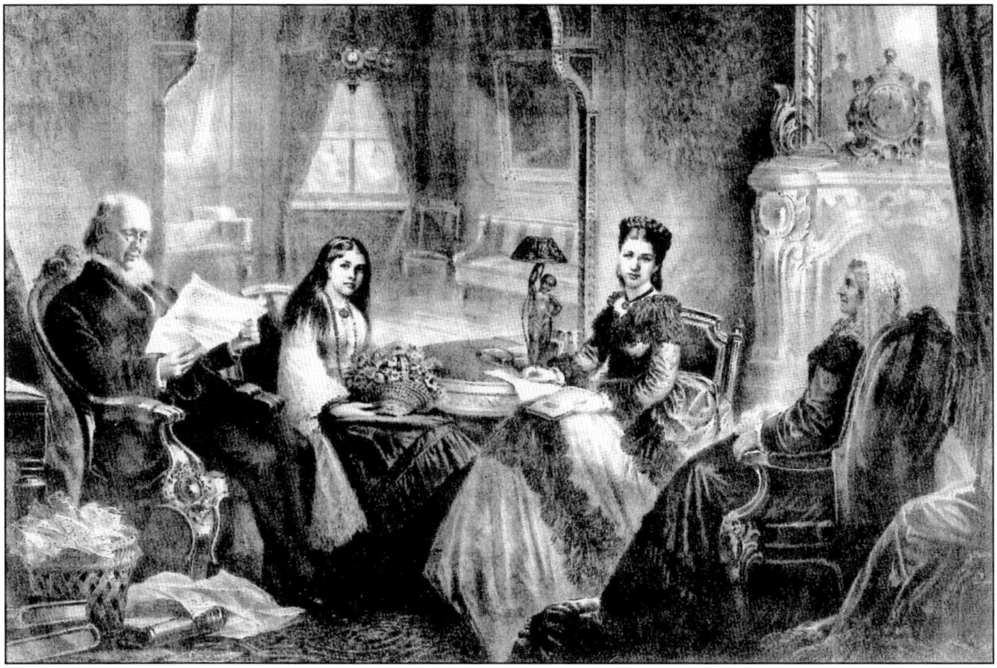

Horace Greeley's campaign for the presidency in 1872 provoked a torrent of photographs and prints, portraying the candidate and his activities in great detail. This family portrait, drawn in a fanciful and more opulent setting than their actual home, shows Greeley and his invalid wife Mary (right) with their daughters Gabrielle, 15, and Ida, 24. By this time the two daughters were the only survivors of the Greeleys' seven children.

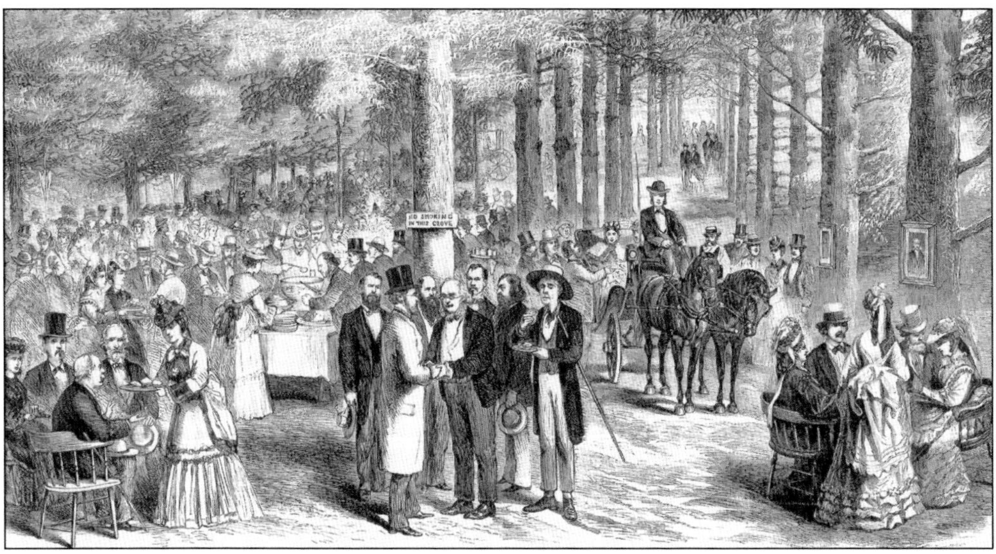

In August, Horace Greeley provided a picnic for 400 friends and supporters in the evergreen grove that he himself had planted on the farm. Several of the trees, grown to majestic size, still survive. Ida organized the picnic and served as hostess in place of her increasingly frail mother. A wide variety of food was served, but no alcohol, tea, or coffee—just lemonade punch, for Greeley was a teetotaler.

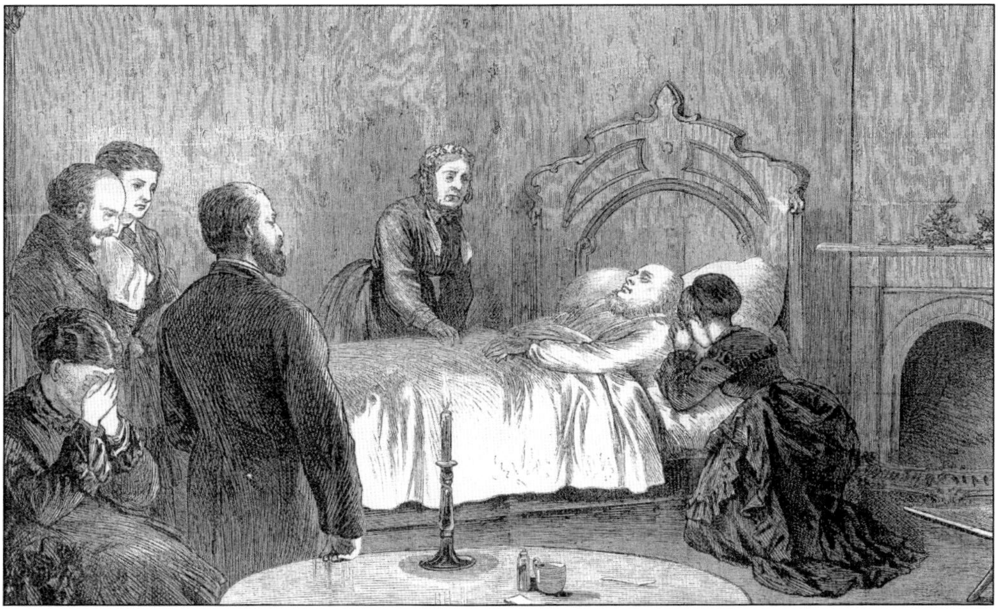

The fall of 1872 brought a triple tragedy. Mary Greeley became terminally ill, and Horace Greeley wore himself out tending to her until her death on October 30. In the election a week later, he was decisively defeated by Ulysses S. Grant, although he seemed more relieved than disheartened by the outcome. Then, a week or so after that, he discovered that he had sold or given away so many shares of *Tribune* stock that he no longer controlled the paper. He collapsed, mentally and physically, and died at Dr. George Choate's sanitarium in Pleasantville (now the Pleasantville campus of Pace University) on November 29, at the age of 61.

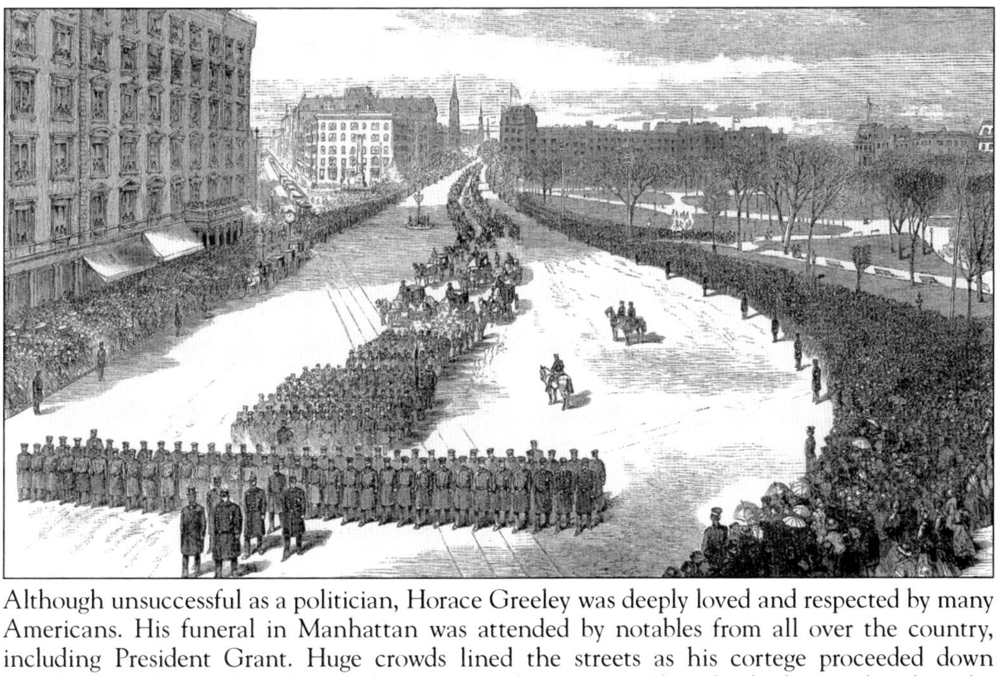

Although unsuccessful as a politician, Horace Greeley was deeply loved and respected by many Americans. His funeral in Manhattan was attended by notables from all over the country, including President Grant. Huge crowds lined the streets as his cortege proceeded down Broadway to the Brooklyn ferry and Green-Wood Cemetery. There his body was placed, in the family crypt, alongside the remains of Mary Greeley and their deceased children.

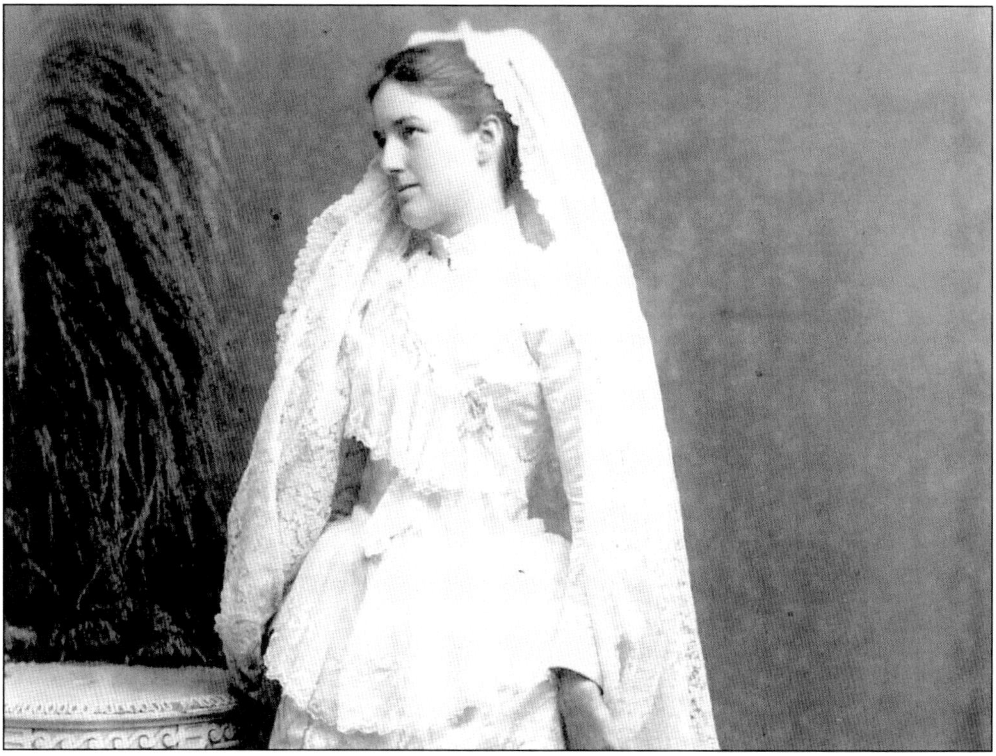

After their parents' deaths, Ida and Gabrielle Greeley continued to live in Chappaqua. Ida married in 1875 and moved away, but Gabrielle took possession of the farm and remained there for the rest of her life. She married Episcopal minister Dr. Frank Montrose Clendenin in 1891, and this photograph shows her in her wedding dress.

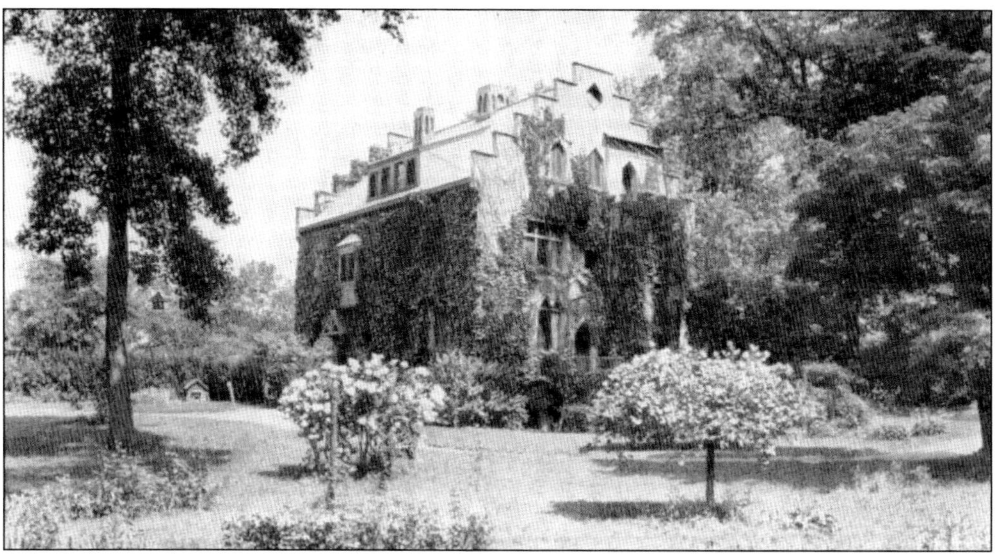

The Clendenins remodeled Greeley's sturdy concrete barn into their home, which they named Rehoboth. It remains a private residence today.

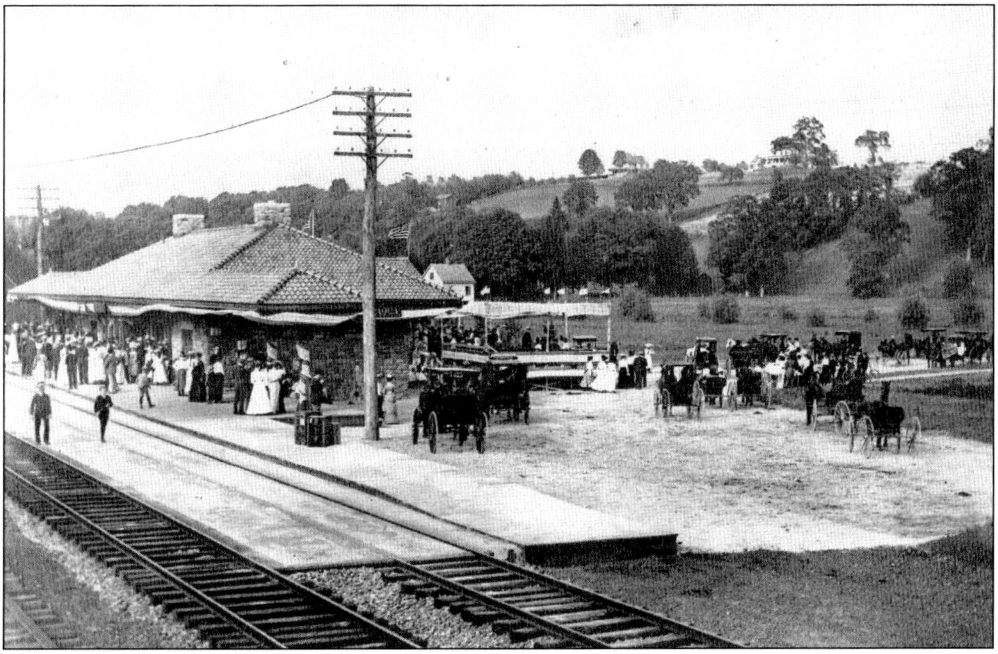

The Clendenins were generous supporters of the community. In 1901, they donated land from the Greeley farm for a new railroad station and an adjacent park. The station was completed and dedicated in 1902. The street leading to it, Woodburn Avenue, was named for Horace Greeley's mother, Mary Woodburn Greeley.

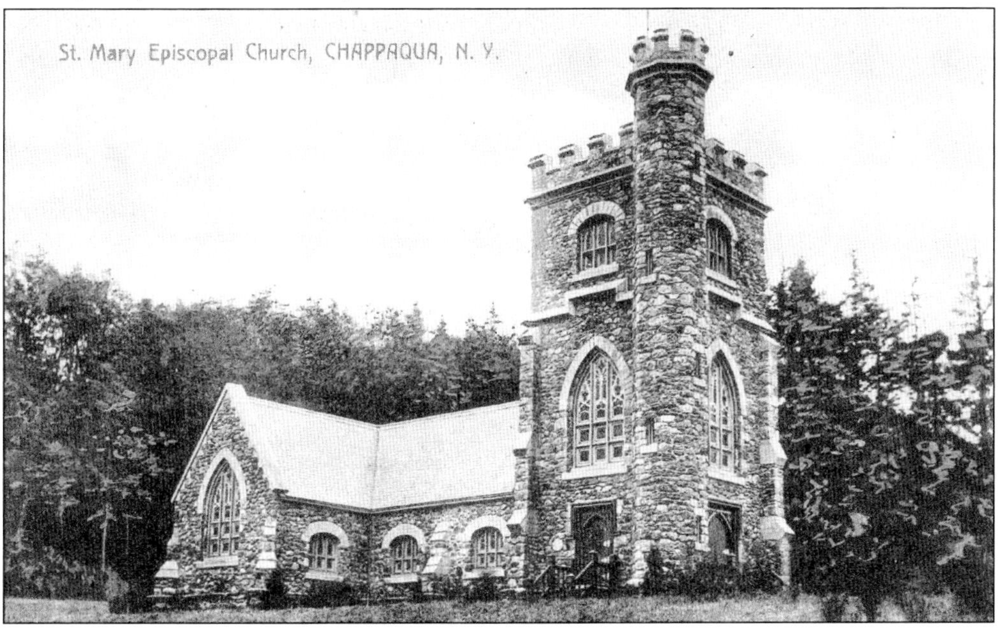

In 1906, the Clendenins erected the Episcopal church of St. Mary the Virgin, dedicated to the memory of their daughter Muriel, who had died in 1903 of polio. Gabrielle donated the land and Dr. Clendenin the building, just north of Greeley's grove of evergreens. Behind the church is a small, enclosed plot containing the graves of Muriel; Frank M. Clendenin, who died in 1930; Gabrielle Greeley Clendenin, who died in 1937; and twins who died in infancy.

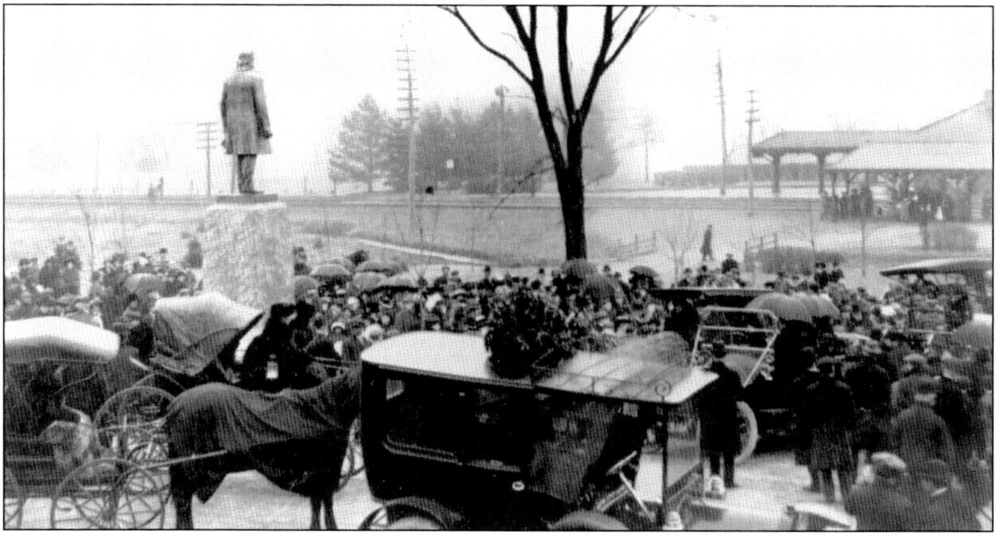

Horace Greeley was born on February 3, 1811. As the centennial of the date approached, local citizens organized the Chappaqua Historical Society and commissioned sculptor William Ordway Partridge to create an over-life-size bronze statue as a memorial to the Sage of Chappaqua. A site directly west of the railroad station, connected to it by a double roadway with a landscaped median, was donated by landowner and developer John I. D. Bristol. The memorial was not ready for the centennial. It was not cast until 1912, and the 10-foot granite base had to be reordered when the original supplier went bankrupt. The monument was dedicated on February 3, 1914. The Clendenins attended, and Dr. Frank Clendenin gave an address. When the Saw Mill River Parkway was constructed in the 1930s, its right-of-way crossed the roadway between the statue and the station, requiring the eventual closing of that approach to the station. Today, the statue is essentially cut off from the village center, and its landscaped area is surrounded by the Mill River Road traffic circle.

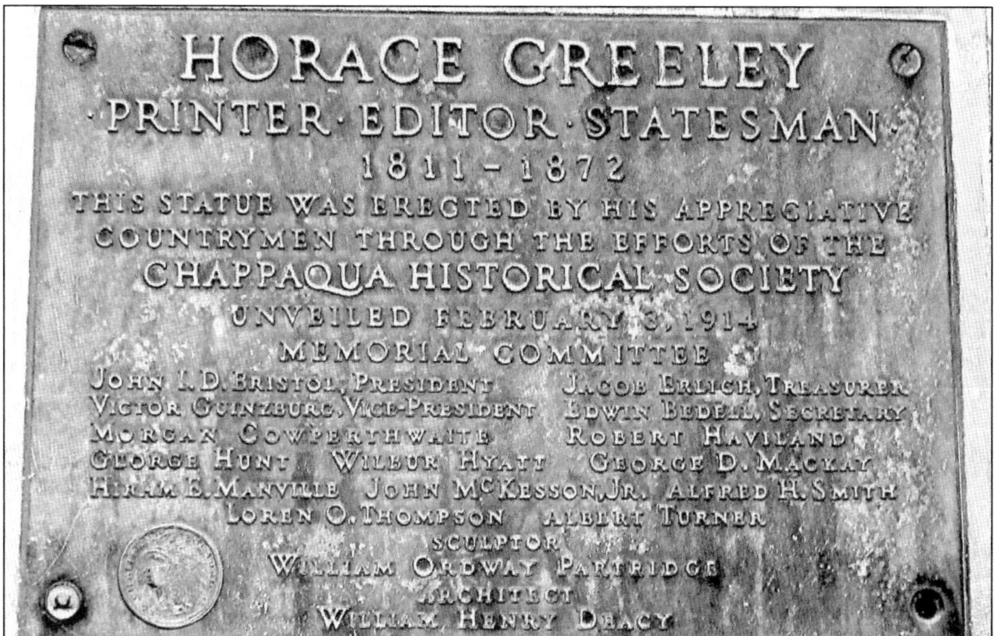

Eight

HILLTOPPERS

THE ERA OF ESTATES

After the New York and Harlem Railroad began to provide fast and convenient transportation between the city and northern Westchester, affluent New Yorkers began to establish country homes in New Castle. Among the first was Horace Greeley, who purchased his Chappaqua farm starting in 1852. By the early 1900s, many other New Yorkers were buying farms to assemble into large estates, where they built imposing mansions. They were known locally as hilltoppers because many placed their homes on the crests of hills, with commanding views of the surrounding countryside.

The hilltoppers introduced a more sophisticated lifestyle to largely rural New Castle and provided some stimulus to its economy. Many of them were public-spirited citizens who contributed significantly to community organizations and institutions. But their influence was limited and temporary, and most of their estates did not endure. Some owners had to sell their estates after suffering financial reverses in the Depression of the 1930s or because of the rising costs of taxes and maintenance. Other original owners died, and their heirs were unable or unwilling to preserve the properties.

But by far the most powerful force behind the breakup of large estates was the pressure of suburbanization. The rising value of property suitable for residential subdivisions provided an almost irresistible temptation for owners to sell all or parts of their estates. The most successful and influential hilltoppers were John I. D. Bristol and his son-in-law Albert Turner, who not only assembled large estates for themselves but also bought several other properties in New Castle that they transformed into suburban developments.

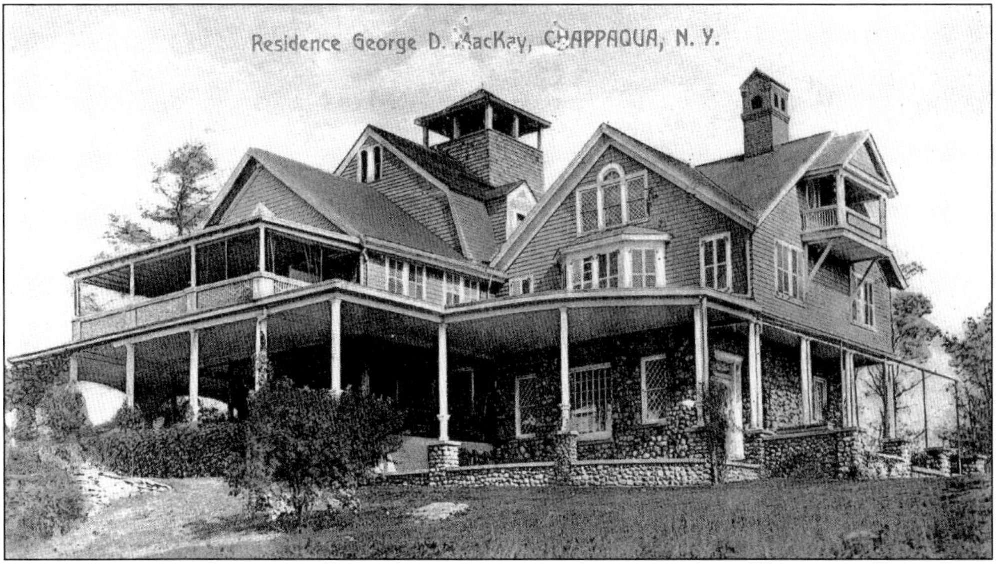

Around 1898, New York City banker George Devereux MacKay (pronounced mac-KIGH) bought a large farm near the crest of the hill on Whippoorwill Road, where it crosses from New Castle into North Castle. It was the original homestead of the Quinbys, who were among the original Quaker settlers. McKay transformed the farmhouse into a rambling, shingle-style summer home for himself, his wife, and their four sons and two daughters. He also built or adapted many of the other buildings on the property to create After Glow Farm, a complex that was at once a gentleman's estate and a working farm.

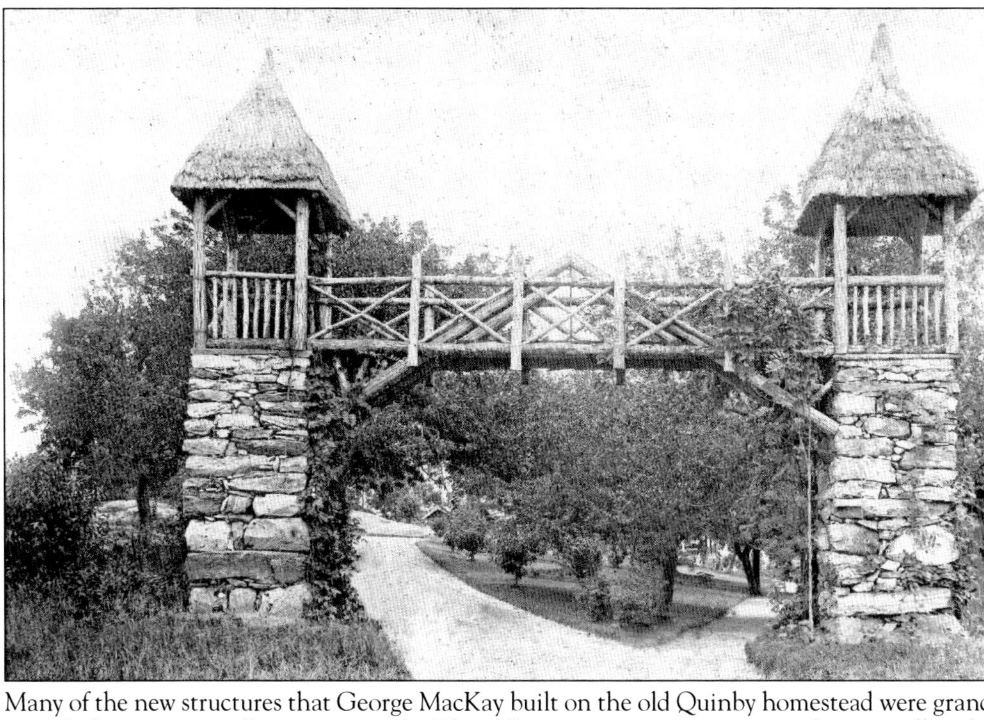

Many of the new structures that George MacKay built on the old Quinby homestead were grand in scale but intentionally rustic in style. The tall entrance gate, suggesting the portcullis of a medieval castle, was flanked by towers of native fieldstone topped by thatched roofs.

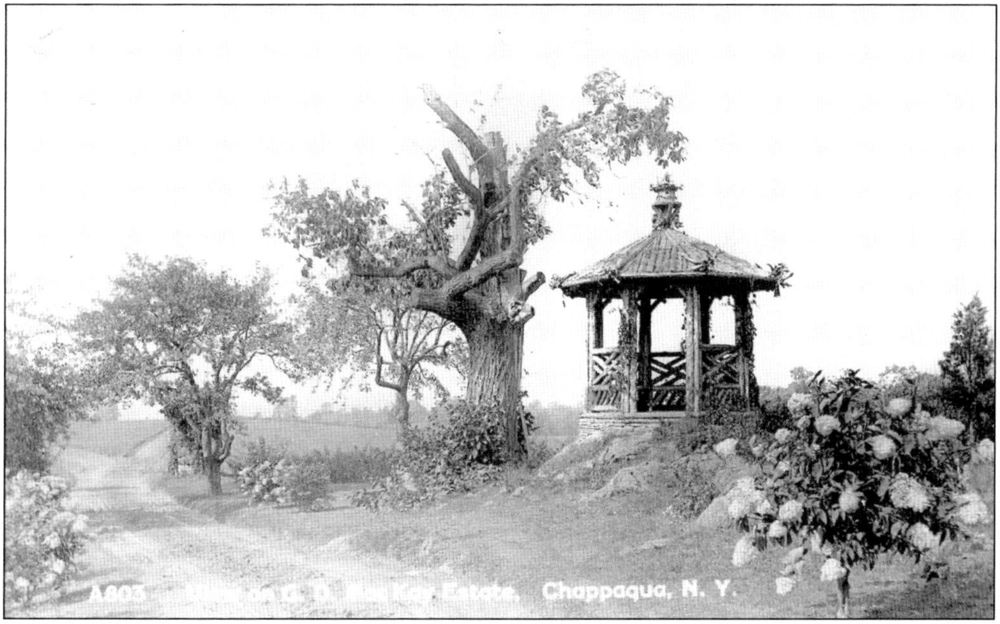

MacKay's name for his country home, After Glow Farm, was perhaps a tribute to the gorgeous sunsets that were a major feature of the hilltop site.

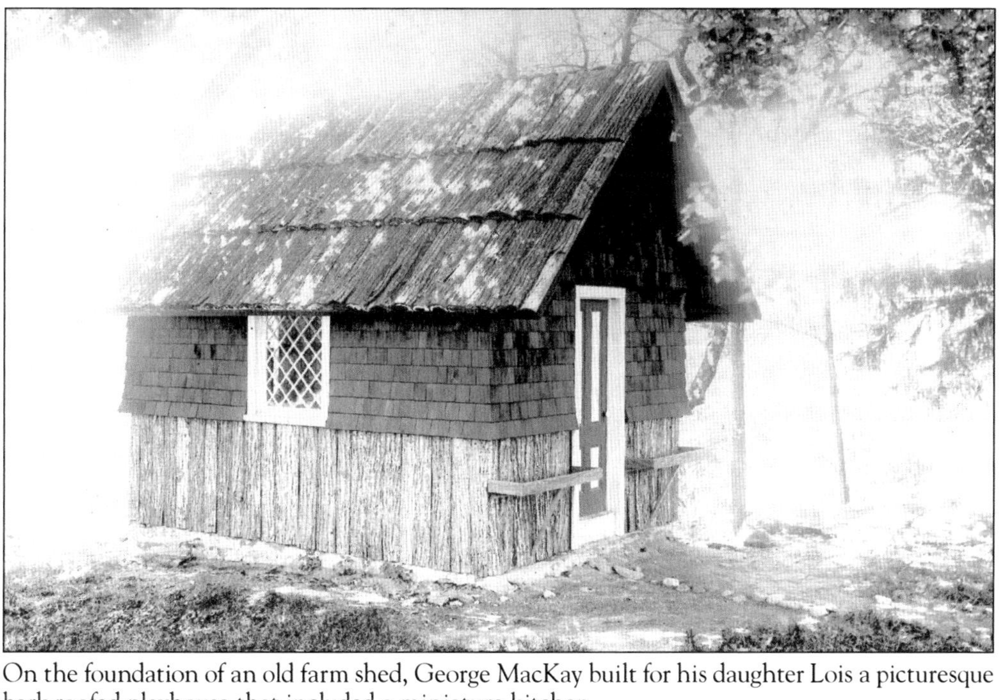
On the foundation of an old farm shed, George MacKay built for his daughter Lois a picturesque bark-roofed playhouse that included a miniature kitchen.

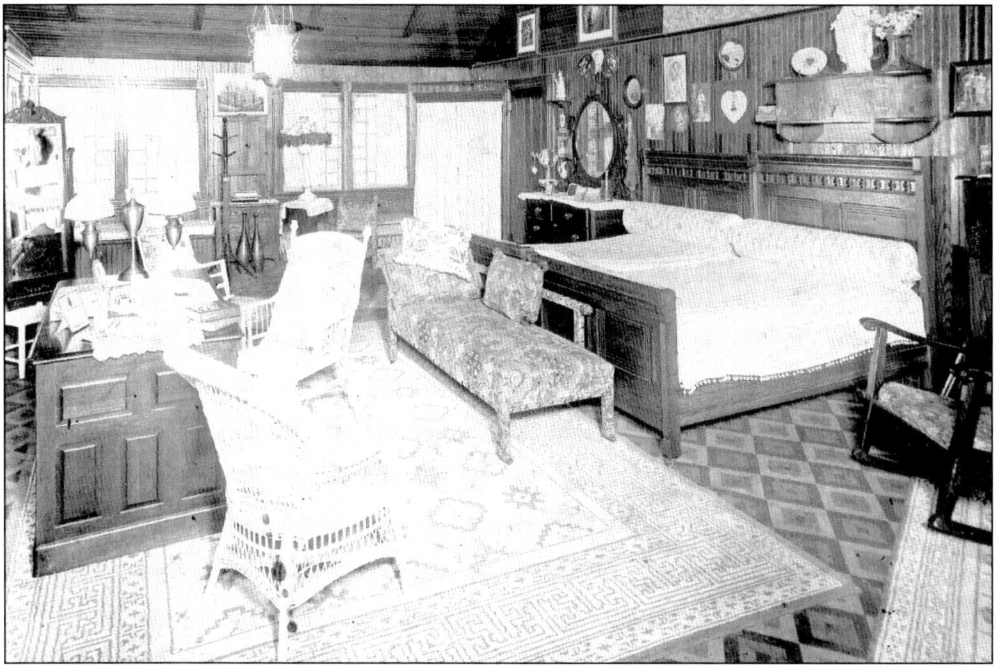

The MacKays' house, though spacious, was not a Gilded Age mansion. The family evidently intended their life in the country to be comfortable yet informal. The walls and ceilings of the master bedroom, for example, were finished in neither plaster nor hardwood paneling but inexpensive beaded planking, and the furnishings were likewise relatively plain and utilitarian.

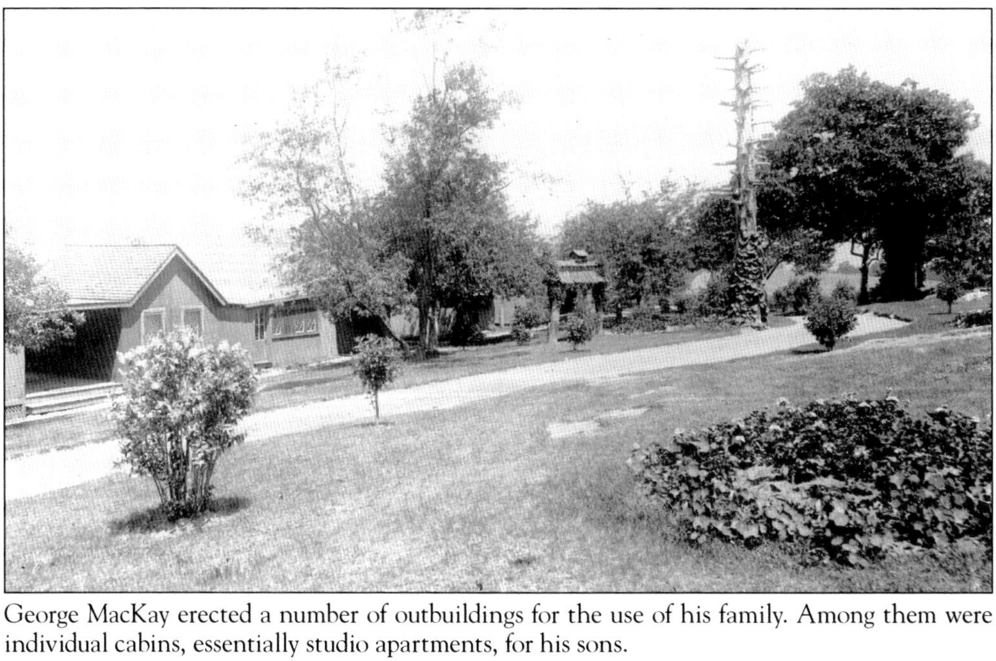

George MacKay erected a number of outbuildings for the use of his family. Among them were individual cabins, essentially studio apartments, for his sons.

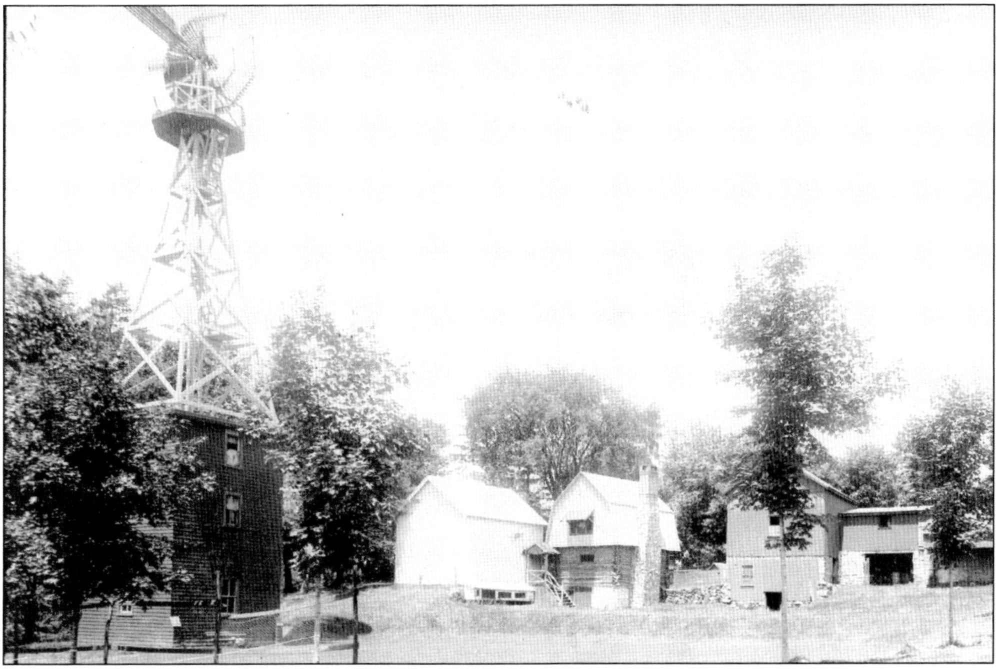

At the same time, George MacKay attempted to preserve the agricultural tradition of the Quinby homestead. He rebuilt and adapted some of the old farm buildings and installed new facilities such as wells, windmills, and water towers.

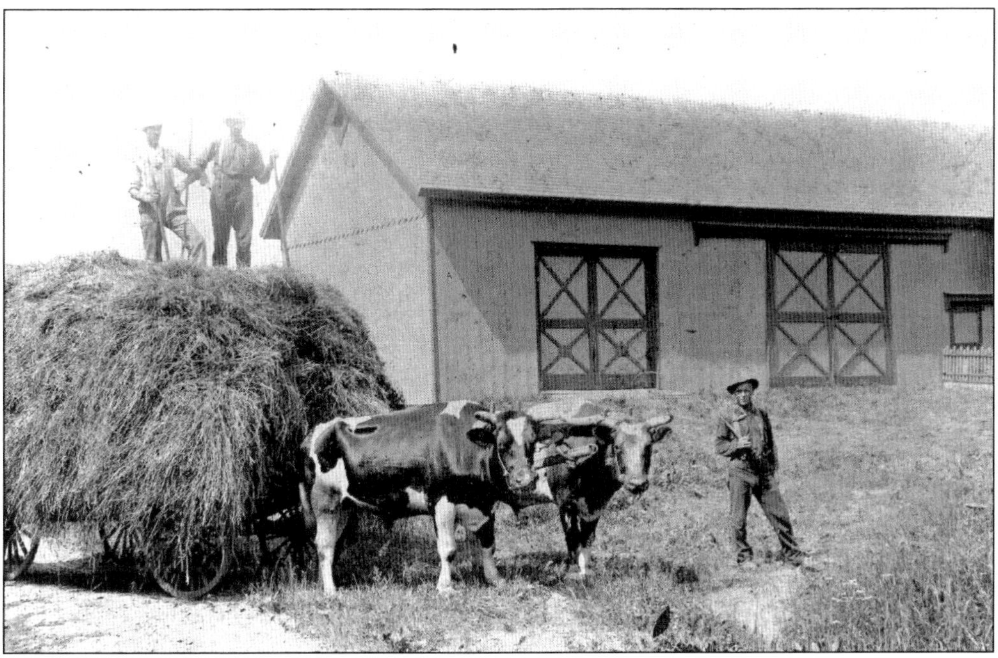

After Glow Farm was basically a dairy farm that required the harvest and storage of large quantities of hay to serve as winter feed for the cows.

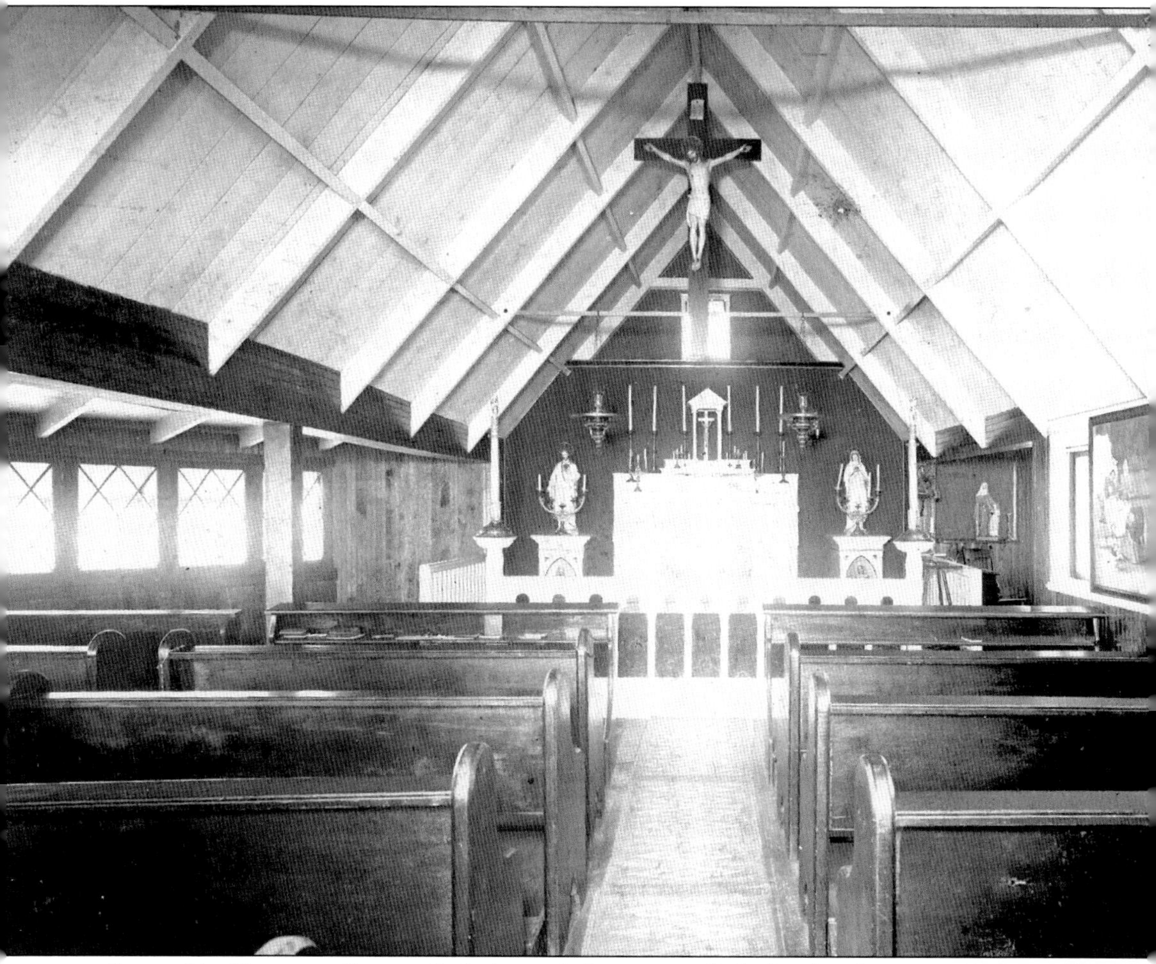

George MacKay was a Roman Catholic, and the nearest Catholic church was in Pleasantville, several miles away. He therefore built a chapel on the property for the use of family and friends, and a priest came weekly from Valhalla to perform Mass. In the early 1920s, MacKay suffered financial difficulties and was forced to sell the After Glow property. A few years later, most of it was acquired by the Whippoorwill Country Club. Almost no traces now remain of the former estate.

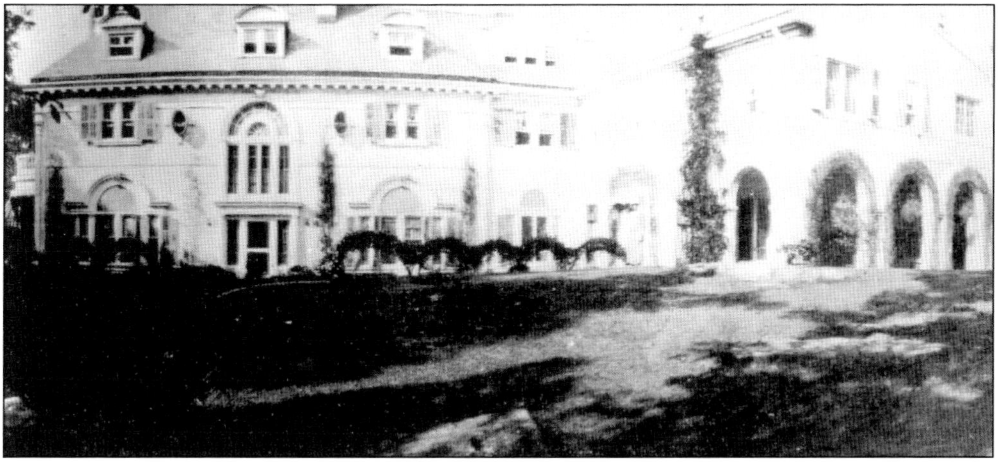

The largest of the hilltop estates in New Castle was 600-acre Annandale Farm, assembled in the early 1900s from several adjoining properties between Bedford and Armonk Roads (Routes 117 and 128). The owner was Moses Taylor V, who was a member of the investment-banking firm Kean Taylor and Company, a vice-president of the Lackawanna Steel Company, and a director of two railroads. At the highest point of the estate, at the end of Taylor Road, he built himself a truly baronial mansion in the fashionable Georgian Revival style.

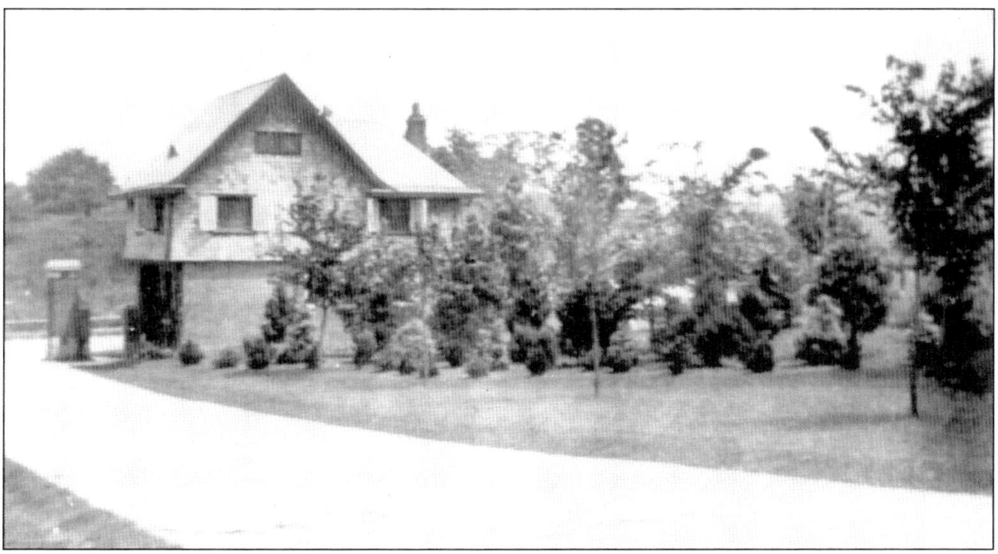

Moses Taylor constructed several other buildings on the estate. Some of them, such as the gatehouse on Armonk Road, still remain.

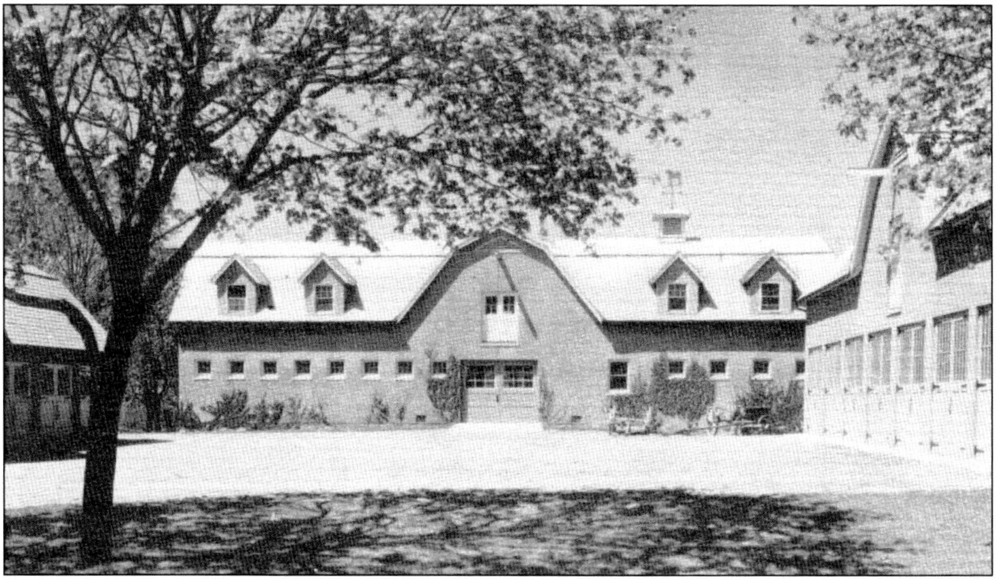

A part of Annandale Farm's elaborate complex of stables and barns also survives as part of the Mount Kisco Country Club.

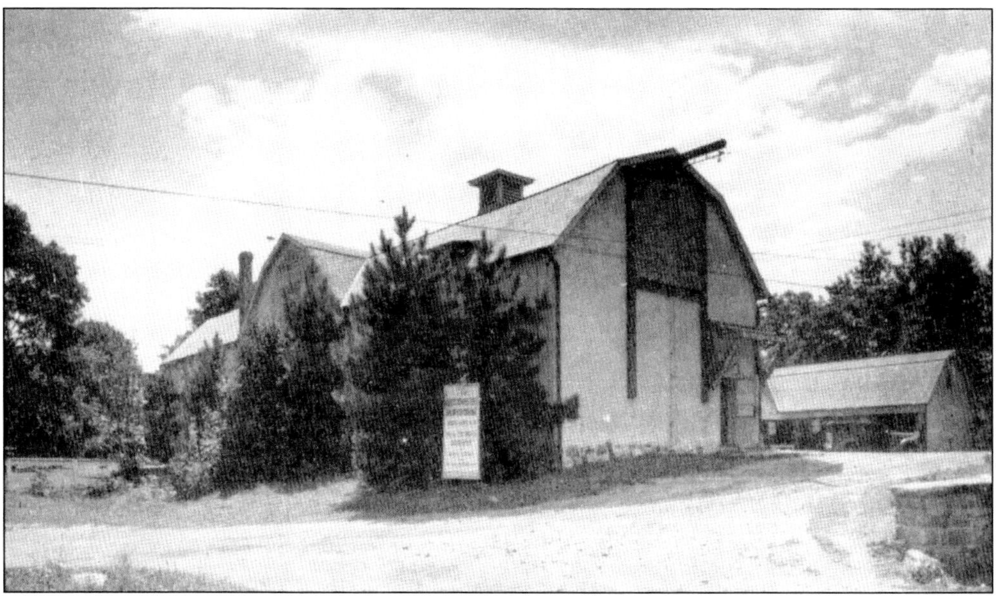

In the 1930s and 1940s, one of the Annandale Farm barns was converted to a summer theater, the Westchester Playhouse. Before air-conditioning became prevalent, Broadway theaters often shut down during the summer months, essentially laying off the actors and actresses who performed there. As a result, many stage stars appeared at seasonal theaters such as the Westchester Playhouse, either as resident professionals or as the leads in touring productions.

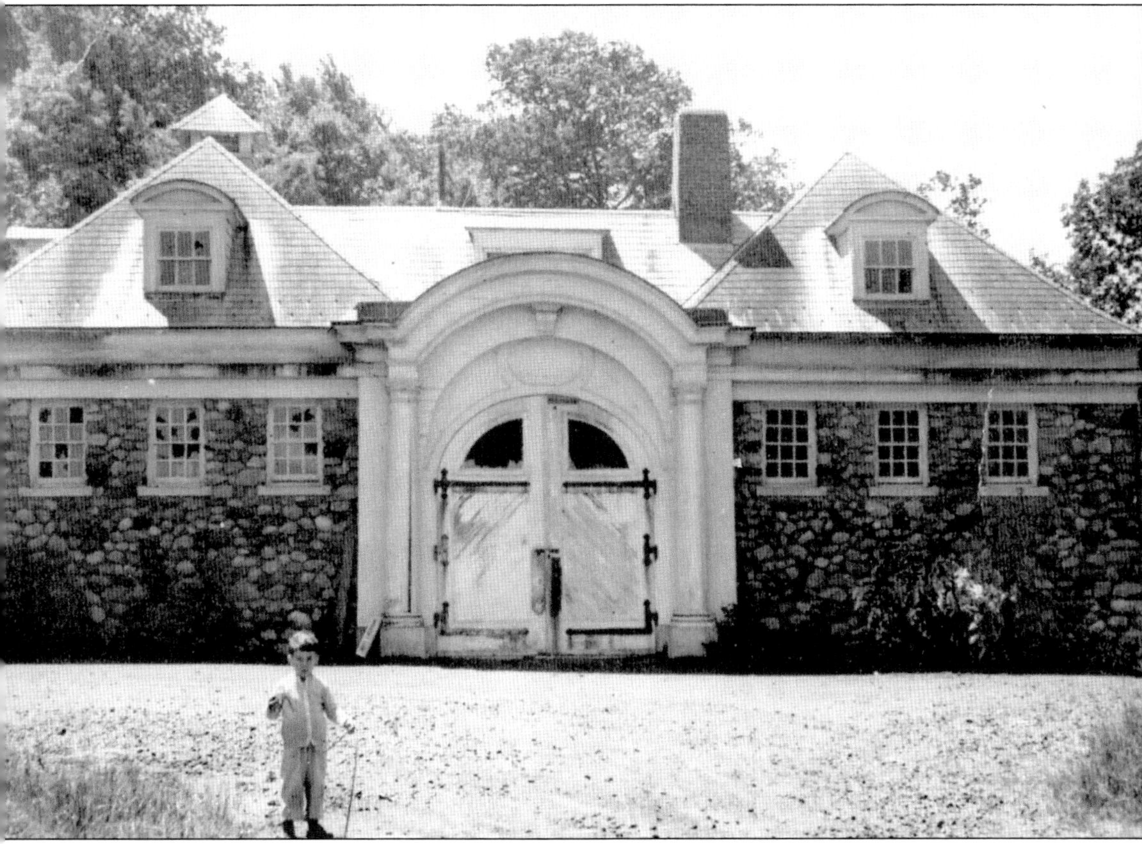

One of Moses Taylor's hobbies was breeding championship dairy cattle, particularly Guernseys. After Taylor's death in 1928, most of Annandale Farm was acquired by the Lawrence Realty Company for the suburban development known as Lawrence Farms. A substantial portion of it became the Mount Kisco Country Club, and the rest was subdivided into residential lots. The mansion was eventually surrendered to the Town of New Castle to pay off overdue property taxes. It proved to be unsellable and was demolished between 1949 and 1950. The carriage house complex (shown here), after a few years of neglect, was renovated as a private home.

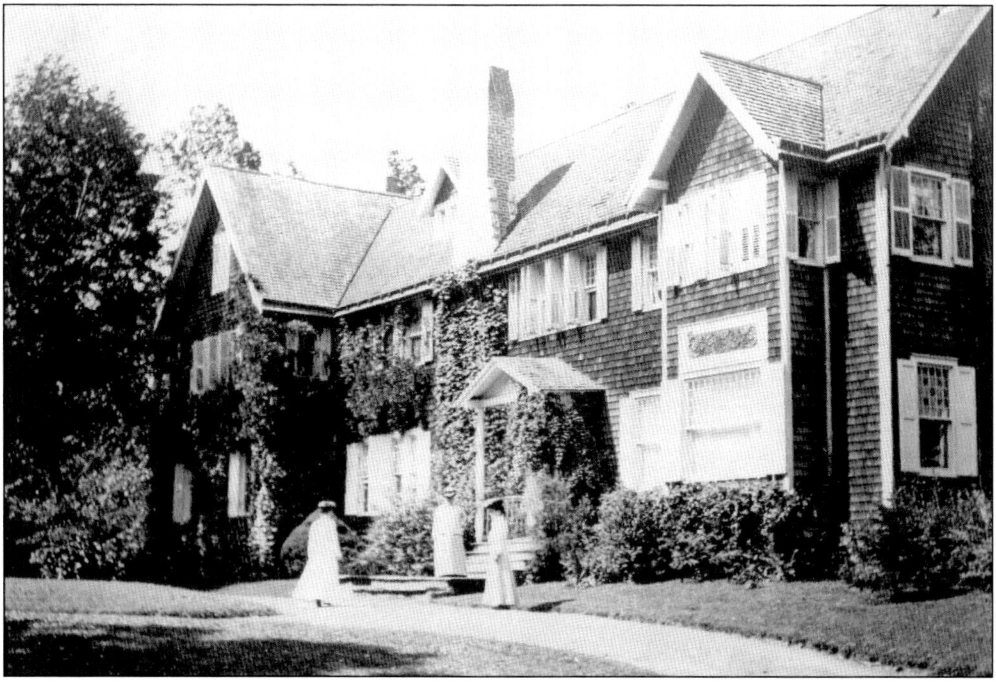

Elizabeth Chamberlain was the daughter of Ivory Chamberlain, editor of the *New York Herald*. In 1897, the Chamberlain family began acquiring property along South Greeley Avenue near the intersection with Bedford Road, and within a decade established an estate called the Orchard, which extended over much of the area between the avenue and the railroad. At the top of the hill, Elizabeth Chamberlain's substantial shingle-style home was built.

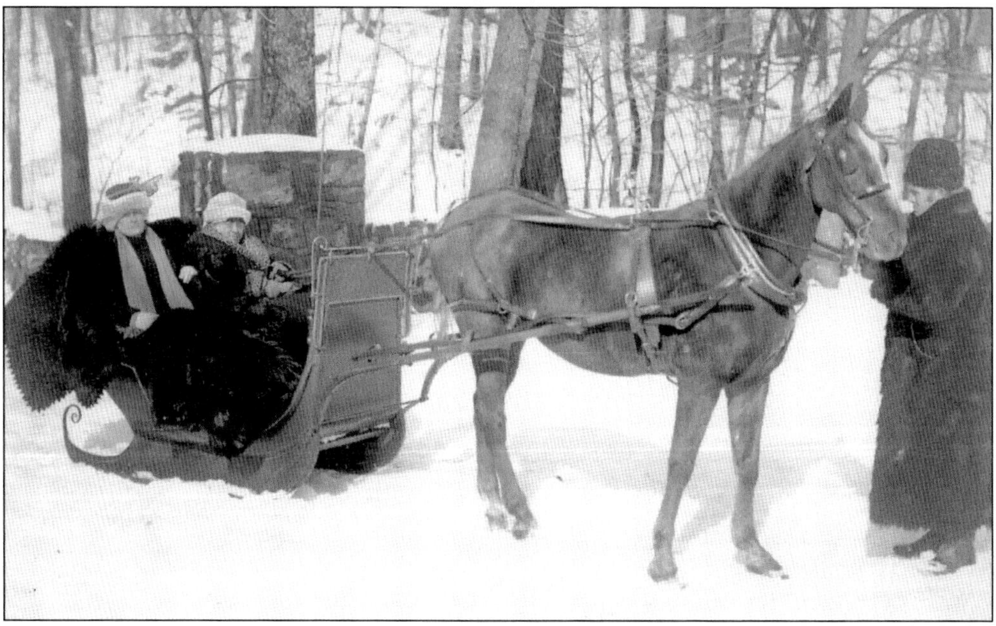

Elizabeth Chamberlain (left) and her life companion, Maria Messinger, are shown riding together in a horse-drawn sleigh. After Chamberlain's death in 1936, Messinger continued to reside in the house until her own death.

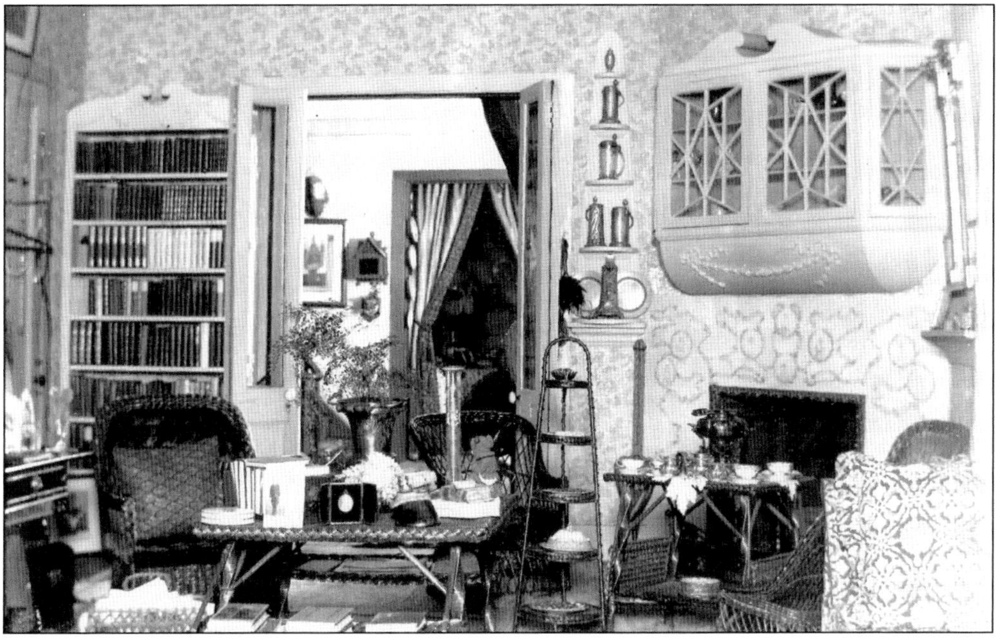

The interior of the house at the Orchard was more representative of the exuberance of the Victorian 1800s than of the more restrained tastes of the 1900s. The rooms were filled to overflowing with ornate furniture, mementos, knickknacks, and works of art.

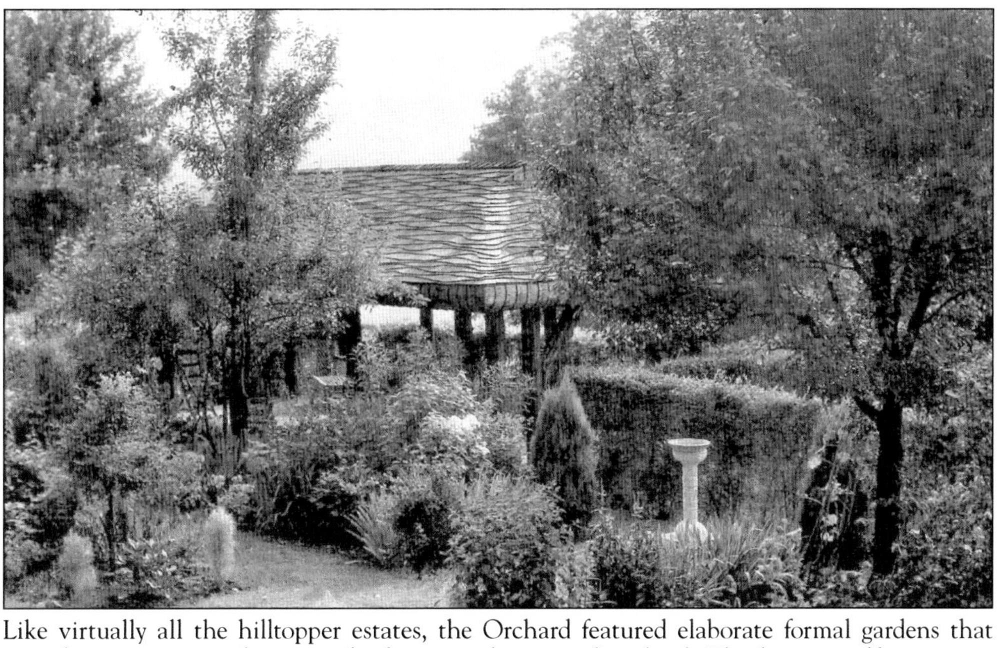

Like virtually all the hilltopper estates, the Orchard featured elaborate formal gardens that served as a transition between the house and surrounding land. The house itself remains a private residence, but most of the estate was sold. Much of the land at the bottom of the hill has become public property—part is occupied by the town hall of New Castle, and an even larger portion serves as the southern parking lot for the railroad station.

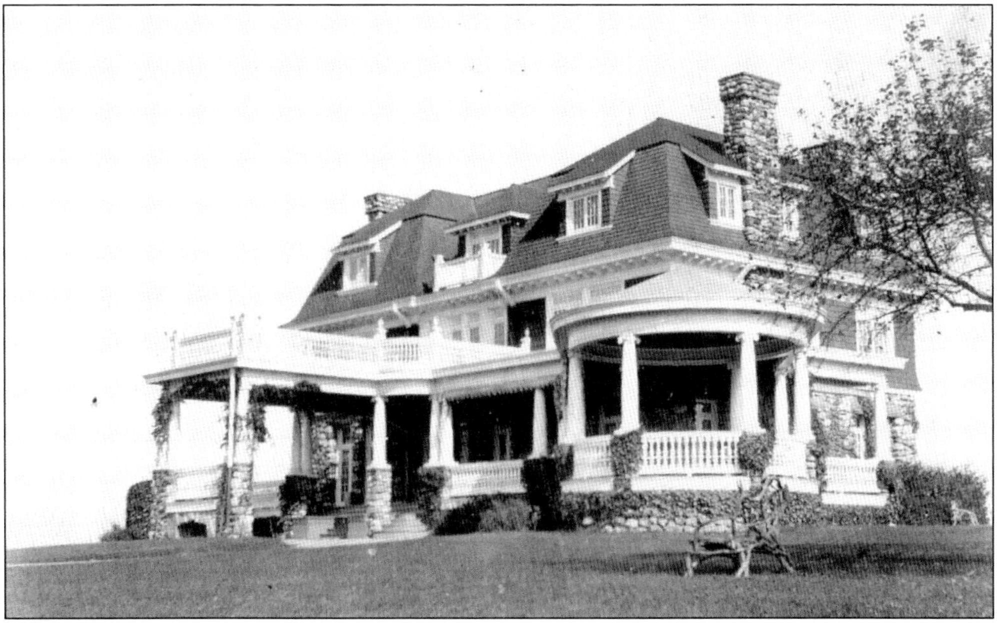

John Isaac Devoe Bristol (1845–1932) was an inventor, writer, and officer of the Northwestern Mutual Life Insurance Company. In 1898, he bought the farm of Joseph M. Valentine on King Street, enlarged the farmhouse to a mansion of more than 10,000 square feet, and named the estate Antiora, from an Indian word meaning "hill in the sky." (Courtesy of Francis Turner Davidson.)

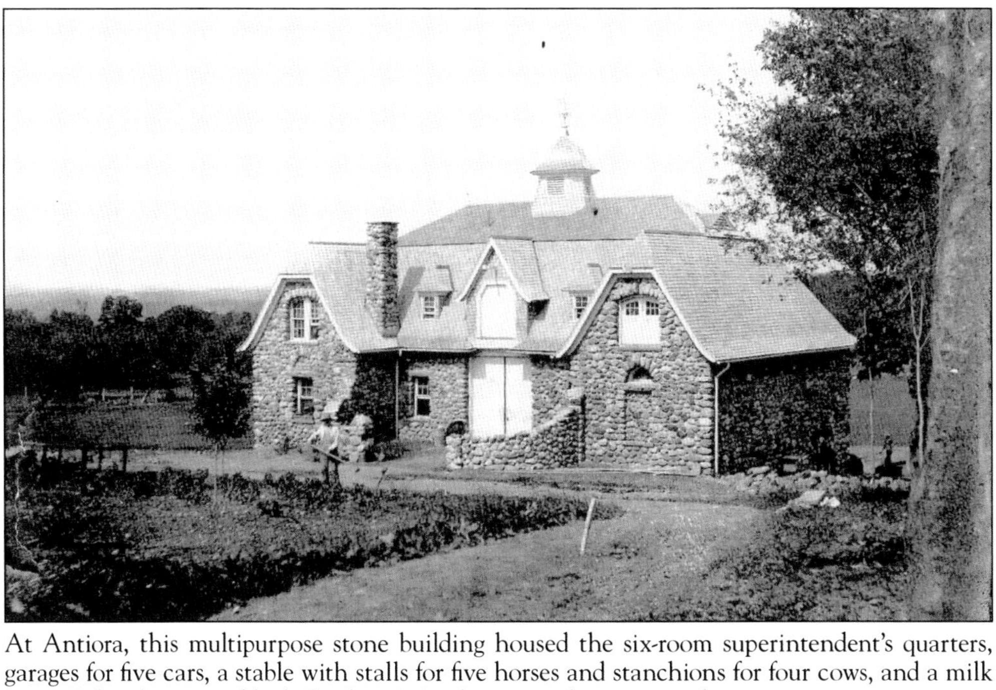

At Antiora, this multipurpose stone building housed the six-room superintendent's quarters, garages for five cars, a stable with stalls for five horses and stanchions for four cows, and a milk room. Behind was a paddock. By the 1940s, the estate also contained a tennis court, a swimming pool, a greenhouse, and extensive landscaping with apple and cherry orchards, pastures for cattle, and a coop for up to 500 chickens. (Courtesy of Frances Turner Davidson.)

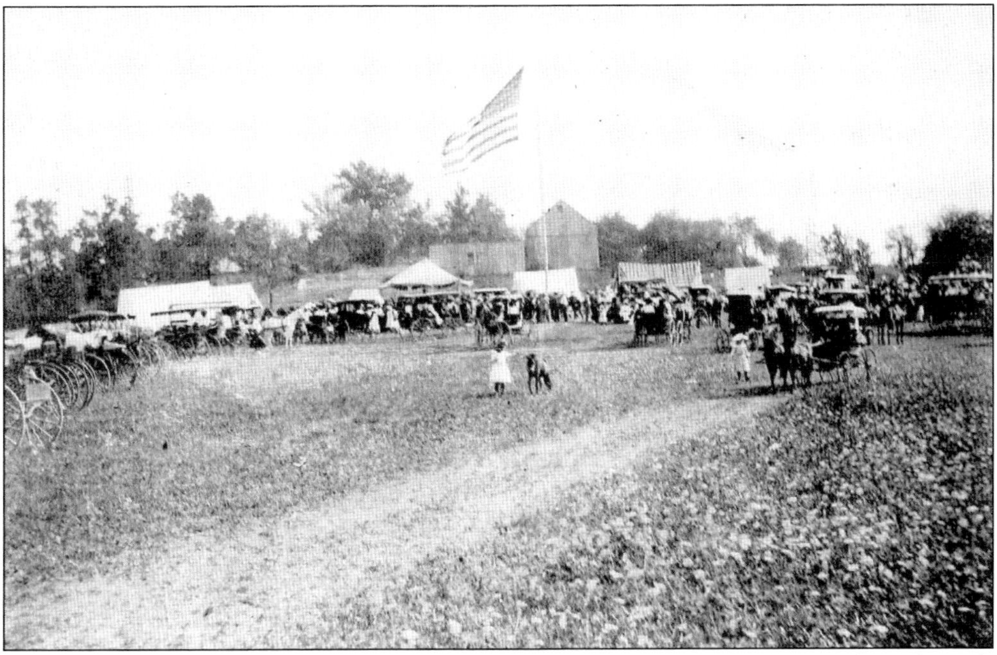

Each summer, an elaborate festival, open to the public, was held at Antiora. These festivals featured livestock displays, games, and refreshments. (Courtesy of Frances Turner Davidson.)

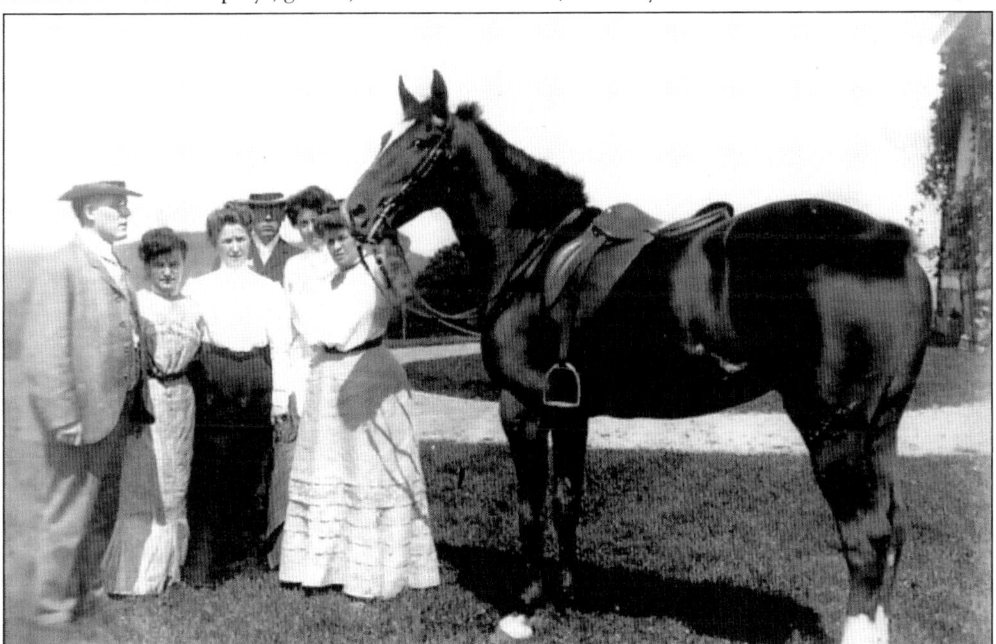

In 1909, John I. D. Bristol began building a home on another estate in New Castle. Antiora then became the home of his only child, Frances (1875–1969), and her husband, Albert Turner (1865–1925). Turner (far left) was a builder and developer and, with his father-in-law, assembled large holdings of land in New Castle for potential development. In the 1930s, his sons Ross and Bain subdivided much of the land around Antiora to create the development of Hillholme and Devoe Road. (Courtesy of Frances Turner Davidson.)

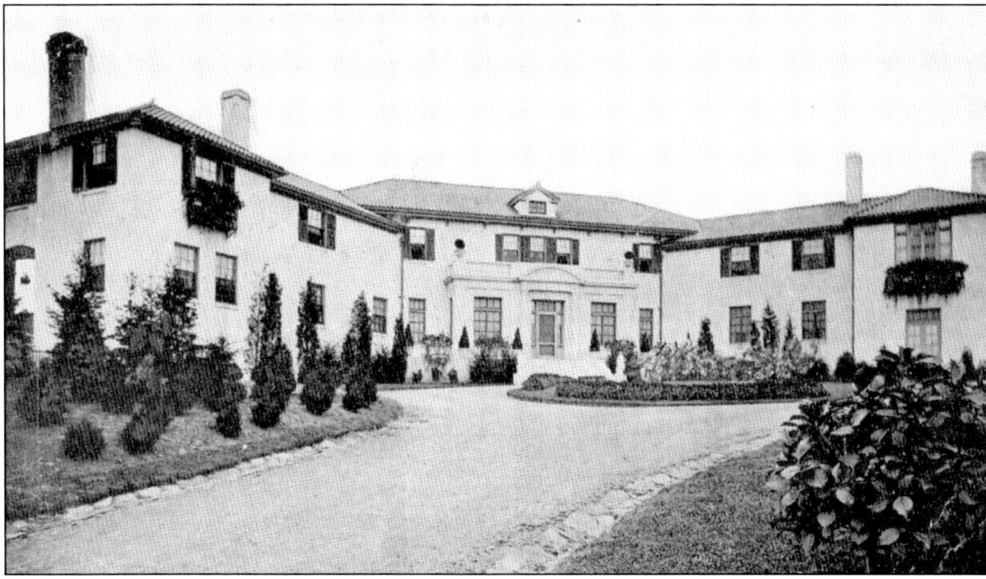

John I. D. Bristol built his new house atop a hill that overlooked the center of Chappaqua. He named the hill Perry Heights and the mansion Villa Perry, in honor of Commodore Perry, the victor of the Battle of Lake Erie during the War of 1812, to whom Bristol was related on his father's side. Several subdivisions developed by Bristol, Albert Turner, and their descendants have names associated with Bristol and his ancestors: Commodore Road, after Perry; Brevoort Road, for Henry B. Brevoort, Bristol's maternal grandfather and a Marine captain in the Battle of Lake Erie; and Devoe Road, from Bristol's middle name.

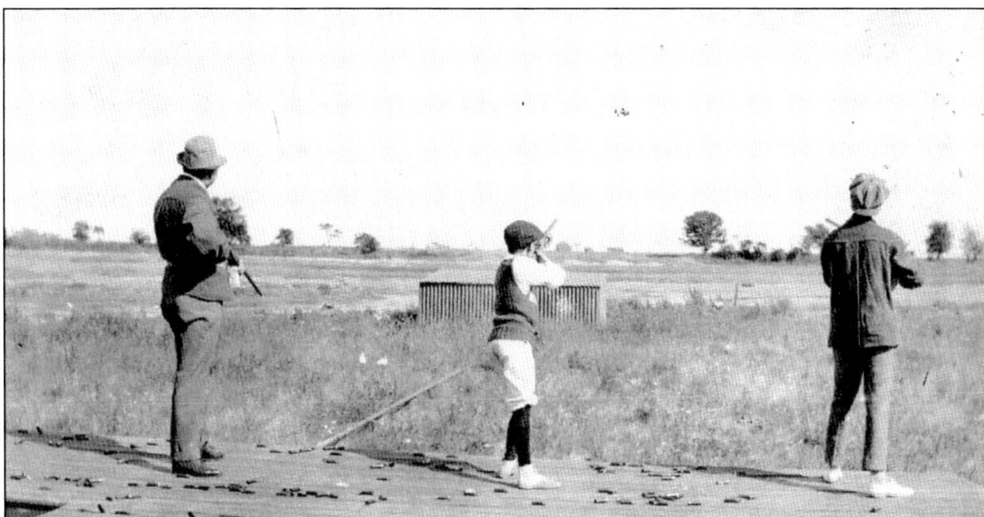

On the hilltop, John I. D. Bristol established the Perry Circle Gun Club for the use of his family and members of the community. It included this platform for trapshooting. Extremely active in the community, Bristol served as vice president of the Chappaqua National Bank and sponsored the J. I. D. Bristol Fire Company, still a unit of the Chappaqua Fire Department. He was a founder and the first president of the Chappaqua Historical Society and donated the land at the foot of Perry Heights on which the society erected the statue of Horace Greeley in 1914. (Courtesy of Francis Turner Davidson.)

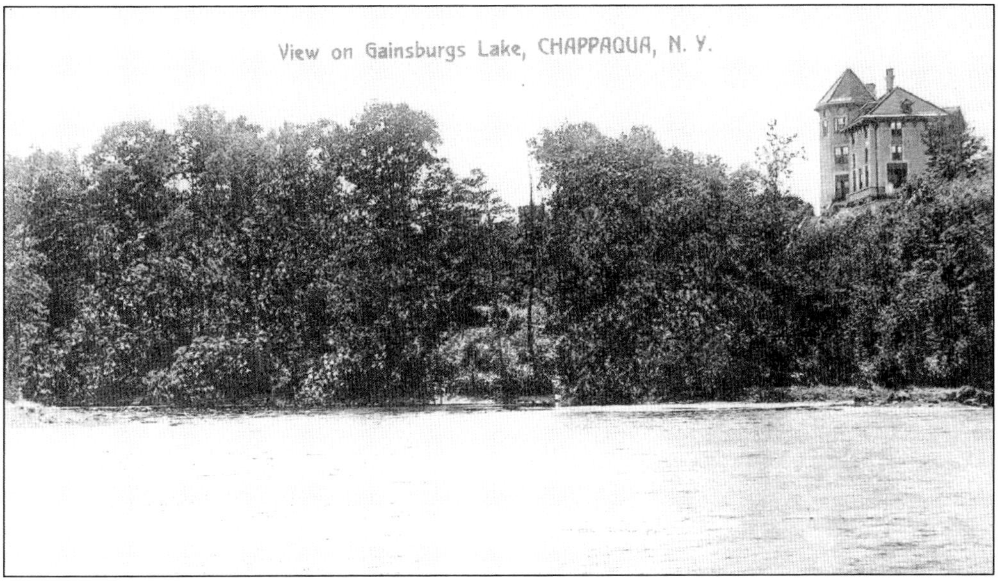

In the 1890s, Victor Guinzburg, president of the Kleinert Rubber Company, assembled a large estate from former farms along both sides of King Street, a short distance south of Antiora. He named the estate Chiselhurst, in honor of his wife, Henrietta, who carved statues in marble. In 1902, Guinzburg began to dam the streams that passed through the property, forming reservoirs to supply water for much of central Chappaqua. He named the first lake Heaptauqua because the project had provoked such a "heap o' talk" among his neighbors. The Guinzburgs, whose original summer home was in Walter Sutton's former farmhouse on King Street, built this imposing, towered mansion on a knoll overlooking Lake Heaptauqua in 1907.

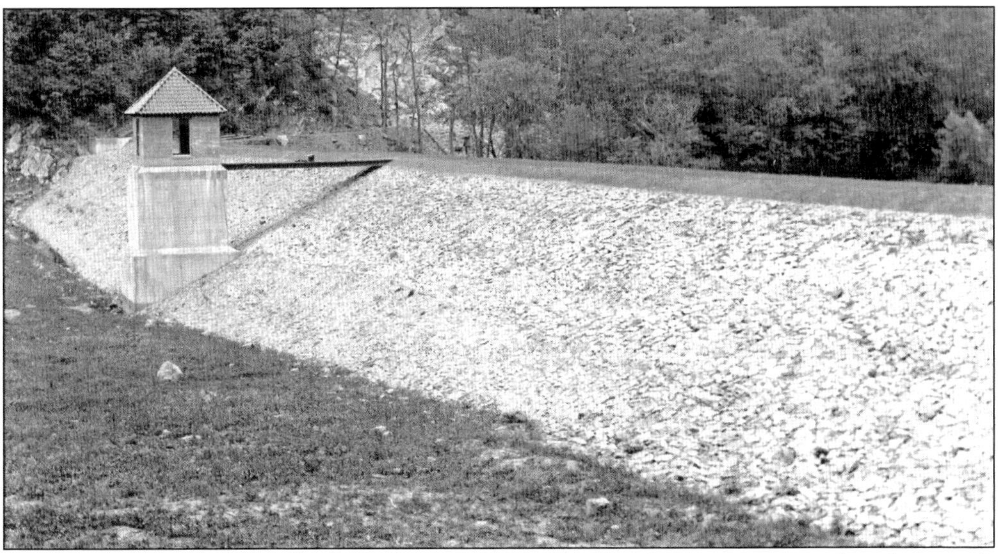

Victor Guinzburg's second reservoir was even larger than Lake Heaptauqua. This photograph shows the dam under construction. Guinzburg also installed pumps, water towers, and pipes down King Street hill to the center of Chappaqua. The Chappaqua Water Company provided water to the community until 1930, when most of the town switched to supplies from the aqueducts serving New York City. The company continued to sell water to individual neighborhoods until after World War II.

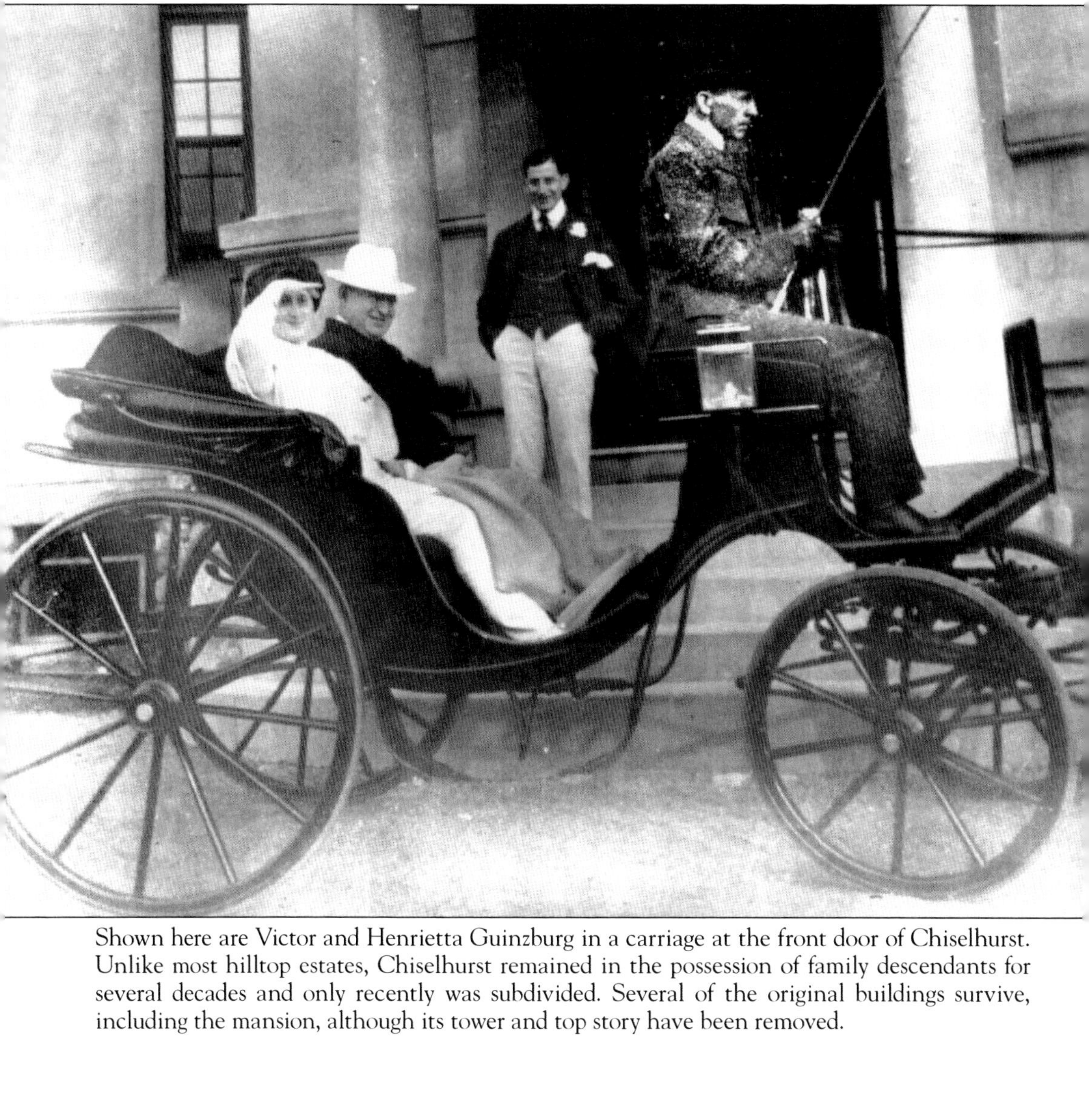

Shown here are Victor and Henrietta Guinzburg in a carriage at the front door of Chiselhurst. Unlike most hilltop estates, Chiselhurst remained in the possession of family descendants for several decades and only recently was subdivided. Several of the original buildings survive, including the mansion, although its tower and top story have been removed.

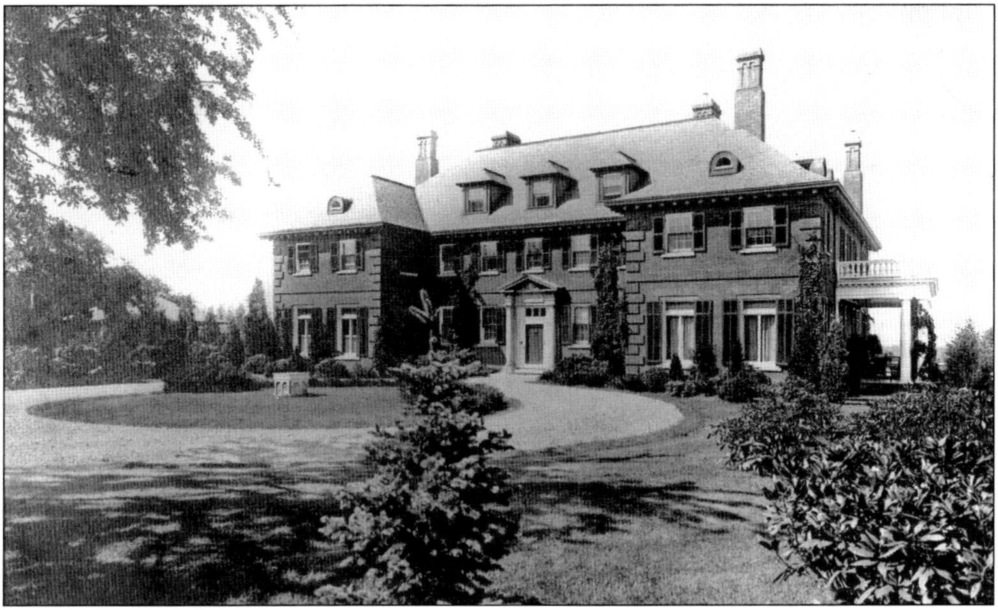

Adjoining Chiselhurst and across King Street from Antiora was Southerleigh, the estate of investment banker Sigmund Neustadt. Neustadt and his wife, Agnes, made this Georgian-Revival mansion their summer home from 1909 to 1949.

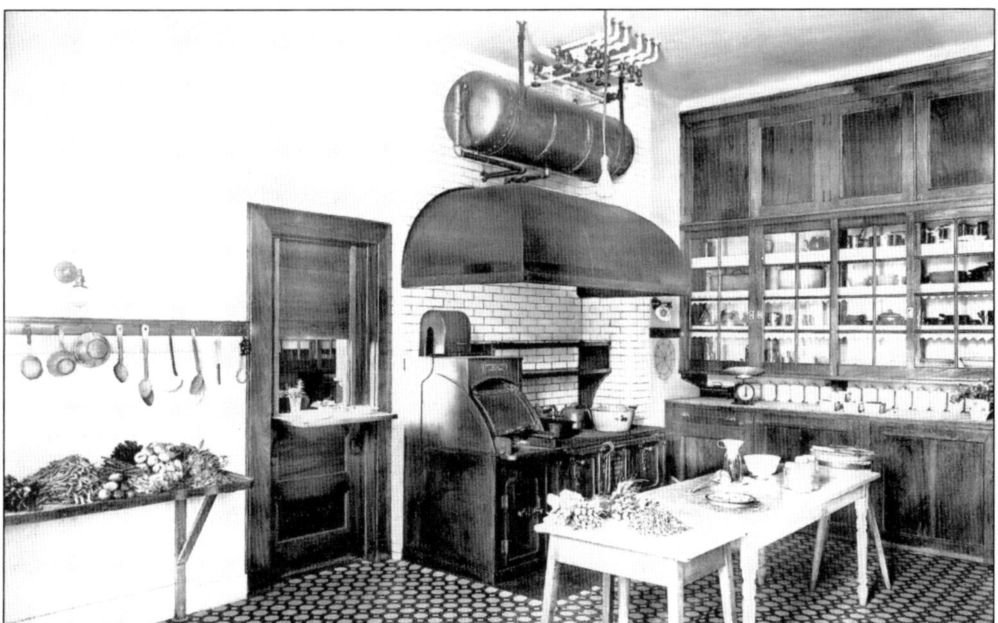

A particularly detailed series of photographs was taken at Southerleigh in the early 1900s, including views of service areas not often recorded. This shows part of the elaborate kitchen, equipped for entertaining on a large scale.

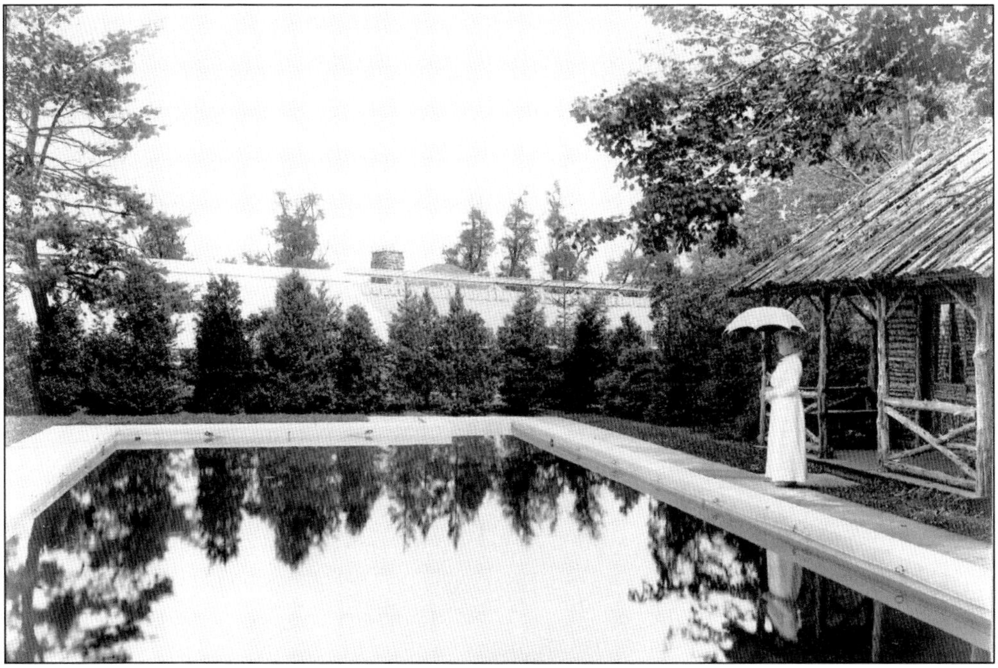

Most estate owners from the early 1900s on considered a swimming pool, preferably surrounded by formal gardens and accompanied by a changing house, an essential component of a proper country home.

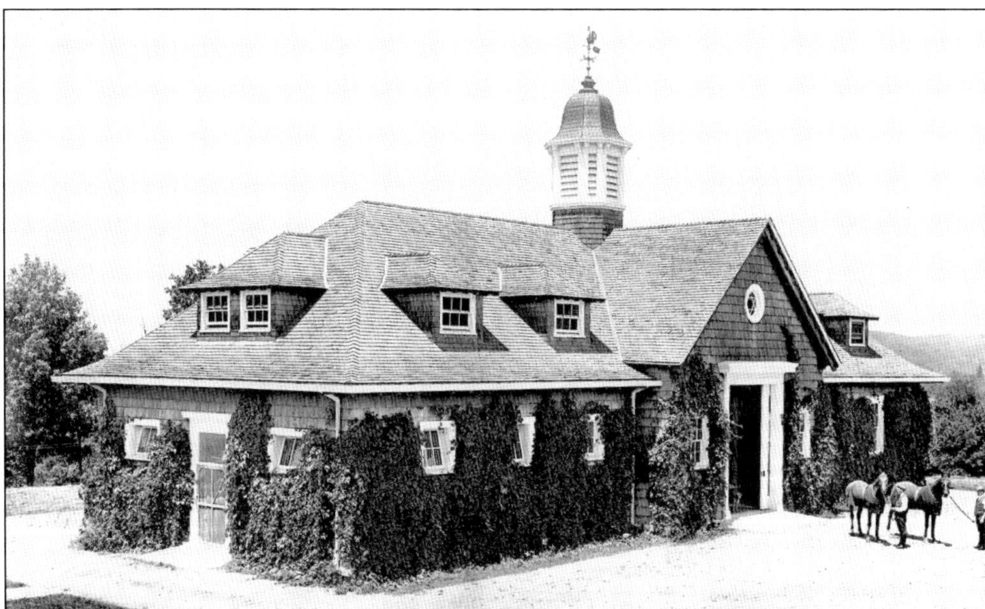

Almost nothing of Southerleigh remains. The mansion was destroyed by fire in 1966. A large portion of the property became the campus of the Douglas G. Grafflin Elementary School, and the rest was subdivided for residences on Old Lyme Road and Neustadt Lane. One survivor was the sturdy barn and carriage house, which was converted to a distinctive house on Old Lyme Road.

Nine

DISASTERS

NATURAL AND OTHERWISE

New Castle has enjoyed a relatively quiet existence over the centuries. But a few disasters, natural and man-made, have been notable exceptions to this placid history. The most dramatic and destructive was the tornado of 1904. Saturday, July 16, was a hot and hazy summer day until about 3:00 p.m. At that time, Walter Sarles was driving with his family from the top of Chappaqua Mountain toward his home on Quaker Street. Black clouds gathered in the valley below, accompanied by a tremendous roar and crash that could be heard for miles. Sarles's horse froze in terror and refused to go on. For 10 minutes the view was hidden by intense darkness, and when the clouds cleared, Sarles realized his family had narrowly escaped a tornado. His home and four others, together with several barns and outbuildings along the stretch of Quaker Street between present-day Gray Rock Lane and Dodge Farm, were destroyed. Several people were injured, including Anna Washburn, who lived next door. Her aged mother died of shock shortly after the house collapsed around them.

The next disaster was the result of human error. On August 31, 1907, a train heading south from Mount Kisco to Chappaqua was mistakenly switched to a track that was under repair. The train derailed, and the locomotive rolled over on its side. The coal and baggage cars tipped over only slightly, and the crowded passenger cars remained upright, so only the engineer and the fireman suffered injuries.

The remaining disasters—repeated floods in downtown Chappaqua—caused significant property damage and dislocation but no serious injury or loss of life. Downtown flooding was remedied in the 1980s by widening and deepening the channel of the Saw Mill River south of the village. Nonetheless, the heavy, sudden rains of Hurricane Floyd in 1999 washed out stretches of two town roads, plus the Duck Pond dam in Chappaqua.

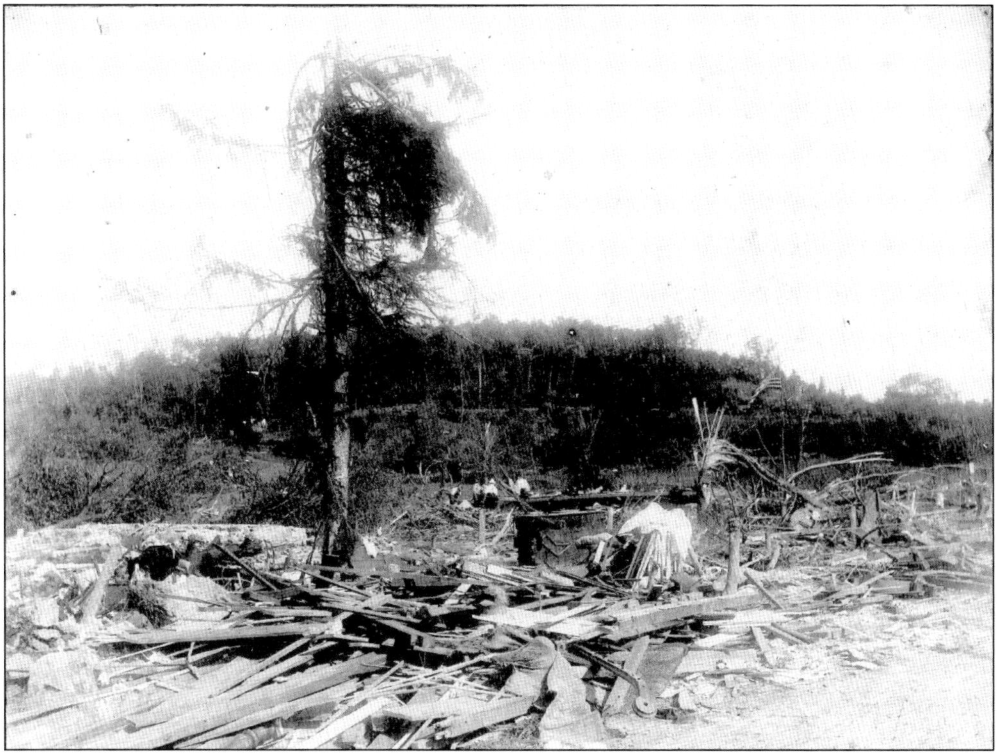

These photographs were probably taken on the day after the July 16, 1904, tornado, when crowds of the curious from as far off as New York City thronged Quaker Street, which extends across the center of the view below to the south from the farmyard of Charles Dodge. On either side of the road are the ruins of the houses and other buildings destroyed by the powerful whirlwind. In the foreground, a pile of hay marks what little remains of the Dodge barn.

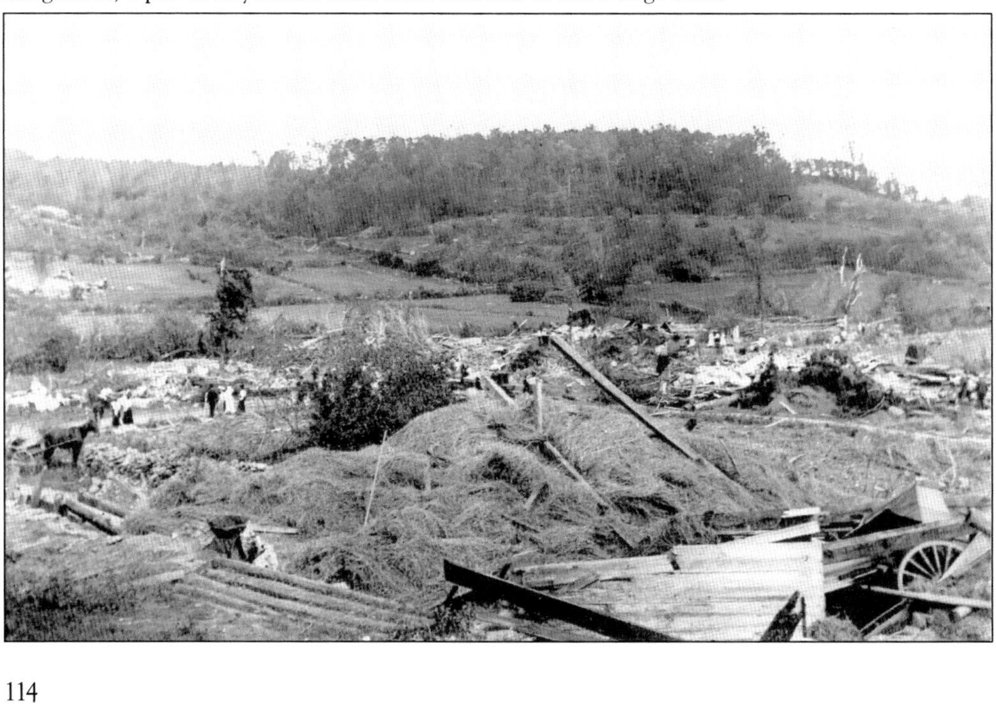

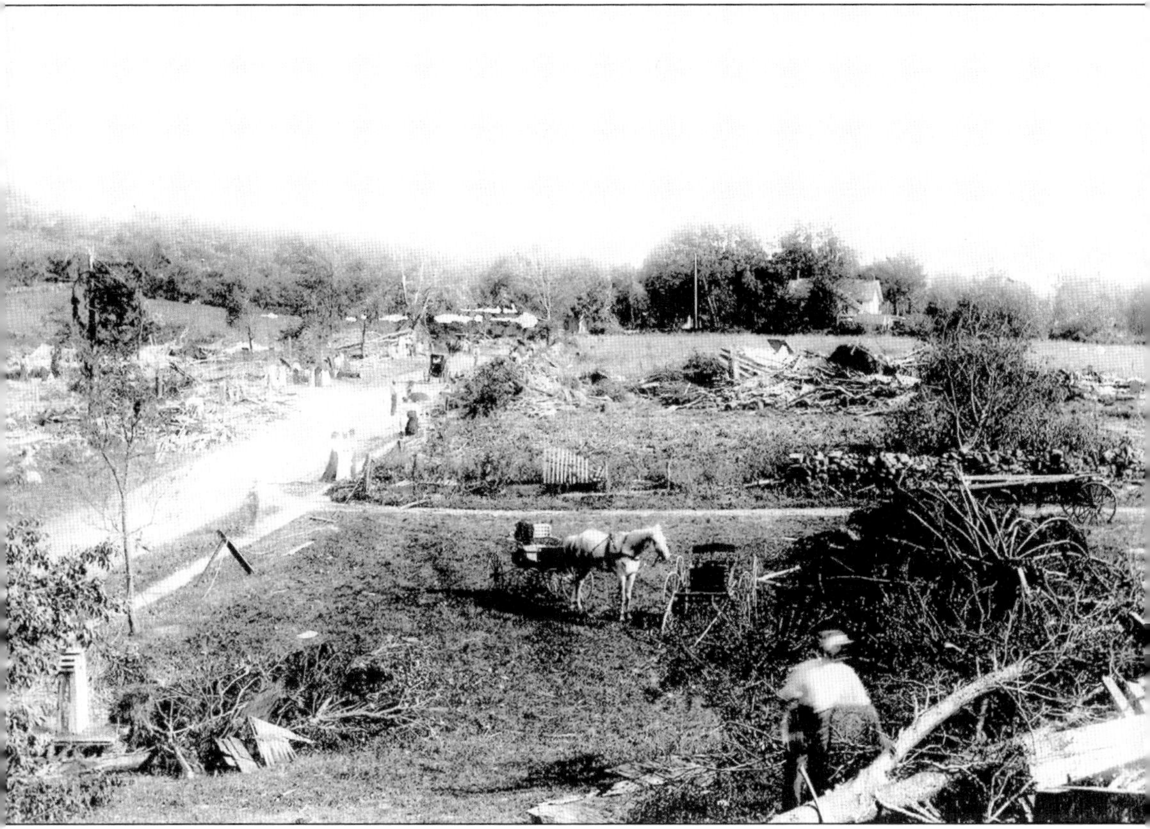

In this similar view along Quaker Street, the old Quaker home of Alfred Underhill (background) can be seen largely undamaged. It still exists at the corner of Gray Rock Lane. The cart track that extends to the right from Quaker Street is now Marcourt Drive, the road through Dodge Farm, developed by descendant Courtney Dodge. Harry Cronk (foreground) saws a fallen tree. The horse and cart belonged to Abram J. Quinby and his wife, who lived across town and were probably looking after their daughter, Mabel Quinby Dodge, who had witnessed the storm from the Dodge house and gave birth to a daughter there the next day. Buildings in the direct path of the 1904 tornado were shredded to pieces. Most of the debris remained on site, but some was scattered over a distance of several miles. A savings passbook that belonged to Warren Tompkins, for example, was snatched up from his disintegrating house and turned up in northern Armonk.

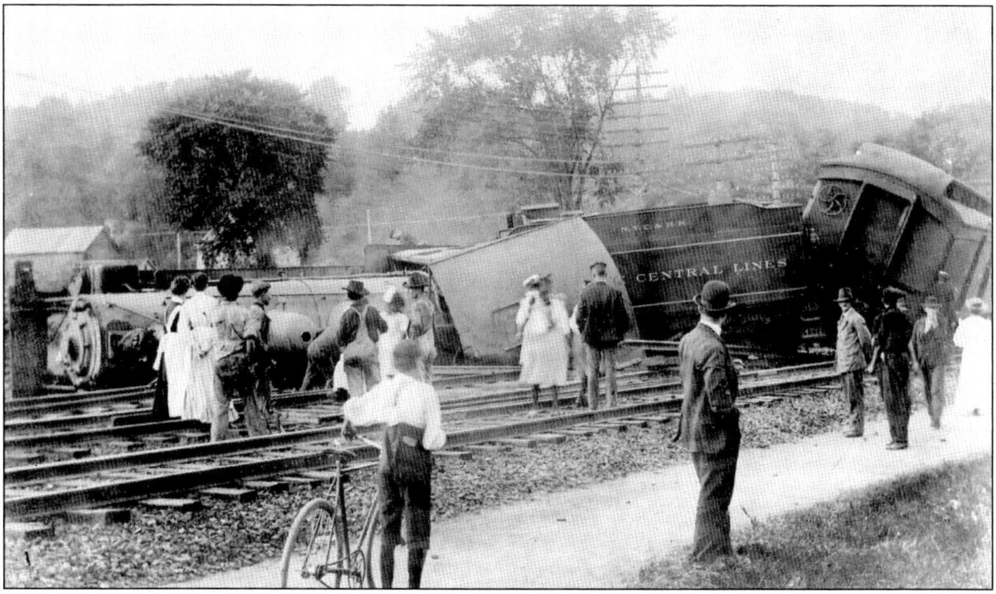

On the afternoon of August 31, 1907, a New York Central train bound for the city was mistakenly switched to a track that was under repair, just north of the Main Street crossing at Chappaqua. The tracks were ripped up, and the train derailed. The accident could have been much worse. The train was already slowing down as it approached the Chappaqua station, and the engineer, Bill Weaver, managed to slam on the brakes and jump from the locomotive before it rolled over. He suffered only minor burns from escaping steam. The fireman, Ed Collins, was more severely scalded, but eventually recovered.

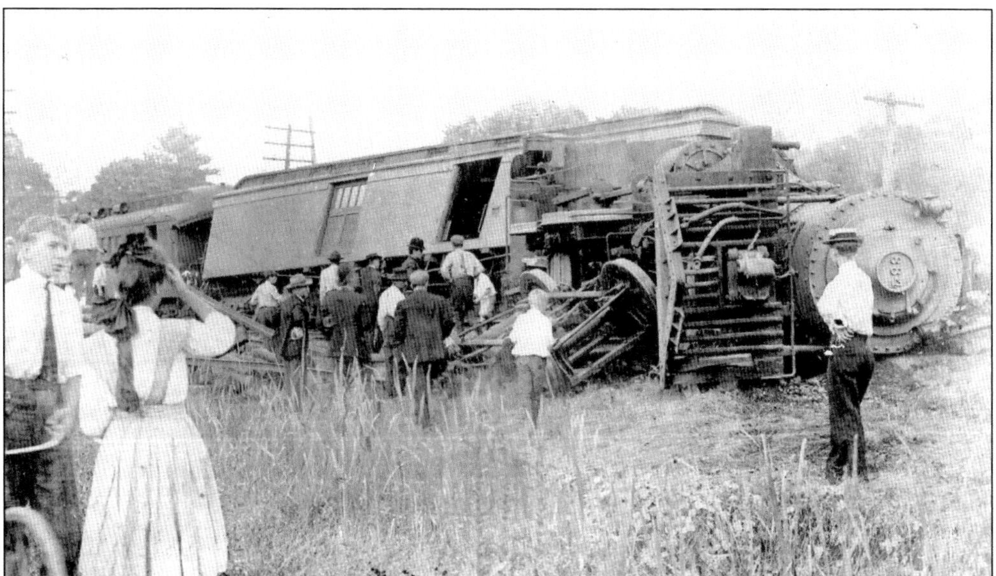

Behind the locomotive, neither the coal car nor the baggage car completely rolled over. Baggage man George Hopkins jumped into the high grass next to the tracks and escaped injury. The four passenger cars remained upright, and the riders were only shaken up.

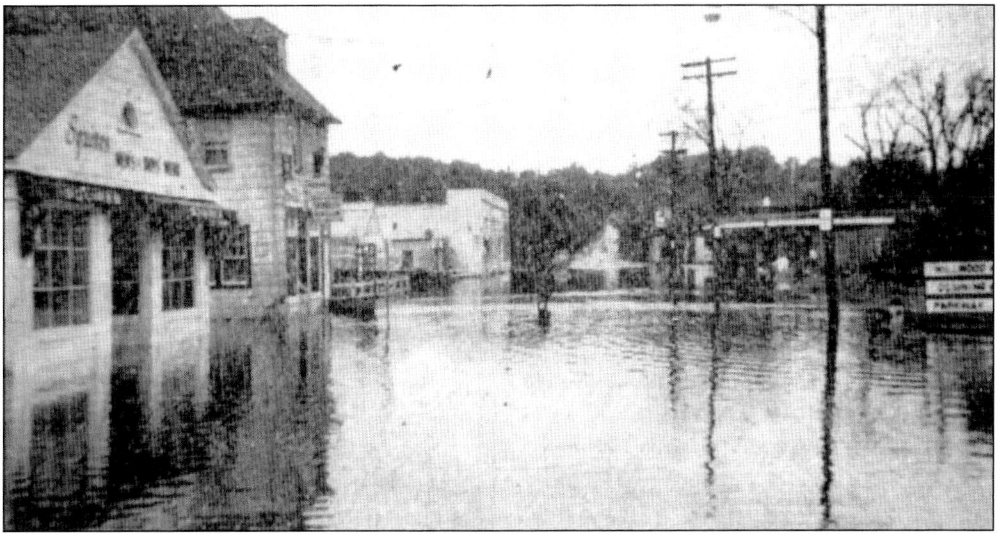

Downtown Chappaqua is located on a flood plain, which is ordinarily drained by the Saw Mill River. But until recent years, heavy rains caused repeated flooding of the area. As early as the 1850s, Horace Greeley made expensive and unsuccessful efforts to dry out his meadow along what is now South Greeley Avenue. In the 1900s, floods became more frequent and more severe. On October 15–16, 1955, South Greeley Avenue was covered in three to five feet of water, and its stores suffered much damage and loss of inventory. Particularly hard hit was Squire's Men's Shop (far left). At the urging of the town, the U.S. Army Corps of Engineers came up with a Chappaqua Flood Control Project to enhance drainage through the Saw Mill River. Implementing the project, however, took several decades more.

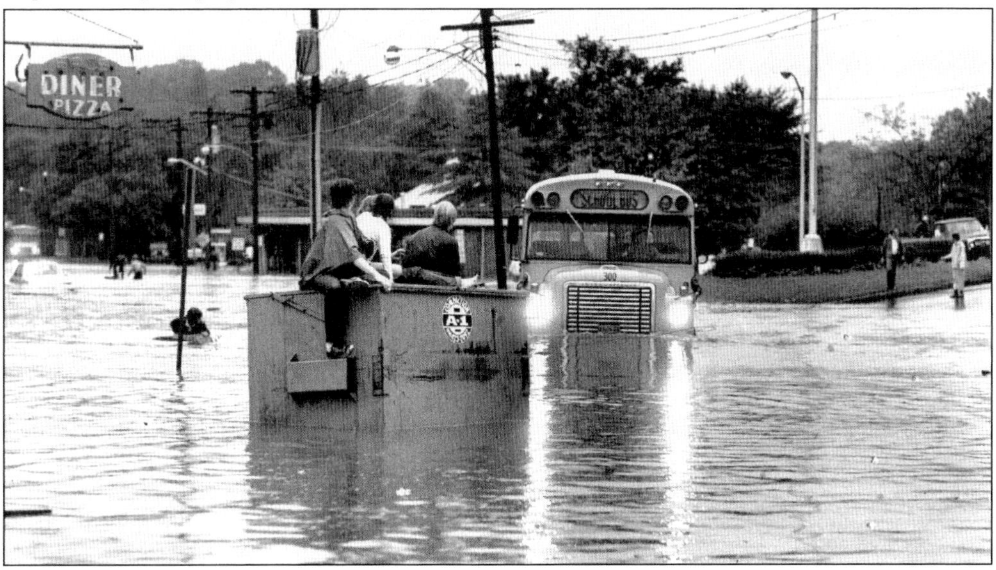

On Friday, September 26, 1975, following five days of heavy rain, South Greeley Avenue was flooded as severely as it had been 20 years earlier. Once again, Squire's lost much of its stock. Here, several young people perch on a floating dumpster, while a school bus, with Joan Corwin at the wheel, nearly stalls as it ferries stranded students and commuters along the inundated street. Despite town pleas, the Chappaqua Flood Control Project was not completed until the 1980s. Since then, downtown flooding has been minimal. (Courtesy of the town of New Castle.)

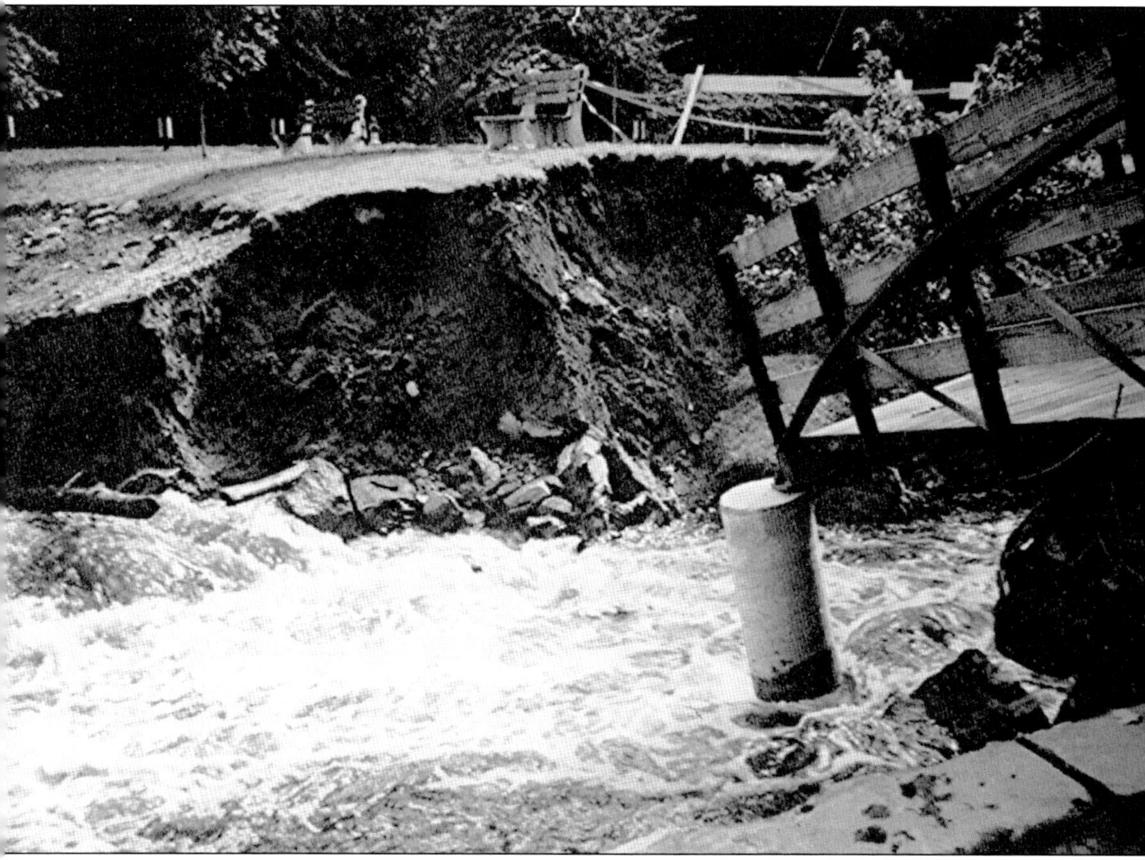

The torrential rains that accompanied Hurricane Floyd on September 26, 1999, caused severe flooding and erosion across much of Westchester County. In New Castle, Roaring Brook Road, Seven Bridges Road, and the Duck Pond between Quaker Street and Douglas Road were particularly affected. At the outlet of the Duck Pond, floodwaters surged over the dam, washing out its abutments and leaving the footbridge to dangle precariously over the stream. What had been a beautiful and much-loved pond became an ugly, eroded gully. Replacing the dam and its abutments and repairing the undermined roads and clogged drains took many months to complete.

Ten

SUBURBAN NEW CASTLE

Horace Greeley would have liked to commute to New York City, but in his day it was not practical. Railroad service from Chappaqua to the city had been available since the 1840s, but the Manhattan terminal was north of the business district, and to reach the *Tribune* office required a long, slow ride in a cab or horsecar. So, Greeley came out to his country home only on weekends and vacations.

Not until the early 1900s, when electric trolleys, elevated trains, and subways made all parts of the city quickly accessible, did daily commuting to the city become common. That was when New Castle, and Chappaqua in particular, began to become suburban. Developers and builders bought up former farms and estates and subdivided the land into residential neighborhoods.

The suburban building boom accelerated after 1910, slowed down during the Depression and World War II, and then exploded in the decades after the war. Census figures for New Castle tell the story: in 1800, the population was 1,555; in 1890, it was 2,210; in 1910, it was 3,573; in 1930, it was 6,792; in 1950, it was 8,802; in 1960, it was 14,338; and in 1970, it was 19,837. Since then, growth has again slowed, but it has never stopped.

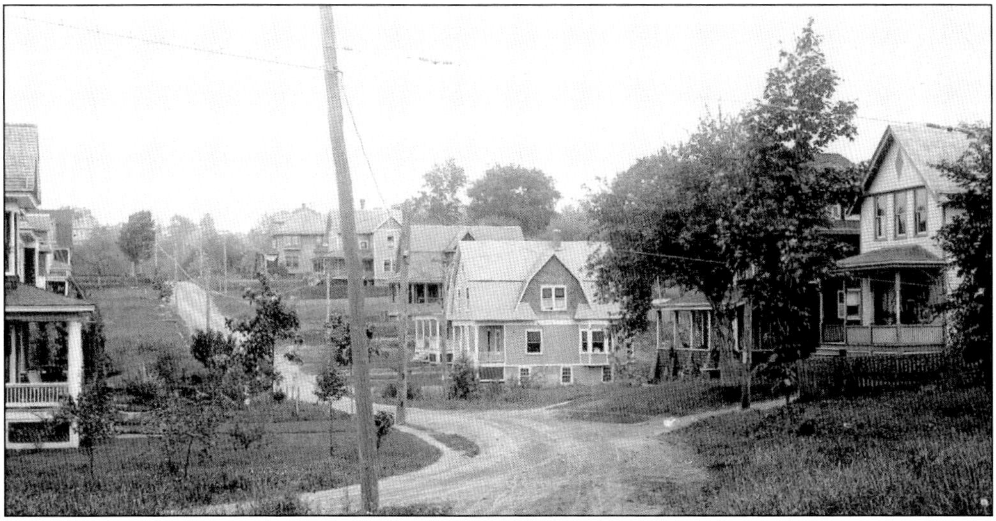

One of the first purely residential subdivisions in New Castle was developed by Abram J. Quinby and his son Sidney Quinby on land they owned southeast of the intersection of King Street and Bedford Road (Routes 120 and 117). They called it by the aristocratic title De Quarmby Park, but the neighborhood is now known by its principal street, Ridgewood Terrace. It was probably not intended to provide homes for suburban commuters, but it was nonetheless within walking distance of the railroad station.

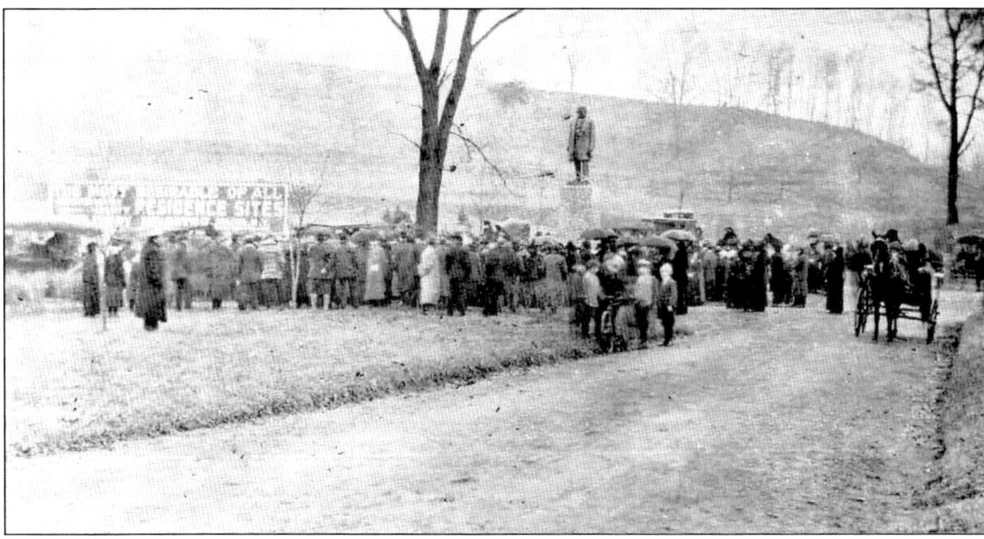

In the 1900s, John I. D. Bristol and his son-in-law Albert Turner were among the most active developers in New Castle. The site for the statue of Horace Greeley, dedicated in 1914, was donated by Bristol. It was located west of the railroad station, right at the entrance to a new Bristol and Turner subdivision called Perry Heights, after one of Bristol's forebears, Commodore Oliver Hazard Perry. In this photograph of the unveiling, a sign at the left advertises "The Most Desirable of All Residence Sites . . . Perry Heights, Chappaqua, N.Y."

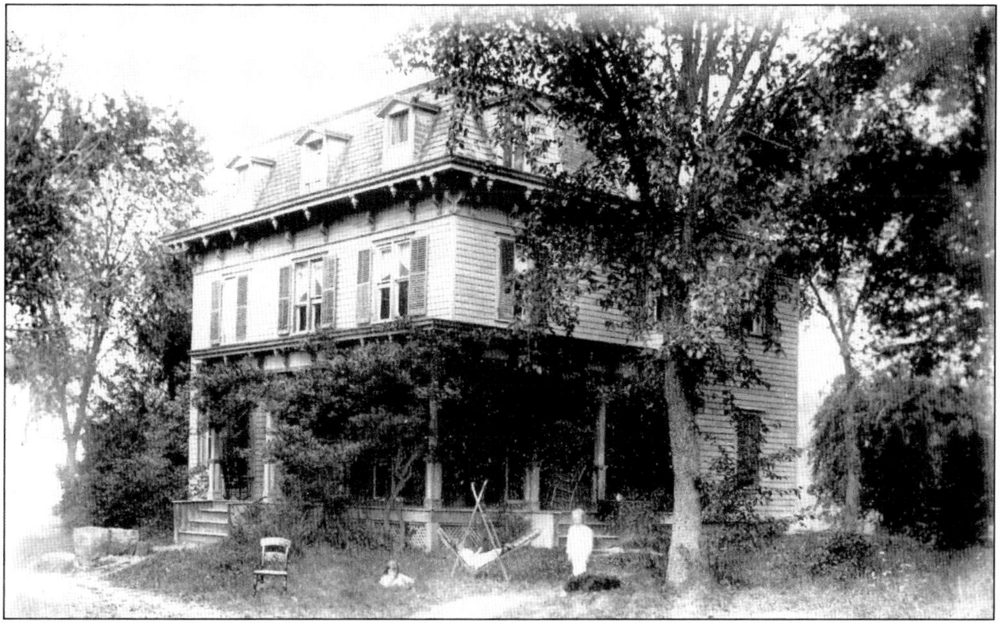

Bristol and Turner bought up several former farms and estates for subdivision and development. One of these properties was the former home of Moses Wanzer, located east of Bedford road near the intersection with King Street. Wanzer's Victorian house was demolished, and the residential development was named Brevoort Road, after Capt. Henry B. Brevoort, another of Bristol's forebears.

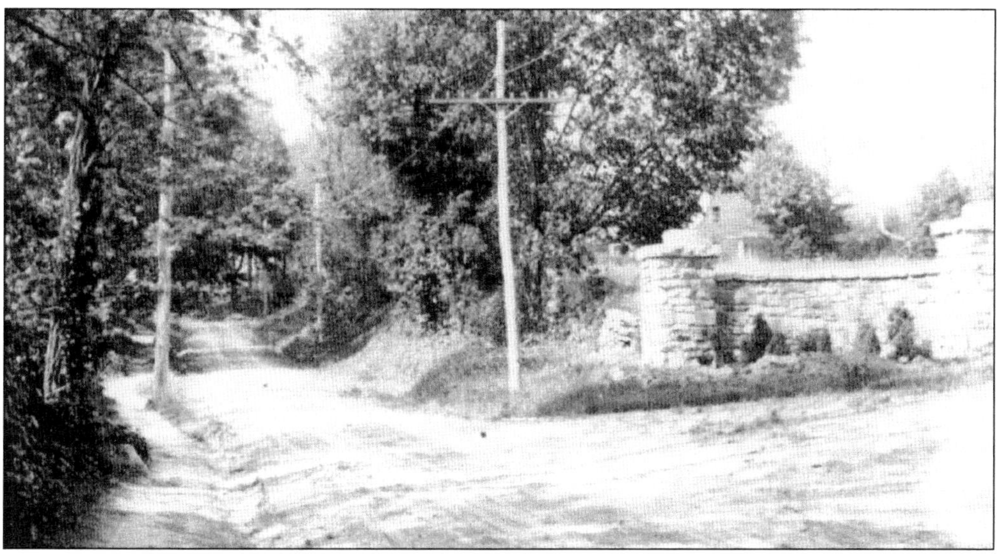

Another Bristol and Turner subdivision was carved out of the Carpenter farm on Quaker Street. It was given the Old-English-sounding name Treeholme, and the road through it was called Commodore Road, after Commodore Perry. At the entrance, the developers erected an imposing stone gateway suggestive of a great estate. Most of the houses in the subdivision, however, were comfortable but unimposing three- or four-bedroom suburban homes.

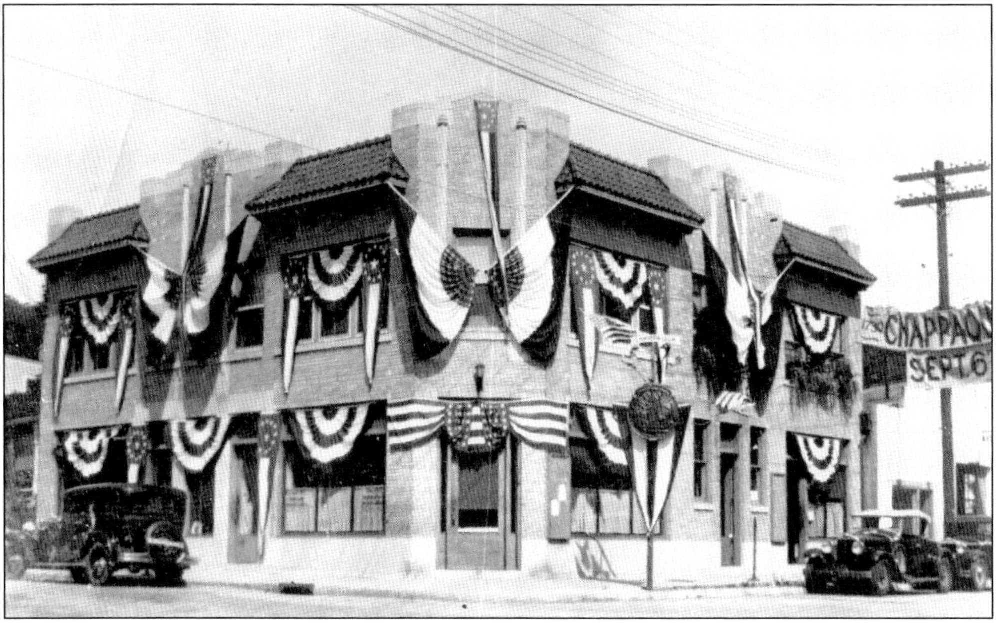

As Chappaqua became more suburban, its downtown became larger, and many of its frame structures were replaced by those of sturdier and more fire-resistant masonry. This building at the corner of King Street and North Greeley Avenue was constructed in 1925 on the site of Amos Tompkins' grain and feed store. This 1930 photograph shows it decorated for the bicentennial of Chappaqua's founding and for the opening of the railroad overpass. At that time, the New Castle town offices were on the first floor and the telephone exchange on the second. Today, the real estate office of Julia B. Fee Real Estate is located here.

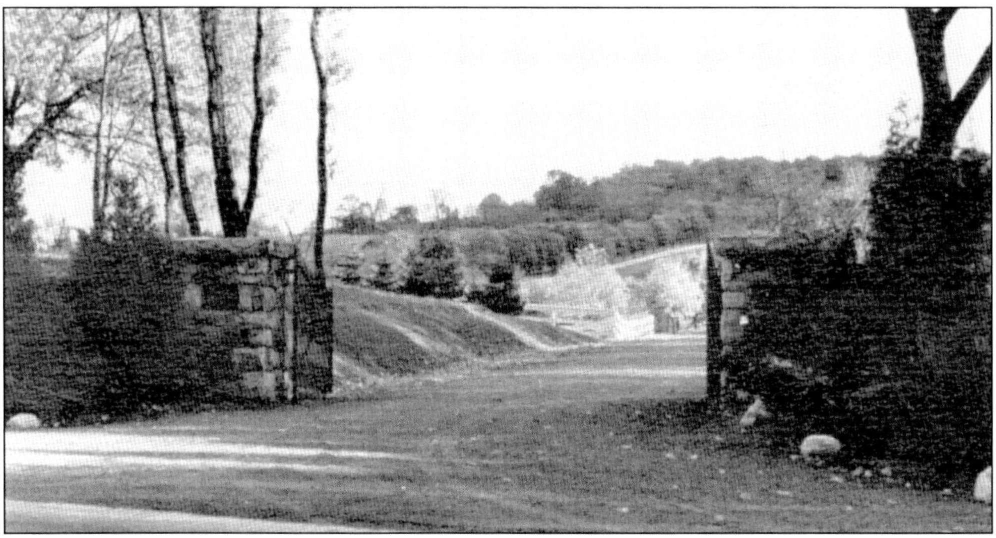

In the 1920s, the Lawrence Real Estate Company, founded by William Van Duzer Lawrence of Bronxville, purchased large tracts of land along both sides of Bedford Road between Chappaqua and Mount Kisco. The largest of these tracts was Annandale Farm, the 600-acre former estate of Moses Taylor V, which extended from Bedford Road to Armonk Road (Routes 117 and 128). Part of the estate was turned into a golf course and country club, and one of the former gateways to Annandale Farm became the entrance to the country club.

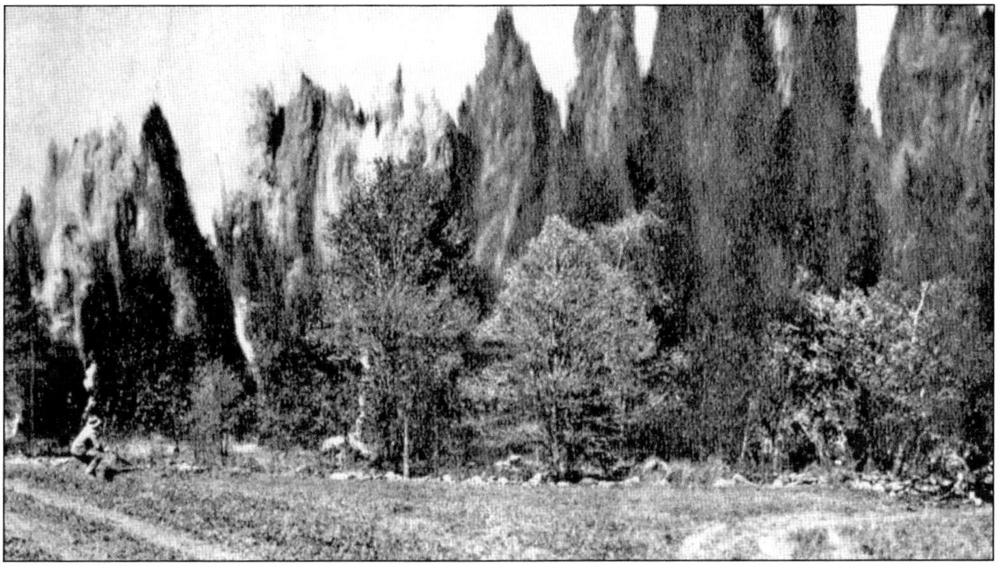

Creating the golf course required some major landscaping changes. For example, 3,500 pounds of nitroglycerine were exploded to lower, by three feet, the bed of the stream that ran through the valley.

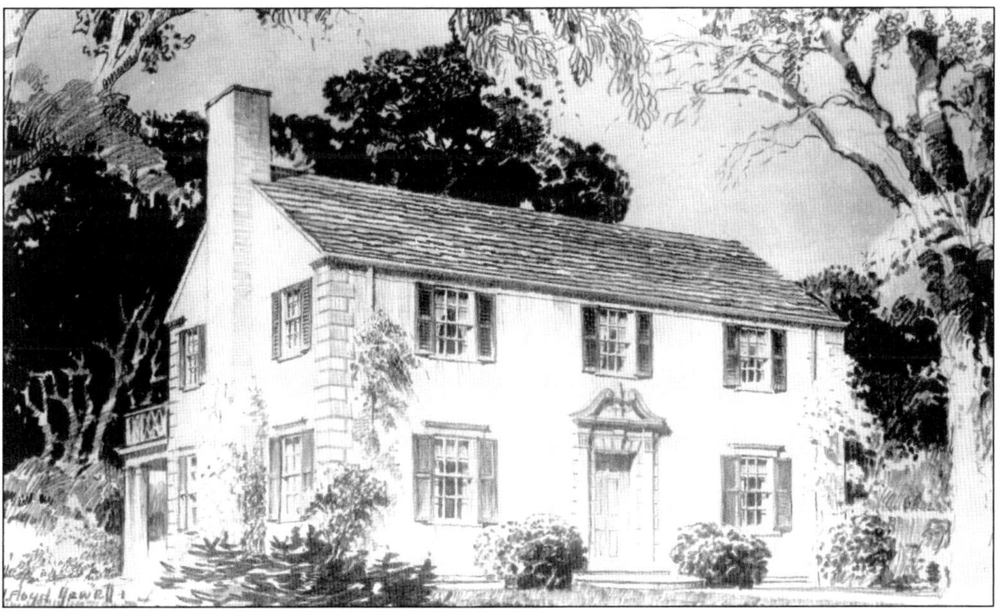

Lawrence Farms was intended to be an upper-middle-class development with substantial houses on relatively large lots. The Lawrence company hired well-known architects such as John Russell Pope and the firm of Delano and Aldrich to design tasteful, if conservative, Colonial Revival houses that would set the tone for the whole neighborhood. (Courtesy of the Westchester County Historical Society.)

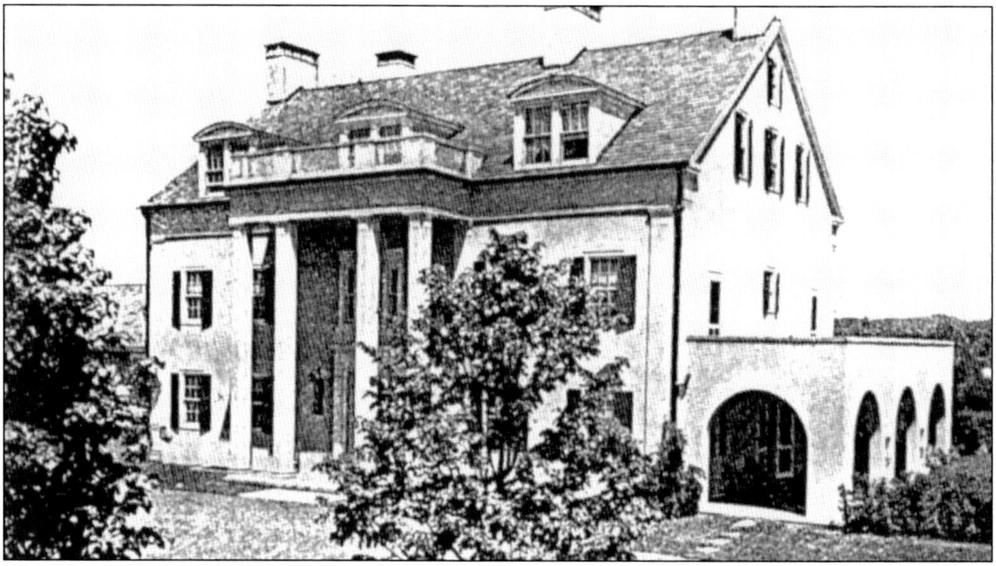

Part of the former Moses Taylor estate was the so-called Kittle House. It had originally served as the barn of Reisig and Hexamer's Ivy Hill Nursery, and in the late 1800s had belonged to the Kittle family. Moses Taylor converted it to a house for his daughter, but she did not care to live in a "barn," and Taylor then used it as a guesthouse for visiting friends. After the Lawrence company acquired the property, it became the Noble School for Girls for five years, as shown in this photograph. It then became the Kittle House restaurant and inn, and has remained so ever since. (Courtesy of John Crabtree.)

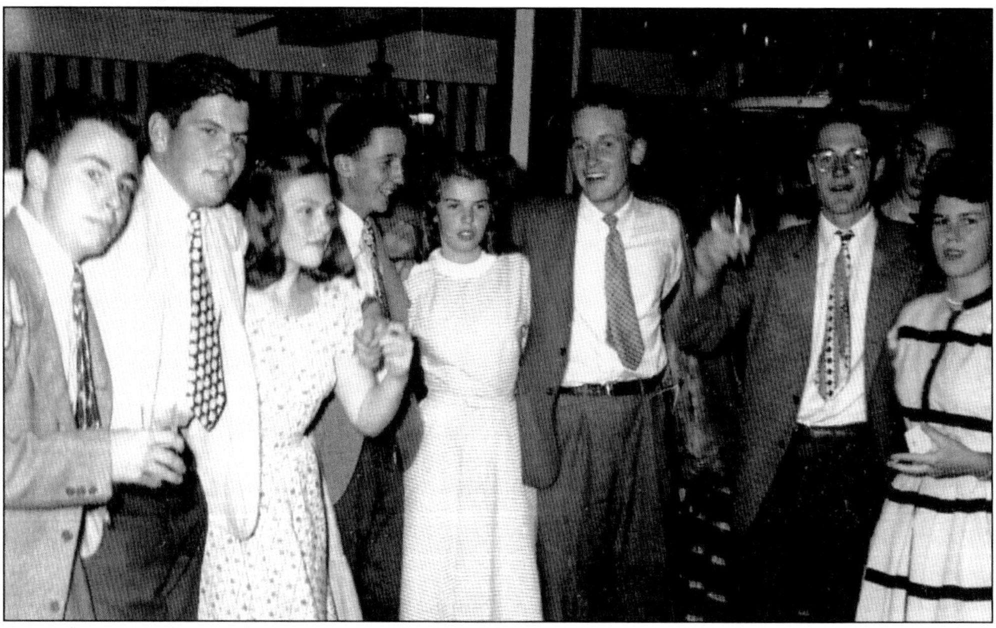

Over the years, the Kittle House functioned as an informal social center for the Lawrence Farms neighborhood. This photograph was taken in 1946 at a private party given by Virginia (Dinny) Lawrence and Corinne "Corky" Cardoff Dailey. From left to right are Edge Quaintence, Carton Clarke, Lucy Jones Berk, Peter Schurman, Corky Cardoff Dailey, Jim Wood, Andy Huber, Peter Bowman, and Jill Fuller. (Courtesy of Corinne Cardoff Dailey.)

The earliest suburban subdivisions in New Castle tended to be on relatively small lots within walking distance of the Chappaqua railroad station. Starting with Lawrence Farms, however, new developments began to appear in areas that were accessible only by car. One of these was Seven Bridges, subdivided and developed in the late 1930s and early 1940s. Its relatively large properties gave the neighborhood a more rural and less suburban atmosphere. (Courtesy of Jane Henzel Kett.)

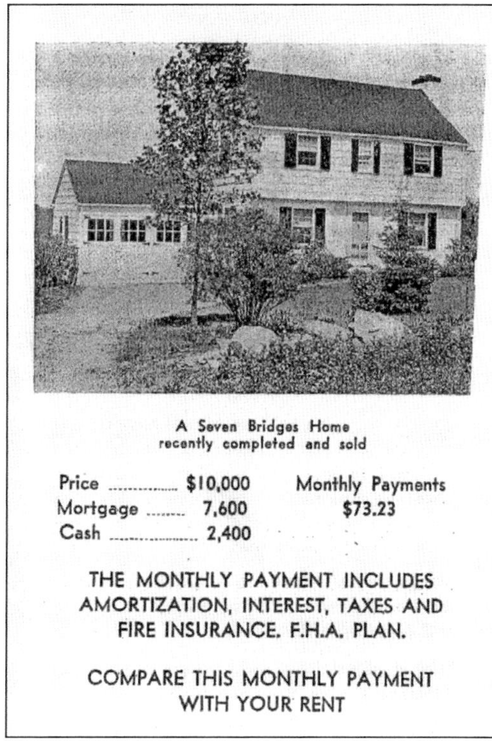

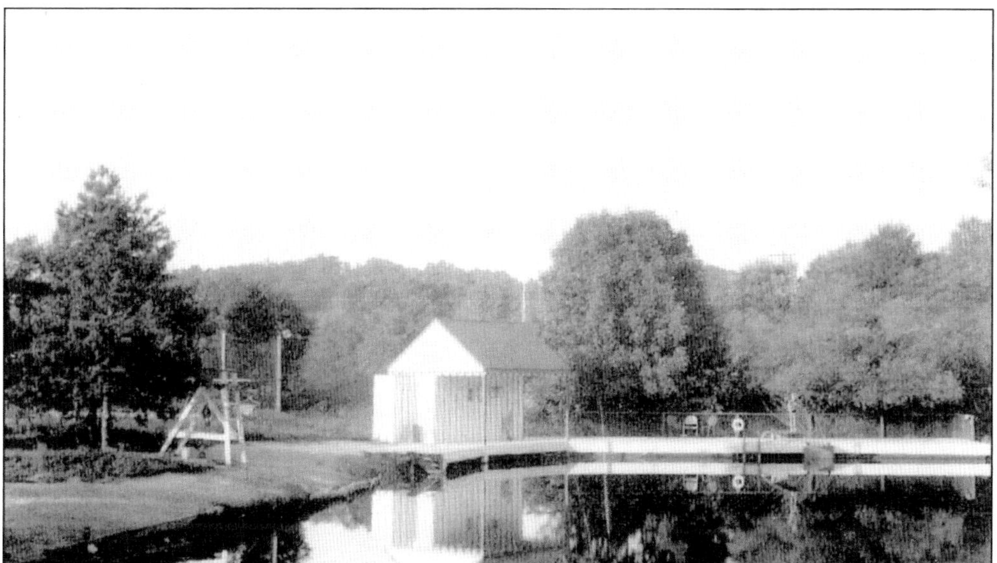

The residents of Seven Bridges formed their own field club, with a swimming pool and tennis courts but no golf course or clubhouse. It became a model for similar swimming and tennis clubs after World War II. (Courtesy of Jane Henzel Kett.)

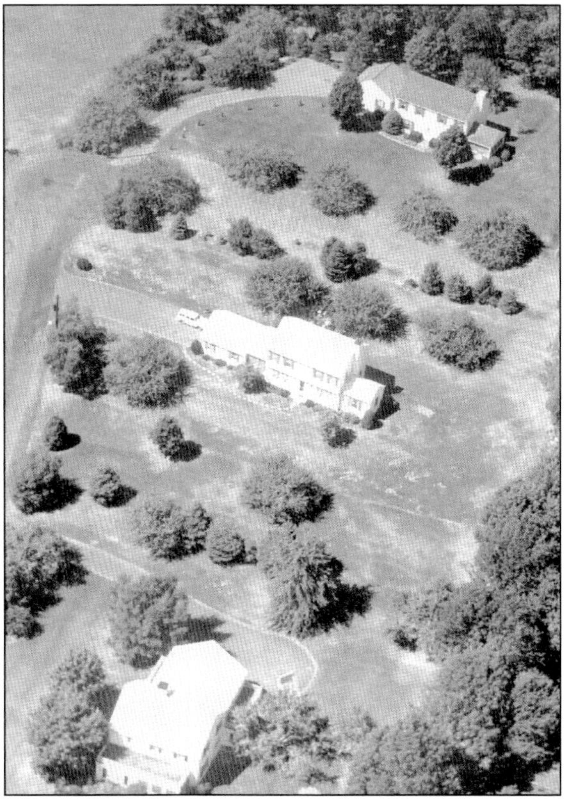

Development slowed down during World War II, when rationing made materials like copper scarce and many construction workers entered the armed services. As soon as the war was over, however, there was a building boom that continued for several decades. A major developer and builder of this period was Stuart L. Bradley, who moved to Chappaqua in 1939. His first two subdivisions, begun in the 1940s, were west of Millwood Road (Route 133). Quaker Village, comprised of Quaker Lane and Gedney Lane, was located on farmlands and orchards that had belonged to the Gedney family. Bradley Farms was developed on the old West Orchard, which in the 1900s had become the estate of David Goodrich. This aerial photograph shows some of the homes built on the subdivision—substantial Colonial-Revival houses on one-acre lots. (Courtesy of Stuart A. Bradley.)

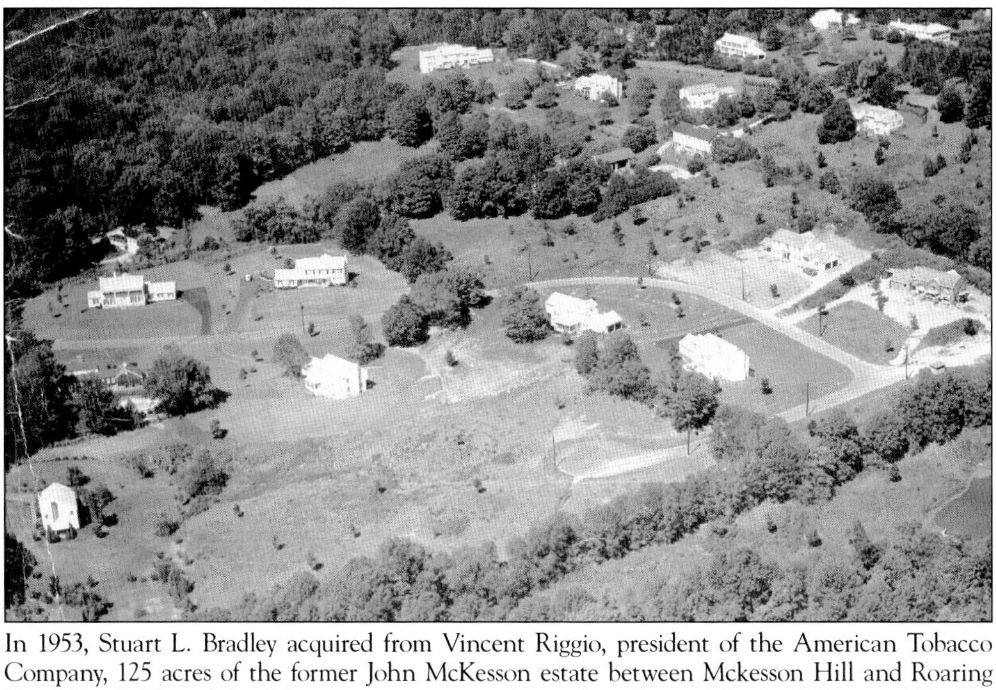

In 1953, Stuart L. Bradley acquired from Vincent Riggio, president of the American Tobacco Company, 125 acres of the former John McKesson estate between Mckesson Hill and Roaring Brook Roads. The subdivided properties were even larger than those of Quaker Village and Bradley Farms, for the area was zoned for lots of at least two acres. (Courtesy of Stuart A. Bradley.)

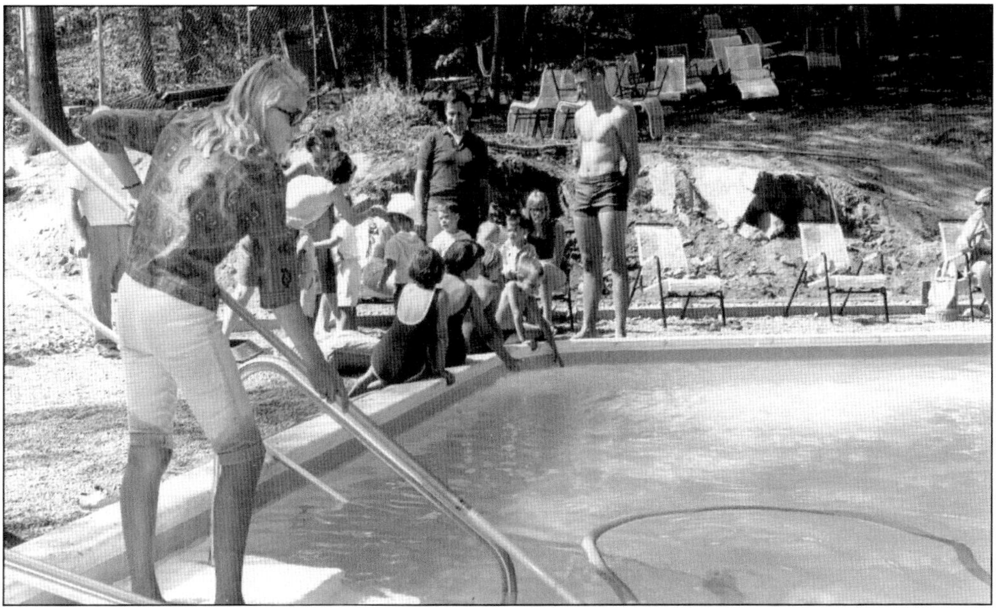

Most of those who moved to New Castle in the postwar decades were families with children, attracted by the reputation of the Chappaqua schools. But these families also sought recreational facilities, particularly swimming pools and tennis courts, that neither the town nor the school district provided. To meet this need, several private swimming and tennis clubs were formed. Construction of the Willow Brook Club swimming pool began in the early spring of 1966, and the pool was ready to open by the following summer. (Courtesy of the Westchester County Historical Society.)

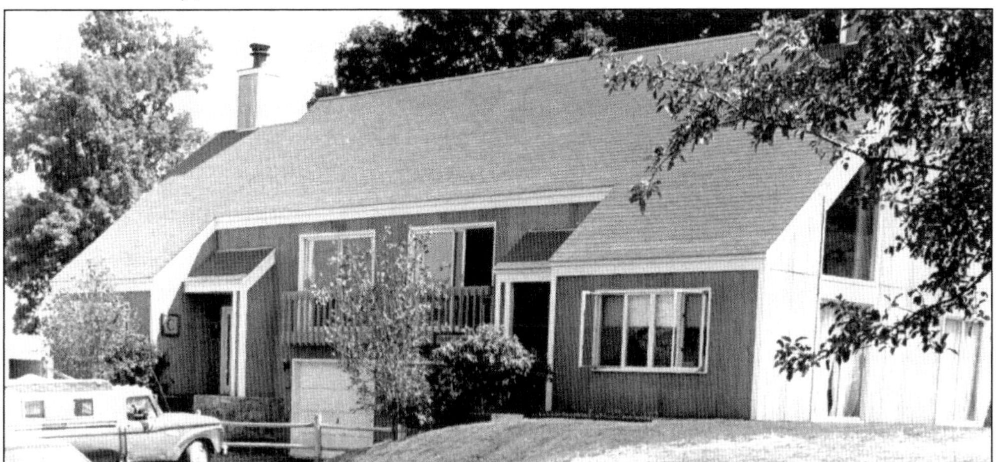

One of the most important changes in New Castle during recent decades has been the gradual introduction of condominiums to a community traditionally composed of single-family properties. The town government, supported by many residents, resisted any such change until a successful lawsuit forced it to accede. Among the first condominium developments was Apple Hill Farm on Bedford Road (Route 117). Opposition to the development was undermined when many of the buyers proved to be people already living in New Castle, who wanted to free themselves of the expense and responsibility of maintaining separate homes, but wished to remain in the community they loved.

CONTRIBUTORS

Stuart A. Bradley, son of Chappaqua developer Stuart L. Bradley, lives at Bradley Farms. He is part owner of a software company.

Jean Cameron-Smith has produced two books published by Arcadia: *Teatown Lake Reservation* and *Yorktown*. The owner of two businesses, she works in Chappaqua as a real estate agent.

Phil Chadeayne is a direct descendant of French Huguenot Jean Chadeayne, who escaped La Rochelle, France, and founded New Rochelle, New York. The family has been in the New Castle area since 1775.

Frances Turner Davidson is a lifelong Chappaqua resident and a descendant of Albert and Frances Bristol Turner, builders of the estates Antiora and Berol Lodge (Whippoorwill Farm). A former nursery school owner, she is currently in the real estate business.

Maura Dunn works in Chappaqua in the real estate field and is pursuing a degree in advertising.

Helen Escoffier, a lifelong Chappaqua resident, has been in the real estate field during most of her professional career. She also owns a business focused on stress management skills.

Michael Fields is the owner of a video and Web site production company that has clients in and around Westchester.

Patricia Gerard currently lives at Apple Hill Farm and serves on the Apple Hill Farm board. She has resided in town since 1984 and has participated in community activities. She works in Chappaqua as a real estate agent.

Emma Hoy, a 10-year resident of northern Westchester, has long been interested in local history. She works in Chappaqua in the real estate field.

Nancy Hutchens came to Chappaqua to work in real estate after spending 20 years as a management consultant. She is the author of two books.

Stacy Levey, a Chicago native, has lived in Chappaqua for the past nine years. She works as a real estate agent in the Chappaqua area.

Rose Marina, a longtime resident of Westchester, has worked in Chappaqua in the real estate field for many years.

Tina Plesset has lived on Brevoort Place and has been active in school and town matters for nearly three decades. A former computer health care consultant, she is now in the local real estate business.

Richard Pogact is the owner of Pogact Excavating, the company responsible for many of the foundations of homes built in New Castle since 1956.

Joanna Rizoulis, a resident of Lawrence Farms East, moved to Chappaqua from Manhattan, where she was a lawyer. She now is the managing director of the Chappaqua and Katonah office of Julia B. Fee Real Estate.

Eric Rosenfeld is the fourth generation of his family in Chappaqua. An original "Greeley-ite," having gone through the entire local school system, he began his career as a business owner and continues today in local real estate.

Janet Short has lived in one of the oldest houses in Chappaqua for more than a quarter of a century. Active in several local groups, she works in real estate and volunteers with the town's meal service program.

Phyllis Weydig, originally from Chappaqua, is a lifelong Westchester resident. She was a local business owner before entering the real estate field two decades ago.

Karl Weydig, a lifelong resident of Westchester, has served as a volunteer firefighter and has been active in the Boy Scouts. He sells real estate in Chappaqua and Katonah.

Gray Williams is the town historian of New Castle, a trustee of the Westchester County Historical Society, and an active volunteer for the New Castle Historical Society. A nearly lifelong resident of Chappaqua, he is a freelance writer, editor, and photographer.

Lynne White, a lifelong Westchester resident, has lived in Chappaqua for 26 years. Her passion is pottery, and her field is real estate.